Schooling
Ordinary Kids

Schooling Ordinary Kids

Inequality, unemployment, and the new vocationalism

PHILLIP BROWN

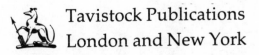

Tavistock Publications
London and New York

First published in 1987 by
Tavistock Publications
11 New Fetter Lane, London EC4P 4EE

Published in the USA by
Tavistock Publications
in association with Methuen, Inc.
29 West 35th Street, New York NY 10001

Typeset by Keyset Composition, Colchester
Printed in Great Britain by
J. W. Arrowsmith Ltd, Bristol

British Library Cataloguing in Publication Data

Brown, Phillip
  Schooling ordinary kids: inequality, unemployment
  and the new vocationalism
  1. Education—Social aspects—Great Britain
  2. Education and State—Great Britain
  I. Title
  370.19'0941   LC191.8.G7

  ISBN 0-422-61490-4

*For my parents
Ted and Lee Brown*

Contents

Acknowledgements

This book is based on my PhD thesis completed at the Department of Sociology and Anthropology, University College, Swansea. I am particularly grateful to my supervisor John Parker for his encouragement and guidance. I would also like to express my thanks to a number of people who have helped in different ways. They are: Betty Arnold, David Ashton, Shane Blackman, Ralph Fevre, Herman Gilligan, Richard Jenkins, Hugh Lauder, Graham Lowe, Mike Nellis, Karen O'Connell, Teresa Rees, Richard Startup, Chris Stray, Angela Vagnarelli, David Webster, and Bill Williams. However, my greatest debt is to Chris Harris who is both an excellent sociologist and a valued friend.

Thanks also to the pupils, staff, and careers officers from Middleport, without their co-operation this study would obviously have been impossible; and to the person who has had to suffer most, but who has constantly offered support and encouragement, a big 'thank you' to Liz.

1 · Introduction

In post-war Britain there has always been a minority of working-class pupils who appeared to accept the school, usually because they believed that by arming themselves with enough qualifications to compete for middle-class jobs, they could get out of their class of origin. Another minority have rejected the school as boring, irrelevant, and frequently repressive. This book, however, is about the 'invisible majority'[1] of 'ordinary' working-class pupils (Kahl 1961; Jenkins 1983) who neither left their names engraved on the school's honours boards, nor gouged them into the top of classroom desks. It explains why these ordinary kids did not conform with the school ethos but were nevertheless willing to 'make an effort', and why they are now at the centre of a major educational crisis.

This crisis is closely connected to broader social and economic changes which have taken place outside the school over the last decade. Britain's economy has been seriously affected by world recession and much of the country's manufacturing industries languish in the shadow of international competition. There have been mass redundancies and unemployment on a scale which even at the time of Callaghan's great debate on education in 1976, were unthinkable. We have also witnessed the rapid expansion of the Manpower Services Commission (MSC) as the problem of unemployment among both young and old alike has become more acute and apparently more intractable. Job opportunities for school leavers have virtually collapsed in many parts of England and Wales. In Britain as a whole only 18 per cent of 16-year-olds entered employment in 1984 compared with over 60 per cent a decade earlier (DES 1985). These changing circumstances outside the school have been accompanied by the rise of Thatcherism and the new right (Hall and Jacques 1983). According to one of its main protagonists, Sir Keith Joseph, Thatcherism represents a political doctrine motivated by a desire to convert 'romantic and out-moded' socialist aspirations into the acceptance of the 'new common ground of reality' (Hillard 1986) which enshrines the principle of individual free enterprise.

It is hardly surprising therefore that the right have sought to define the present educational crisis as a consequence of ill-conceived egalitarian liberal democratic reforms in the post-war period, which they argue has resulted in an unprecedented decline in educational and moral standards. They also identify the educational system as having contributed to the massive increase in youth unemployment as a result of teachers inculcating anti-business and industrial attitudes into pupils who, as a result, are believed to be grossly ill-prepared for the economic realities of the late twentieth century. Consequently the Thatcher government has engaged in a major programme of educational reform in an attempt to ensure that the educational system meets the needs of industry. This 'new vocationalism' (Bates *et al.* 1984; Ranson *et al.* 1986) has manifested itself in a number of recent programmes such as the Technical and Vocational Education Initiative (TVEI); the Certificate of Pre-Vocational Education (CPVE); and more recently the launch of twenty City Technology Colleges (CTCs).[2]

The conclusion of this book, however, will be that the right's account of the educational crisis and arguments for the new vocationalism are not supported by the evidence. It will be argued that while the new vocationalism undoubtedly represents a major challenge to the principles of comprehensive education, it is motivated more by an attempt to maintain (indeed extend) educational and social inequalities than to equip pupils for adult life. This is occurring, furthermore, at a time when the economy and labour market are being restructured, and when the old educational settlement – the conditions under which compliance to the school was ensured – between teachers and the ordinary kids is breaking down. The current crisis in schools results from the fact that there has been a widespread collapse of the types of jobs which enabled the ordinary kids to 'get on' in working-class terms and become adult in a respectable fashion. Its conclusion is not that these pupils must be educated once more to know their place; it is that they already know their place but are less likely to see the school as useful in attaining it.

The classroom crisis among respectable working-class youth, therefore, dramatically highlights the contradictions which underlie the schooling of all working-class youth, and it will be argued that if we are going to meet the educational challenge of contemporary social and economic change, we will require social and educational policies that are geared towards breaking down social and educational inequalities. This will require the development of an alternative politics of education to that which underlies the new vocationalism, because the new vocationalism represents an attempt to subordinate concern about the provision of equal educational opportunities for the working class to 'making the preparation for a place in the occupational structure the *raison d'être* of public education' (Grubb and Lazerson 1982).

The study of ordinary kids also challenges a lot of what sociologists have hitherto told us about education and the working class. Much of the previous research on working-class responses to school has focused on either the high flyers or, more typically, the school rebels (Hammersley and Turner 1980). The very fact that the ordinary kids have been regarded by teachers and indeed by other pupils as *ordinary* has tended not to make them an intrinsically appealing object of sociological enquiry, and there has been little demand for such studies from teachers because they have not, at least until recently, been seen to be a cause for concern. Among sociologists, the ordinary kids' relative quiescence in school (when it seems contrary to their class interests to be so), has led to them being seen as blindly conforming to the whims of teachers. This view has been expressed in a number of sociological studies, including Willis' impressive book *Learning to Labour* (1977). According to Willis any working-class pupils who do not rebel against the school – this includes ordinary kids – constitute a further reminder of the ideological spell under which large numbers of working-class pupils are duped.

Such accounts of so-called 'conformist' responses are both deterministic and 'over socialized' (Wrong 1967), and are in fact grossly inadequate for understanding the way in which ordinary kids experience school life. It will be shown that the way the ordinary kids responded to school was as much a working-class cultural response as the one which led to its rejection. The ordinary kids' willingness to make an effort in school, albeit limited, was part of an authentic attempt to maintain command of their own lives; to maintain a sense of personal dignity and respect (Sennett and Cobb 1977) in circumstances where they were not academically successful; and, on their own terms, to enhance their chances of making a working-class career when they left school (Ashton and Field 1976).

A further reason why the ordinary kids have been largely ignored and misunderstood is because their 'invisibility' and apparent conformity has been associated with female pupils. The study of gender and schooling has recently become a major topic within the sociology of education and the belief that girls are the passive recipients of the school's formal and hidden agendas has correctly been questioned by a number of writers (Davies 1984; Griffin 1985). This study will show clearly that boys as well as girls fall within the category of ordinary kids, and that despite important differences in the way they experience school they adopt a similar orientation, which in turn highlights a number of issues about the relationship between class and gender for understanding working-class educational behaviour.

A study of ordinary kids, and the way their responses to school differ from other groups of pupils, also leads to the twofold conclusion that the educational system neither simply fails the working class, nor do the working class simply fail themselves, as Willis appears to imply. It is the moving encounter between identities and institutions (Abrams 1982) which enables us to understand why the ordinary kids bother to make any effort in school; why some working-class pupils have successfully utilized school as a way of 'getting out' of their class of origin; and why unemployment has brought to a head the contradictions underlying the schooling of ordinary kids. The argument of this book is that the structure and organization of schooling *does* make a difference to the way ordinary kids respond to school, and if it is indeed the case that the working-class demand for education is to be understood in terms of an interplay between identity and institutional structure, then there is nothing inevitable about the contemporary pattern of working-class educational behaviour. These ideas are elaborated in the next chapter, but to begin with, a brief description of the Middleport study is required.

THE MIDDLEPORT STUDY

The study was conducted in a large urban settlement in industrial South Wales. In order to maintain the confidentiality of the pupils and schools involved, it has been called Middleport. Middleport is socially and culturally divided into distinct 'north' and 'south' areas. The north is characterized by middle-class private housing, while the south has retained much of its appearance and identity as a traditional working-class area (Jackson 1968; Willmott 1966), although much of the original industrial base has now disappeared. It was in the south of Middleport that most of the research was conducted. The Welsh language is rarely spoken in this town, and coming from a small working-class town in England's Home Counties, I was struck as much by the similarities as by the differences in the dispositions and outlooks of the people in the two settings.

Middleport provided an ideal location for studying the impact of unemployment on the way the ordinary kids responded to school and their struggle to find employment. As with the rest of industrial South Wales, Middleport has experienced large-scale redundancies as the heavy engineering and steel industries in the area shed labour or simply went out of business. What new jobs have been created are to be found in the service sector, particularly in the retail industry, junior clerical work, cleaning, and light manufacturing. These jobs tend to recruit a large proportion of female labour, a trend which motivated one local newspaper to herald the age of the 'petticoat workforce' (sic).

In the early 1980s Middleport's official unemployment rate was approximately the same as the rest of Wales, which had doubled from 7.3 per cent in 1979 to almost 16 per cent in 1983. This unemployment rate was also comparable to many other unemployment blackspots in the North of England and the West Midlands (Central Statistical Office 1985), and the study can therefore claim a degree of typicality. Another common characteristic of these areas is that the young have been especially hard hit by changing economic circumstances (Jackson 1985; Raffe 1987). In Wales more than one-third of the unemployed were between the ages of 18 and 23 (MSC 1985a), and a growing proportion of these young adults are still experiencing long-term unemployment. The situation for school leavers is even bleaker. In Thomas High School which I will describe below, those who left school at 16 years of age in 1983 had only one-quarter of the chances of getting a job which their predecessors had enjoyed in 1979, and only one-eighth of a chance of an apprenticeship.

Middleport also provided an interesting case study of the impact of unemployment on the school, because of the time-honoured assumption that working-class parents and children in Wales have a greater respect for, and interest in, education than is the case in England. In 1979 a report on Welsh education noted:

> Traditional attitudes and expectations . . . impinge in a marked way on the education service of the Principality. Historically education offered for the academically able a way out of the industrial rut. This phenomenon had the effect of investing academic education with a measure of esteem and respectability and this attitude still persists in

some measure to the disadvantage of more technical or practical areas of learning. (p. 2)

The characterization of Wales as the great exporter of teachers and preachers is not without an element of truth, but the idea that there is a consensus about the virtues of academic study, which is distinctly *Welsh*, should be treated with caution. Belief in the existence of this consensus has invariably been based upon the fact that Wales once produced a higher proportion of academic achievers than England. However, since the late 1970s this has ceased to be the case. Indeed, what the later statistical comparisons between the two countries in fact highlight is the larger proportion of children from Welsh schools who are entering the labour market with no formal qualifications at all (Rees and Rees 1980).

The belief that academic study is highly valued throughout Wales must also be treated with caution because it ignores regional variations in educational performance within the principality itself. There may well be important differences in educational attitudes between the rural and the urban industrial regions. However, even making a distinction between rural and urban areas in this rather simplistic way tends to underplay differences in educational ambitions among people living in the same 'local social structure' (Rogoff 1961; Urry 1981). It will be shown in this study that within the working-class districts of Middleport, striving for academic success as a way out of the industrial rut is in fact a minority pursuit.

In other parts of Britain there are already signs of a growing disaffection with school, particularly among black youth (Jenkins and Troyna 1983). What this study offers is the chance to examine how unemployment has affected the educational responses of an almost exclusively white, traditional working-class neighbourhood. Thus, if there is evidence of a growing disenchantment with school among the ordinary kids described in this study, then the same phenomenon is quite likely to be taking place in similar regions throughout the rest of Wales and England.

Thomas High School was therefore chosen as the *main study school* because of a desire to examine a co-educational comprehensive school which was of average reputation in the town; neither particularly rough nor particularly academic.

Thomas High School was built in the early 1970s as a community school to service the people living in the south of

Middleport. The school was located in a densely populated working-class neighbourhood of terraced housing, interspersed with a generous quantity of corner shops, public houses, and chapels. Thomas High School had a fairly good reputation among local people, 'as schools go'. The staff were relatively young and progressive in their attitudes towards their job. They frequently espoused a belief that in this sort of area the academic curriculum was irrelevant to the lives of all but a small minority of pupils, and therefore that they had an important *socially* educative role to perform. However, the only manifestation of this philosophy which occurred while I was at the school were the daily tutorial periods of 30 minutes each. I was told that attempts had once been made to remove the streaming of pupils when they entered the school, but that this idea had been abandoned after a number of complaints from local parents. Finally we should note that pupils entered Thomas High School at the age of 14 from two feeder junior high schools, and that it also had a small academic sixth form.

Data was also collected from two other schools in Middleport, which I have called St Birinus and Greenhill High. St Birinus was situated close to the town centre, and was similar to Thomas High School in that it also catered for pupils from a working-class background between the ages of 14 and 18 years. It had once served Middleport as a grammar school before reorganization had turned it into a comprehensive and its austere appearance reflected these origins. Unlike Thomas High School it contained many older members of staff who had become disillusioned with teaching after the school's intake began to include non-academic pupils. By way of contrast, Greenhill High was selected precisely for its distinctiveness from the other two schools. It was situated in the middle-class district of Middleport, and catered mainly for the children of professional and business people living in the north of the town. Greenhill was the largest of the three schools catering for approximately 1,500 pupils between the ages of 11 and 18. The school was surrounded by a large area of attractive park-land which was in stark contrast to the location of the other two schools. The staff and many of its pupils (past and present) prized the school's reputation for being good for sport, and it boasted a 'respectable' record for sending pupils on to Oxbridge.

The selection of the three schools was not intended to provide a representative sample of the attitudes and experiences of all pupils in Middleport comprehensive schools, although there is little to suggest that the pupils involved in this study were particularly different from the pupils in any of the other comprehensive schools in the locality. It was, however, intended to ensure that the data collected from the main study school, Thomas High, was not peculiar to that school (particularly in regard to the way its pupils were responding to youth unemployment).

In order to understand the way working-class pupils were responding to school and to assess the gap between pupil aspirations and labour market realities, it was decided to combine questionnaire data which would give the study breadth and ethnographic data which would give it depth. The combination of these two approaches is favoured by many research methodology textbooks, but is rarely adopted in practice for a variety of professional reasons. My deployment of qualitative and quantitative methods is therefore unlikely to please purists on either side of this methodological debate, whether they are of the persuasion that the only data worth collecting is that which captures the subjective world of the social actors, or of the persuasion that in gleaning knowledge of what working-class pupils think about school and how unemployment will affect their attitudes only random samples of large populations will do. I personally do not regard these research methods as being in competition with each other, and they are in fact mutually advantageous given the issues that this study has sought to address.

All fifth-form pupils from Thomas High School and St Birinus were asked to complete a questionnaire, along with selected classes of O level and CSE pupils from Greenhill (primarily in order to include an 'academic' section of pupils from a middle-class background). Table 1.1 shows that these schools provided a sample of 451 male and female pupils, all of whom were sent a postal questionnaire approximately two years later. In total, 318 of

Table 1.1 *The make-up of the sample*

Thomas High School	200
St Birinus	153
Greenhill High	98
Male	223
Female	228
Total	451

the 451 pupils in the original sample returned questionnaires. This represented a 75 per cent response rate, once those who did not receive a questionnaire by virtue of being untraceable, were excluded.

Although the information provided by these questionnaires proved to be invaluable, it is necessary to get behind the ticked boxes if a fuller appreciation of the processes and shared cultural understandings of *being* a working-class pupil in school is to be achieved. A number of semi-structured and unstructured interviews were therefore conducted in all three schools. In Thomas High School I spent time observing lessons and at lunch times I worked in the youth wing tuck shop. My job in the tuck shop provided access to the informal pupil culture, and was an invaluable source of information about how different groups of pupils responded to one another.

The main focus of my observations was a group of thirty male and female middle-band pupils studying for CSEs, together with a small group of non-examination pupils who constituted a conspicuously male anti-school subculture. At the end of the first phase of data collection twenty O level pupils, thirty-four CSE pupils and a group of approximately twelve non-examination pupils from Thomas High School had been interviewed individually and in small groups. The interviews with O level and CSE pupils were conducted with both male and female pupils in approximately equal proportions. A small number of ordinary kids from Thomas High School were also re-interviewed approximately two years after leaving school.

To find out whether the attitudes and experiences of pupils from Thomas High School were substantally different from those expressed by pupils in other schools in Middleport, twenty male and female CSE pupils were also interviewed from both St Birinus and Greenhill, and a further twenty academic O level pupils from Greenhill were interviewed to allow a comparison between pupils in the academic bands from different social backgrounds.

Finally, in a modest attempt to gauge teacher responses to the changing context of schooling in the 1980s, a number of informal discussions also took place with teachers and, in addition, ten teachers were interviewed formally, along with a head teacher and two deputy head teachers, all of whom were from Thomas High School.

The combination of different research methods requires me to say something about the way in which the book is organized, particularly Chapters 3 and 4. Although invaluable, the combination of different research methods does create problems of presentation, which is why the questionnaire data is used to inform Chapter 3 and the interview data Chapter 4. The two chapters should however be read in conjunction, because although they use different sources of data they both describe the ways in which ordinary kids have responded to school, and the consequences of unemployment for their collective under-standings of being a working-class pupil. Indeed the whole book is organized in a way that is intended to capture the interplay between micro and macro processes, between identities and institutional life.

The articulation of a framework which will permit us to capture this interrelationship between the private troubles of pupils and school leavers, and the public issues of social structure (Mills 1970) is a task undertaken in the next chapter, while the empirical Chapters 3–6 go on to explain who the ordinary kids are and how youth unemployment had affected their response to school. They also seek to explain the intended and unintended consequences of the ordinary kids' actions for the reproduction of social and moral divisions among working-class pupils. The political and classroom context of the new vocationalism is then examined and an assessment is made of its likely consequences for both ordinary kids and teachers (a theme which remains central to the rest of the book). The empirical Chapter 6 shifts attention away from the school to the labour market, revealing what has happened to the ordinary kids since leaving school, and indicating how the moral divisions which once distanced the ordinary kids from other pupils in school may now be growing among the ordinary kids themselves, as competition for the few available jobs grows ever sharper.

The concluding chapter reassesses the contribution of existing sociological accounts of schooling the working class in post-war Britain in the light of the Middleport study and discusses the political strategies necessary to get a better deal for ordinary kids, and for meeting the educational challenge of the late twentieth century. The new vocationalism and the politics in which it is grounded are emphatically not the answer, and it is my hope that this study will contribute to a wider appreciation of their limitations, and to the kind of policies which will effectively counter them.

2 · Schooling the working class

The relationship between education and social class is a central problem in the sociology of education. The reason for its discussion in this chapter is not to provide another review of contemporary theories and interpretations, but to demonstrate why an adequate account of the educational experiences of ordinary working-class pupils can only be achieved by transcending existing theories. The purpose of this chapter is to outline what the available literature has to teach us, why its lessons are inadequate, and what an alternative interpretative framework needs to look like.

Most of the writings on education and the working class have been presented within a wider debate about social justice, inequality, and equality of opportunity. In post-war Britain pupils from a working-class background are consistently found to gain fewer academic qualifications, to be under-represented in institutions of higher education, and to end up in jobs offering little opportunity for social advancement. Whatever form of sociological explanation is offered to account for these findings, the educational system is seen to play a key role because it is the school which has been given the task of the *socialization* and *selection* of future generations of workers and citizens (Parsons 1961; Althusser 1972), and because educational performance is a major determinant of future life-chances (Venn 1964; Bowles and Gintis 1976).

The post-war debates about social class and educational performance, dominated by liberal democratic approaches in the 1950s and 1960s and by Marxists since the mid-1970s, have focused on *why* the school operates to the disadvantage of children from a working-class background, and what measures can be taken to improve educational opportunities, rather than on showing the way in which working-class pupils experience the school and how this results in educational under-achievement. Despite the radically different ways liberals and Marxists view the functions of the school and its potential for achieving greater social justice, both offer *structural* accounts which have failed to elucidate the schooling *process*. What little attention these structural accounts give to describing educational processes leads to strikingly similar explanations of what the school 'does' to pupils in terms of what will be called the process of *educational* differentiation. These *structural* theories may be contrasted with *cultural* explanations which have gained attention as a result of Willis' *Learning to Labour*. This alternative understanding of how working-class pupils fail academically in school is centrally concerned with what will here be called the process of *cultural* differentiation. Such understandings involve the rejection of any structural accounts as deterministic and giving no place to human agency. They claim, instead, that middle- and working-class pupils have different culturally based aspirations and ambitions. In so doing they seek to explain educational outcomes, not as the product of the school's selection processes but as the result of social processes operating outside of the school. Pupils from a working-class neighbourhood do not value academic success because they have developed social and occupational identities which lead them to reject the school and middle-class life styles as irrelevant. After examining these different approaches this chapter will argue that structural and cultural explanations are not so much competing as one-sided, with the former emphasizing school structure and the latter, cultural agency. Both are inadequate because they fail to listen to what the other is saying, and fail to provide an adequate account of the educational experiences of ordinary kids.

THE PROCESS OF EDUCATIONAL DIFFERENTIATION

The sociology of education in Britain grew out of a liberal democratic commitment to establish equal educational opportunities for all children. As a consequence sociologists were more concerned with the demonstration rather than the explanation of institutional sources of inequality in education (Bernstein 1975). In a review of the sociology of education in 1958, Floud and Halsey outlined a new agenda for enquiry. They suggested that sociologists must become concerned with more subtle aspects of social inequality than the poverty, squalid housing conditions, and malnutrition which had traditionally provided the focus of their attention. The problem was increasingly seen to be one of working-class 'educability', which had somehow to be remedied before pupils from a working-class background could take advantage of increasing levels of educational provision:

> The educability of an individual, given his [or her] personal endowment and unique life-history, represents his [or her] socially determined *capacity to respond* to the demands of the particular educational arrangements to which he [or she] is exposed.
>
> (Floud and Halsey 1958: p. 183, emphasis added)

The focus on working-class educability led to an examination of cultural, emotional, and psychological consequences of material and social disadvantage (Plowden Report 1967), the enduring features of which were believed to be manifest in class inequalities in educational attainment. This way of understanding the issue of education and the working class not only had a significant impact on liberal attempts to explain the persistence of educational disadvantage despite greater equality of opportunity, but also had important consequences for educational policy. By defining the problem of working-class educability in terms of an inability to respond to the school, and class differences in educational attainment as a consequence of the continuation of educational inequalities, it provided a political lever for the further expansion and reorganization of secondary education.

The argument for increasing social justice was reinforced by the economic argument that Britain could no longer afford to waste the talents and skills of working-class youth if it was to compete in the international market. Therefore the political motivation for establishing the opportunity for all pupils to be candidates for every position in adult society rested on the twin objectives of increasing economic efficiency and enhancing social justice (Silver 1973; Bernbaum 1977).

The continuing concern of liberal democrats to *demonstrate* why the working classes were continuing to be fed into working-class jobs, rather than seeking to explain the exact nature of the schooling process, is noted by Bernbaum (1977):

> It is clear that a sociology of education which adopts essentially functionalist perspectives to explain in general terms the relationship of the educational system to the wider society is also likely to be a sociology of education which will concentrate at the specific level upon those areas which seem to inhibit the free movement of talent and the creation of talent. Thus in education the major work is on social class and educational opportunity, on family socialisation and selection. (p. 26)

This concentration on factors which inhibit the free movement of talent has important consequences for explaining the functions and process of schooling. Underlying liberal democratic accounts are a set of assumptions which relate closely to structural functionalism. There is a belief that social stratification is an inevitable feature of all advanced industrial societies, but also a recognition of compelling social and economic reasons why equality of opportunity is desirable. Again Bernbaum notes:

> At a societal level, education can be seen as the crucial investment, the condition for sustaining economic growth. At an individual level, education can be seen as the key to social mobility. (p. 25)

Inequalities in educational attainment are not seen to be the manifestation of an unequal and unjust social structure which requires the transformation of the whole society, but as a *technical* problem which the educational system has the potential to overcome. Liberal democratic approaches also share an assumption that there is a common culture which has created a universal demand for education and middle-class occupations. Given the existence of a normative value system it is assumed that class differences in educational attainment must result from an *inability* of working-class pupils to respond to the school, and therefore represent class inequalities in educational opportunity.

These underlying assumptions of liberal democratic accounts have at least two related consequences. First, there is a failure to take seriously class *differences* in educational aspirations. Second, attempts to explain class differences in educational attainment do so by reference solely to the process of *educational* differentiation. Such approaches emphasize the decisive role of the school's sifting, sorting, and selection processes in determining how pupils from a working-class background are channelled into the lower streams (or bands) of the school, and fed into the labour market for working-class jobs. Marxist structural accounts challenge many of the underlying assumptions of the liberal democrats, but they fail to advance our understanding of exactly how working-class educational failure occurs.

By the mid 1970s the optimistic belief that the educational system could generate equal educational opportunity was regarded with growing scepticism (CCCS 1981), for it had by then become apparent that the introduction of comprehensive schooling and programmes of compensatory education had not significantly improved the academic performance of working-class pupils. Early scepticism quickly grew into a tide of criticism from those on the political left and right. Both accused the liberal democrats of everything from naïvety to politically motivated projects in social engineering and ideological mystification. Marxist writers rejected any idea of the school as a liberating force, offering the 'royal road' to social mobility:

> It is probably cultural inertia which still makes us see education in terms of the ideology of the school as a liberating force . . . and as a means of increasing social mobility, even when the indications tend to be that it is in fact one of the most effective means of perpetuating the existing social pattern.
>
> (Bourdieu 1974: p. 32)

Rather than attempt to explain the educational failure of working-class pupils in terms of individual and collective class attributes which handicap them in their capacity to respond to educational opportunities, the concern among Marxist writers has been to show the unequal nature of capitalist societies and to demonstrate the *inevitability* of working-class educational failure. From this standpoint the school is primarily a means of reproducing the existing structure of social and economic inequalities:

> The educational system, basically, neither adds to nor subtracts from the degree of inequality and repression originating in the economic sphere. Rather, it reproduces and legitimates a pre-existing pattern in the process of training and stratifying the workforce.
>
> (Bowles and Gintis 1976: p. 265)

There are important differences within Marxist accounts of schooling in capitalist societies, particularly in the degree of 'relative autonomy' given to the educational system from the demands of capitalist production. The idea of a direct correspondence between school and industry which is offered by Bowles and Gintis has been rejected by those Marxists who prefer to emphasize the relative autonomy of the school from the factory, and to focus on the way the educational system successfully legitimates (sometimes not until the last instance), its selection process, so that those it fails see their failure as the result of a 'fair' rather than a 'fixed' contest. Despite such differences, the Marxist attack on liberal democratic approaches derives less from a judgement concerning the inadequacy of previous under-standings of the attributes and ambitions of working-class youth or the schools' selection processes, than from a different theory of the nature of the society in which we live, and a different understanding, therefore, of the structural location of the educational system (see also Young 1971).

Despite the important differences between liberal democratic and Marxist structural explanations they share important similarities when it comes to explaining the *process* of schooling rather than the functions of schooling. Both tend to interpret the process of schooling in terms of the functions of the education system according to their theory of the society of which it is a part. It may also be argued that both assume the existence of a common or dominant culture, when attempting to explain working-class educational experiences. Marxist accounts, although they make a clear distinction between the values, attitudes, and interests of the working and middle classes, none the less see both classes as sharing bourgeois ways of thinking and acting as a result of the inculcation of a dominant ideology. An attendant feature of approaches which rely on the notion of a common or dominant culture is, as previously noted, that they assume a universal demand for education across all classes and also that all pupils share similar educational and occupational aspirations. This has led to a failure to take seriously the possibility of class differences in pupil aspirations, and to an attempt to explain social class differences in educational success and failure in terms of differential class access to socially agreed goals, rather than as representing cultural differences in the very *definition* of desirable goals. Explanations of this type, therefore, focus on the school as the site of what has been called the process of *educational* differentiation. The school is a sifting and sorting mechanism which, given existing inequalities in the selection process, ensures that pupils from middle- and working-class backgrounds arrive at educational and occupational destinations appropriate to their class membership.

A further objection to accounts which explain working-class educational failure in terms of the process of educational differentiation is that the development of the individual's social identity, of which occupational identity is a central feature, is not seen to have any bearing on how pupils perceive the school and its value. Indeed, the process of occupational preferences and decision making is seen to be a by-product of educational performance. Occupational preference, when it is considered, is viewed in terms of the capacity of the educational system to instil realistic occupational goals and to successfully 'cool-out' (Hopper 1971) those pupils who are unable to gain access to middle-class jobs. An example of this kind of account is Roberts (1975) who, although not a Marxist, emphasizes the environment of constraint which confronts working-class school leavers. He then explains how working-class pupils accept their working-class jobs through a process of adaptation which is achieved by pupils evaluating their abilities and accomplishments against those of their peers. Estimation of their life-chances leads pupils to structure their educational and occupational aspirations in accordance with those expectations, which is why Roberts believes there is a close relationship between occupational preferences and scholastic attainment. At the same time occupational aspirations are seen to be a consequence of school performance which disadvantage working-class pupils as a result of class inequalities operating within the school. Therefore, the school not only ensures that working-class pupils will be the least-qualified school leavers but also that by the time they leave school they have adapted preferences and expectations to a life in working-class jobs. A similar understanding is evident in the Marxist writings of Bowles and Gintis (1976) who inform us that:

> The educational system helps integrate youth into the economic system . . . through a structural correspondence between its social relations and those of production. The structure of social relations in education not only inures the student to the discipline of the work place, but develops the types of personal demeanour, modes of self-presentation, self-image, and social-class identification which are the crucial ingredients of job adequacy. (p. 131)

So far it has been argued that liberal and Marxist structural approaches have dominated accounts of education and social class. It has been shown that despite presenting radically different theories of the structural location and functions of the school, both share important failings when it comes to describing working-class educational failure. Schooling is understood in terms of the process of educational differentiation which represents little more than the translation of class inequalities into differences in educational attainment and the 'cooling out' of unrealistic expectations. They are also functionalist in that they interpret what happens in schools simply in terms of the functions the school must perform for 'society' as they conceive it. Little attention is given to the consciousness and action of the pupils themselves, and these approaches provide little conceptual space for the study of the groupings, relations, and practices of pupils and educators in contemporary capitalist societies.

THE PROCESS OF CULTURAL DIFFERENTIATION

There are a number of writers who have tried to explain working-class educational underachievement in terms of class cultural differences in the demand for education. It is worth noting that in the late 1970s a book about perspectives in the sociology of education (Reid 1978) notes that explanations of the relationship between education and social class in terms of class differentials in the values, interests and aspirations of pupils, had no major representative in the sociology of education. Such a representative was, however, to be found in a Marxist class cultural study by Willis (1977). This account of how working-class pupils get working-class jobs has dominated recent discussions of working-class educational failure. Willis disputes the claim that working-class pupils have no choice about what happens to them in school as being not only deterministic, but also as involving a misunderstanding of the often unintended consequences of working-class responses to education, which themselves lead into working-class jobs. His argument acts as an important corrective to those accounts which explain working-class educational and labour market experiences solely in terms of the process of educational differentiation, and no apology is offered for discussing his valuable account at a number of points in this book. What does need to be said here, however, is that the prime assumption on which class cultural explanations such as that of Willis are based, is a belief that working- and middle-class people have distinct and largely self-contained sets of values and practices which are in opposition to each other. Turner (1964) notes that exponents of this approach, which he calls 'subcultural', assume that:

> each class is to some degree a self-contained universe, developing a distinctive set of values which guides its members' way of life. While these class subcultures are constrained by the necessity to maintain working relations with other classes within a general national framework, the subcultures of different classes are in important respects mutually contradictory. Objects which are positively valued in one class subculture may be negatively valued in another. . . . According to this view, the classes have different conceptions of what objectives are worthy of pursuit and what qualities entitle a person to the esteem of his fellows. (pp. 9–10)

In America a number of studies of social stratification and

cultural values sought to explain the apparent lack of working-class social mobility in class cultural terms. Inequalities of educational access and provision were rarely completely denied in such works and were acknowledged to maintain the existing social structure. However, there were believed to be others of a:

> subtle psychological nature which have not been illuminated and which may also work to perpetuate the existing order. It is our assumption that an intervening variable mediating the relationship between low position and lack of upward mobility is a system of beliefs and values within the lower classes which in turn reduces the very *voluntary* actions which would ameliorate their low position.
>
> (Hyman 1953: pp. 426–7)

Explanations of these distinctive value and cultural systems vary, but all assume that the extent to which academic achievement and social mobility are sought by working-class pupils cannot be taken for granted and must be regarded as problematic. In class cultural explanations of working-class educational underachievement, it is not so much the class bias in the school's selection process which is emphasized but the process of *cultural* differentiation. Such accounts recognize that working-class pupils may be *unwilling* rather than *unable* to respond to what is on offer in the school, given a collective understanding of school success as having little effect on systems of status (Becker 1961). Whereas the process of educational differentiation leads to understandings of pupil ambitions as the by-product of educational performance, the process of cultural differentiation recognizes working-class social and occupational identities to be a product of different world images (Bulmer 1975), which leads them to reject what is taught in school because it has little meaning or relevance to their present and future life. Therefore, if you want to understand working-class underachievement it is not the school's but the *pupils'* selection processes which hold the key.

In earlier non-Marxist class cultural accounts, it was the socialization of the child within the family which was believed to be the main determinant of pupil ambitions. It is fair to say that these writers, such as Carter (1962) and Ashton and Field (1976) were primarily interested in the transition from school, and in differences within working-class aspirations. Such differences were explained in terms of working-class family 'types'. Carter (1966) distinguished the 'home-centred' and aspiring (which he subdivided into 'traditional respectable' and 'newly affluent') from the 'solid working class' and what he calls the 'rough' or 'disreputable':

> These three types of background exert distinctive influences upon children as they approach the end of their school days and prepare to enter the world of work. Job aspirations and general attitudes towards work, knowledge about work, and the ability to take steps to smooth the transition from school to employment are all profoundly affected. (p. 41)

The importance of family background was such that each family 'type' was assumed to have a distinct set of attitudes, values and predilections towards education and employment, which made contact with the school unlikely to have much impact on pre-existing social and occupational identity. Those differences in occupational preference which existed among working-class youth were believed to reflect internal differences *within* the working class rather than the result of the school's selection process. Ashton and Field also traced differences in working-class ambitions and labour market achievements to family background. They distinguished the 'careerless' from families where the father was in semi-skilled or unskilled jobs; those who made a 'short-term career' with school leavers from a skilled working-class background; and those who made an 'extended career' with the middle and lower middle classes. These differences in family background led to different world images which were reinforced within the school, rather than produced there. In their account of the 'careerless', for example, they argued that:

> In terms of their orientations to the world, their experience of school merely reinforces the attitudes transmitted within the family, for these young pupils (unlike others) are not offered any future rewards for successful performance, there are no educational certificates for them. (p. 52)

Marxist cultural accounts have questioned theories of social class and social values which place a premium on family 'types' as an explanation of differences in working-class images because, among other things, they tend to emphasize what Marxists see as superficial differences within the working-class neighbourhood, and thereby serve to obscure the significance of a *class* cultural explanation of how working-class pupils get working-class jobs. In *Learning to Labour* Willis wants to preserve a holistic view of the working class and working-class culture, which stands in a position of both subordination and opposition to the dominant middle-class culture (Hall and Jefferson 1976). Those who adopt the counter-school culture of 'the lads', the group of youngsters on whom Willis' study focused, are not simply conforming to a particular script learnt during childhood in a particular type of working-class family; their resistance to the school has important *class* significance in that it results from a form of cultural penetration; an insight into the conditions of existence confronting working-class people. A critique of Willis' account of the counter-school culture will be reserved until later; what needs to be noted here is one contribution and two problems with Willis' cultural explanation.

Willis does not present the process of schooling simply as a story about what the school 'does' to pupils. His main contribution is the recognition that it is only possible to make sense of class differences in educational responses if they are viewed in the light of the pupils' own experience within their own culture, which may lead them to interpret the school and their place within it in different ways. The problems are firstly, that by emphasizing the *active* role which pupils play in the reproduction of their own subordination he is inadvertently led to a voluntaristic explanation of working-class educational failure. He seriously underplays the importance of class differences in power and privilege which permit the middle class to manipulate educational and labour market processes in order to maintain social and material advantages in a society where only a few can 'make it', regardless of whether all pupils share the same educational and occupational aspirations.

Second, Willis does not deal adequately with the full complexity of the question which is central to the sociology of education, as well as to his own study, namely the question of educational failure among the working class. This is a legitimate question because there are undoubtedly major differences in educational and occupational attainment between working- and middle-class youth, and these differences have correctly been a major concern to sociologists in this field. However, *not* all working-class pupils do fail academically. Some do go on to higher education and into the professions. Moreover, even among those who do not escape the working class, there are major differences in response to the school and labour market (Ashton and Field 1976; Jenkins 1983). If we are to take class differences in aspirations seriously, which we must, and accept that such differences may have an important impact on the process of schooling and the transition into the labour market, then it is equally necessary to take seriously the possibility of different cultural responses *among* working-class pupils. The recognition of variations in responses to school within the working class not only opens the way to a more adequate understanding of working-class responses to education and unemployment in general, it also illuminates the reasons for the failure of sociologists adequately to grasp the relationship between class and schooling in post-war Britain.

EXPLAINING DIFFERENCES IN WORKING-CLASS RESPONSES TO SCHOOL

The difference between the explanations put forward by structural and cultural accounts is illustrated by the contrasting approaches of Hargreaves' *Social Relations in a Secondary School* (1967) and Willis' *Learning to Labour*. A comparison of Hargreaves and Willis clearly shows how explanations couched, respectively, in terms of the process of *educational* and *cultural* differentiation understand variations in working-class educational experiences. This comparison and a more detailed examination of Willis' contribution will provide a basis for spelling out why an alternative interpretative framework is needed and what it might look like.

We begin with Hargreaves' *Social Relations in a Secondary School*. Hargreaves was interested in showing how educational processes worked to the disadvantage of working-class pupils. He recognized that, within the secondary modern school, pupils from a similar social background were streamed and treated differently by teachers depending upon their position in the scholastic hierarchy, and that pupils reacted to their situations in different ways. Hargreaves found that pupils in the A and B streams were more likely to exhibit pro-school attitudes and pupils in the C and D streams to exhibit a strong dislike for school, and that this differentiation led to the development of an anti-school subculture. He argued that in the early years most pupils conform to the normative order of the school. It is only as pupils move through the secondary school that they begin to evaluate their school performance against those of their peers and assess future life chances. The polarization of pupil subcultures is the direct result of the hierarchical ordering of pupils which the adolescent understands to represent a corresponding hierarchy of social worth. Within such a regime Hargreaves argues that pupils in the lower streams experience failure and rejection, for which the anti-school subculture offers compensation:

> When the school system is viewed in the setting of societal values, the upper stream members are 'successful' and their efforts and values are rewarded by the status they derive. The low stream boys are 'failures'; they are status deprived both in school and in society; their efforts meet with little success. Their problem of adjustment is solved by rejection of societal and teacher values, for which are substituted a set of peer group values, and status derived from conformity to a reversal of societal and teacher values. (p. 176)

The anti-school subculture is believed to result from the problem confronting a large proportion of male working-class pupils due to their inability to succeed in terms of the 'middle-class measuring rod'. Scholastic failure is assumed to require the collective solution made possible by the anti-school subculture, offering a way of compensating for failure on educational and societal criteria. In Hargreaves' account differences in educational and occupational aspirations are seen as resulting from differences in school performance, which in turn present pupils in the lower streams with the problem of coming to terms with a future in semi-skilled and unskilled employment. Willis alternatively argues that the difficult thing to explain about how working-class pupils get working-class jobs is not how the school allocates these pupils to the lower bands, but why working-class pupils voluntarily 'fail' themselves. Rather than attempt to explain educational failure in terms of the available *means* to succeed within the school, and the polarization of pupil subcultures as resulting from the process of *educational* differentiation, we have already noted that Willis viewed middle- and working-class kids as culturally distinct. What happens in the school is simply an expression of cultural differences which originate outside it.

The basic contention of Willis' approach is that the development of a counter-school (non-conformist) culture, is not a *consequence* of educational failure as implied by Hargreaves but a *cause*. In the attempt to explain how the process of *cultural* differentiation occurs within the school, Willis starts from the assumption that all pupils are more or less conformist until the third year of secondary school, a view shared by Hargreaves and others. It is at this time that pupils engage in an 'opportunity–cost' assessment of what conformity to the school can offer. According to Willis, the result of this assessment is relatively independent of the pupil's location within the school. Working-class pupils do not evaluate their relationship with the school in terms of what the school might offer, given their location in the academic order, but in terms of the consequences which academic success has for *being* a working-class adult. It is the class cultural definition of a future in manual labour offering little intrinsic reward, he argues, which leads to the basic exchanges on offer within the school – knowledge for qualifications, qualified activity for high pay and pay for goods and services – to be rejected. Willis outlines two basic features of the counter-school culture: an opposition to teacher authority and a distinction between 'the lads' and the 'ear 'oles' (conformist pupils). The lads' opposition to the school and other groups of pupils is expressed as a style, centring on clothes, cigarettes and alcohol. These serve to separate the lads from other groups of pupils and lead to a direct opposition to the authority of the school.

Accordingly, the school is seen as an arena for perpetual conflict and resistance – 'a fight between cultures' (p. 18). This way of understanding the counter-school culture leads him to bestow considerable political significance on its styles and actions. Indeed, Willis argues that the counter-school culture represents working-class *impulses* (particularly the rejection of individualism) which allows them an insight into the conditions of the working class in capitalist Britain, leading:

> towards an exposure of inequality and the determining relationships of capitalism and the construction of a possible basis of collective action for change by the social group concerned. (p. 174)

However, these class cultural 'penetrations', as he calls them, are rarely uncontaminated. Indeed it is the rejection of the aims of the school and teacher authority which, in contradictory and unintended ways, ensures the social reproduction of the most disadvantaged group of manual employees: their self-damnation is experienced 'as true learning, affirmation, appropriation, and as a form of resistance' (p. 3). What is of immediate interest is Willis' lack of an adequate explanation of why large numbers of working-class pupils do not reject school. This major flaw in his analysis results from his identification of the counter-school culture as the *normal* working-class response to school. This is due to a characterization of the middle and working classes as culturally distinct, and to the assumption that the development of pro- and anti-school responses are a manifestation of these cultural differences. By identifying the counter-school culture as the *normal* working-class response, Willis is left with the problem of explaining why some working-class pupils do not develop an anti-school subculture yet still fail, and why some are academically successful.

The problem with Willis' account of the counter-school culture stems, in part, from a desire to avoid an 'over-socialized' or individualistic account of school 'failure'. We have seen that Willis rejects any attempt to explain working-class educational experiences in terms of family 'types'. He also claims that educational performance has little influence on who will engage in the counter-school culture, since he sees it as a *cultural choice* operating independently of educational experience. He is consequently led to an explanation of other working-class responses to school – lumped together as conformist responses – as the results of the ideological incorporation of such pupils into bourgeois modes of thought.

The problem with this account is that Willis restricts the possibility of a 'truly' working-class response to the 'cultured few' who reject the school. This ignores the possibility that some pupils may comply with the school without being conformist, and that certain types of compliance *may be as much an authentic working-class response as that which leads to a rejection of the school.* Such a possibility is absent because he shares with other Marxists the assumption that, because the school is a middle-class institution, any compliance with it amounts to a sell-out of one's class membership. Such compliance, therefore, has no significance for Marxist writers, including Willis, beyond showing how successful the bourgeoisie have been in incorporating large numbers of working-class kids into the school and securing acceptance of their subordination beyond the school gates. Hence, a further problem with Willis' explanation of differences in working-class responses is that while he recognizes autonomy and creativity in the affairs of the rebellious minority he does so at the cost of refusing to recognize the same human qualities in the majority of working-class pupils who do not become one of 'the lads' (sic).

Despite the contribution which Hargreaves and Willis have made to our understanding of working-class responses to school it is necessary to transcend explanations which centre on *educational* or *cultural* differentiation *alone*. Hargreaves' reliance on explaining differences in working-class responses to school in terms of the process of educational differentiation leads him to mark off a pro- and anti-school subculture on the basis of educational performance as indicated by their membership of the upper or lower streams or bands. Such an approach is inadequate because it assumes that pupil subcultures are a *consequence* of educational location which generate corresponding subjective evaluations among working-class pupils as either 'successes' or 'failures'. This has all the problems of the structural accounts already described and in particular it understands class cultural differences in orientations to school merely as attributes to which teachers react as indicators of (in)educability. This ignores the possibility that working-class pupils may actively limit their involvement in the school well before pupil subcultures are manifest and may not share the same definitions of success and failure as those of the teacher.

The interest generated in Willis' class cultural explanation results from the suggestion that the counter-school culture is not a *consequence* of educational failure, but a *cause*. This is, however, to replace one *over-simple* explanation of working-class educational experiences with another *equally* simplistic account. It is perfectly legitimate to argue that reference to educational location is inadequate as a means of explaining why pupils adopt different pupil subcultures, but to suggest that the development of an anti-school subculture can itself be taken as the sole means of *explaining* working-class educational failure vis-à-vis middle-class pupils is equally inadequate. The reason why Willis' account cannot provide a proper basis for understanding differential scholastic attainment between working- and middle-class pupils is simple; by the time the process of cultural differentiation is under way (around the third year of secondary school) the *real* battle (i.e. access to O level examination routes) is reaching its conclusion! If a cultural explanation of the sort advanced by Willis is to have any validity, if it is the case that the best way of explaining working-class educational failure is to understand why they 'fail themselves', it would be necessary to demonstrate that the process of *cultural* differentiation begins on entry to school rather than almost a decade later.

He offers neither an account of the factors which determine who joins the rebellious lads rather than the conformist ear'oles, nor an explanation of why some remain true to their class membership and reject the school, while others sell out and conform to apparently middle-class definitions of school, which is the only sense Willis can make of working-class pupils who do bother to 'make an effort'. This understanding of pupil careers is therefore ahistorical, because it takes no account of pupil location in the academic order, and previous educational experiences. Consequently Willis' account fails to provide an adequate explanation of why working-class pupils respond to the school in different ways, because it ignores the possibility that there may be other school structure/class cultural relations which lead pupils from a working-class background to 'make an effort' in school rather than totally rejecting it, and because the very qualities of human agency and creativity which Willis portrays as indispensable for understanding the counter-school culture of the lads are completely absent in his account of other working-class pupils and school leavers.

BI-POLAR MODELS OF MALE PUPIL CULTURES

Two further problems need to be noted which are common to both Willis and Hargreaves. Firstly, both accept that pupil culture can be described in terms of a bi-polar model of conformity/ nonconformity; anti/pro-school. This assumption is not without its critics. Woods (1980), and Hammersley and Turner (1980) have criticized writers who adopt a bi-polar model of pupil culture for presenting a simplistic account of the day-to-day experiences of schooling. Woods (1980) has gone so far as to argue that the concept of *conformity* is at odds with interactionist concerns and should be understood as *one* form of negotiation (p. 15). Equally, Hammersley and Turner (1980) have noted that:

> Once we recognize the multiplicity of orientations which even 'official' school values can produce, and also the existence of multiple alternative values and interests, it becomes clear that the pro/anti schema does not adequately capture the complex patterning of pupil perspectives. (p. 31)

I have a great deal of sympathy with Hammersley and Turner's criticisms of the descriptive validity of bi-polar models of pupil culture, but to move from the inadequacy of such models to focus on the shifting moment-to-moment features of school process loses more than it gains. For example, in Woods' book, *The Divided School* (1979), a typology of pupil adaptations is outlined of which we are told 'there are bits of all of them in most people' (p.

78). This may be true, but which bits are most commonly adopted by which pupils? The attempt to specify the origins of pupil adaptations leads Woods to introduce a bi-polar distinction between 'conformist' and 'dissonant' pupil subcultures, which he admits are the 'immediate source or origin of pupil adaptations' (p. 82). It surely follows, therefore, that we must begin with pupil subcultures to specify the range of adaptations which these generate.

The problem appears to be that those who rightly reject the 'phenomenal' simple mindedness of 'bi-polarism' seek to remedy it by more detailed analysis of the process of meaning construction within the school as an interactional context, while those who, like Willis, transcend this narrow focus by referring to processes in culture and society outside the school, still resort to a bi-polar view of the meanings generated within it. This draws our attention to the necessity of devising a theoretical framework which not only allows us to do justice both to the complexity of meanings generated within the school and their relation to wider societal processes, but also gives a proper place to both agency and structure in the determination of educational experiences.

Secondly, in order to account for the full range of working-class responses to school Hargreaves and Willis can also be criticized for conducting studies of boys which ignore gender differences in educational and labour market experiences. The fact that girls and boys may experience the school in different ways is well documented (Deem 1978; Delamont 1980). This recognition owes much to feminist researchers who have noted the absence of half the school population in accounts of education and the working class. These writers have made an important contribution to the existing male-dominated literature, but it seems to me that what remains to be fully explored is the interrelationship between class and gender (see Chapter 3).

What remains to be done in this chapter is to outline an interpretative framework which goes some way towards overcoming the opposition on which current explanations of working-class educational behaviour are premised; which force a choice between explanations in terms of educational or cultural differentiation; of pupil acceptance or rejection.

WORKING-CLASS FRAMES OF REFERENCE (FORS)

In the search for an approach which links class location and educational experience in a way which is sensitive to variations in working-class responses to school, Bourdieu's notion of *habitus* (1977) appears to have some explanatory potential. Bourdieu attempts to explain how symbolic modes of domination are generated and how social inequality is reproduced, particularly through the school because of its role in legitimating the existing structure of power and class. Bourdieu and Passeron (1977) recognize that pupils' minds on entry to the school are not *tabulae rasa*, that they bring with them distinct cognitive structures which are the result of an 'unconscious' calculation of life-chances characteristic of particular social groups or classes. Habitus, Bourdieu suggests:

> represents a sort of deep-structuring cultural matrix that generates self-fulfilling prophecies according to different class opportunities.
>
> (Swartz 1981: p. 370)

The self-fulfilling prophecies are learnt by the child in the early years of life and are systems of durable, transposable dispositions (Bourdieu 1977, p. 72) which operate as a 'generative principle' lasting throughout life and in different social settings such as the school and the workplace. The unconscious calculation of life-chances leads those practices and future experiences which are most improbable to be excluded:

> either totally without examination, as *unthinkable*, or at the cost of the *double negation* which inclines agents to make a virtue of necessity, that is, to refuse what is anyway refused and to love the inevitable.
>
> (Bourdieu 1977: p. 77)

It is in the latter sense that Bourdieu would probably interpret the fetishization of manual labour power among the working-class male youth studied by Willis.

The problem with the way in which the habitus is constructed by Bourdieu need not detain us, but the way Bourdieu and Passeron use it in their study of social class and schooling deserves some attention. In their study of social class and schooling, one would have expected them to show how the internalization of restricted educational and employment opportunities would lead pupils to show little interest in school. If differences in the habitus of working-class children and the way in which the structure and organization of the educational system acts to reinforce or trans- form it had been clearly specified, the idea of habitus might have offered a way of overcoming approaches relying either on the process of educational or on cultural diffentiation. But as a result of identifying the school as the central institution in the legitimation and reproduction of social inequality, habitus became understood as little more than a bundle of values and attributes which predispose children unequally to master the middle-class culture taught in school.

Much of Bourdieu and Passeron's analysis is then devoted to explaining how the school must *convince those it fails* that they have *chosen* the destinies 'which social destiny has assigned to them in advance' (p. 208), the presumption being that the school has to legitimate *its* exclusion of working-class pupils. However, these authors do allow some degree of autonomy to the pupils themselves, since they distinguish between what they call 'deferred self-elimination', which appears to mean failure in examinations, and 'immediate elimination on the basis of a forecast of the objective chances of elimination' – not bothering to work for examinations because they do not think they have any chance of being successful. Apparently, therefore, some working-class pupils are failed by the school in competitive examinations with middle-class pupils, but others fail themselves because of a cultural understanding of school as irrelevant to their future lives. This attempt to give pupils themselves a role in determining the outcome of their education runs against the main tenor of Bourdieu and Passeron's account. If the unconscious internalization of working-class life-chances leads pupils from a working-class background to develop extremely limited expectations of what the school has on offer for the 'likes of us', why should the school have to legitimate the exclusion of working-class pupils from higher education and middle-class jobs, and why should Bourdieu and Passeron feel that the educational system is increasingly having to resort to the 'soft approach' (p. 209), of 'cooling out' pupils through examination failure? They claim that the school is increasingly a 'symbolic government condemned to disappoint in some the *aspirations it engenders in all*' (pp. 209–210, emphasis added). Unfortunately, these variations in the way the school has to legitimate educational failure are for Bourdieu and Passeron nothing more than the time required for the excluded to persuade themselves of the legitimacy of their exclusion (p. 209).

Although the concept of habitus has the potential for demonstrating the interrelationship between class location and educational experience, Bourdieu and Passeron's concern to demonstrate that the educational system functions as a key institution in advanced capitalist societies for the reproduction of social inequalities leads to a naïve structural account of working-class educational experiences. Moreover, there are at least two further reasons why a different conceptual schema is needed. Firstly, when the idea of habitus is related to concrete situations, it becomes difficult to unravel what the concept is being used to describe or explain. Swartz (1981) notes that 'habitus' presents a number of conceptual and empirical ambiguities and that its conceptual versatility, which permits the movement between different levels of abstraction, 'frequently renders ambiguous just what the concept actually designates empirically' (p. 346). Secondly, the problem for Bourdieu, which he shares with Willis, is how to explain variations in working-class orientations to school and employment. The way the working-class habitus (or culture?) is understood by Bourdieu represents an extreme form of social and occupational closure. Jenkins (1982) has correctly noted that Bourdieu's understanding of the working-class habitus relies on

> an almost lumpen model of the working class which ignores that class's internal differentiation and stratification and underestimates the importance of the *possibility* of mobility limited in scale and scope, in the legitimation of patterned domination. (p. 278)

In this study it will be shown that among working-class pupils at least three different ways of *being* in school and *becoming* adult can be identified: 'getting in', 'getting on' or 'getting out' (see Chapter 4). An important minority of pupils reject school as boring, irrelevant and frequently repressive. Here there is a concern to 'get into' the culture proper: away from a world of school kids and into the world of working-class adults and employment at the earliest possible opportunity. Others are more willing to accept the demands of school life and 'swot' for examinations, usually because they believe that by arming themselves with enough qualifications to compete for middle-class jobs they can 'get out' of their class of origin. Yet the majority of ordinary working-class pupils neither simply accept nor reject the school, but comply with it. It will be shown that the ordinary kids made an effort in school because they believed that modest levels of endeavour and attainment, usually leading to CSEs, would help them 'get on' in working-class terms. In the working-class neighbourhoods of Middleport 'getting on' usually meant boys being able to find apprenticeships and girls entering clerical and personal service jobs.

Getting in, getting on, or getting out represent different focal concerns among working-class youth and will be called working-class *frames of reference* (FORS). The idea of a FOR is intended to fill the conceptual space between pupil orientations and strategies in school and class location. Anchoring the idea of pupil frames of reference between class location and classroom processes enables us to make the connection between the way pupils respond to school and how these responses relate to wider social processes. Before elaborating the notion of FOR in more detail, it is necessary to say something about the term 'working-class'.

While there is a vast literature on the concept of class and its use in social research, and much debate about its meaning and heuristic value, there is universal agreement that class refers to the economic aspect of inequality. Moreover, regardless of how it is defined theoretically, when it is used in social and educational research occupation is taken as an indicator. In this study in Middleport, South Wales, the two comprehensive schools which provide the major source of data are both in working-class neighbourhoods, where the majority of employed fathers are in skilled and semi-skilled manual occupations; it is by virtue of these occupations that they can be treated as part of the working class. Having identified the class location of most of the respondents of this study, in this somewhat crude manner, it is possible to explore different aspects of the category thus defined, and these aspects need not necessarily be economic. The term 'social class' (Marshall 1950) is frequently used in the British literature to refer to hierarchically ranked cultural groupings. Rosser and Harris (1965) suggest in their study of family life and social change in South Wales that it is probably more fruitful to think of social classes primarily as broad cultural groupings which cannot be reduced to distinctions between occupational categories, because there are also important regional factors to be taken into account (Massey 1985).

Another reason why it is more fruitful to understand occupational categories in terms of broad cultural groupings is that snapshots of occupational categories ignore the fact that the working-class neighbourhoods of Middleport have their own history which provides a fund of knowledge and experience about what it means to be a working-class pupil or to be unemployed in a given locality. This historical dimension of social class is crucial. As Thompson (1977) has expressed it, 'to understand class we must see it as a social and cultural formation, arising from

processes which can only be studied historically' (p. 12). Therefore, the attitudes, values and conduct of working-class pupils
and school leavers in Middleport are not wholly invented *de novo*
by them; 'they draw upon a fund of experience built into their
lives outside the school and built up historically within working-
class communities in general' (Giddens 1986: p. 299).

The significance of this approach will become apparent in the
following discussion. Of note here is that the cultural resources,
which include the communication of different ways of *being* in
school and *becoming* adult, reflect past processes rather than the
present experiences of increasing numbers of working-class
adults due to the large-scale redundancies and plant closures
which once provided the ordinary kids with the opportunity to
'get on' in working-class terms (Harris *et al.* 1987). An
examination of the way working-class pupils and school leavers
are now making sense of the role of the school and their future
employment is a major task of this study, but it is readily apparent
that the cultural resources available to working-class children in
Middleport in the 1980s may equip large numbers of working-
class pupils to cope with the prospects of a livelihood which many
of them will no longer be able to attain.

Having argued that it is necessary to maintain the idea of a
working-class culture in Middleport which involves particular
ways of thinking, feeling and acting, and which are the historical
product of sharing the same location in a set of class relations, it is
a mistake to conclude that this must have led to a consensus
among the working class as to the role and purpose of the
educational system. It did not. Not only did working-class pupils
respond to the school in different ways, so too did their parents.
Some parents thought that school was a total waste of time, while
most appeared to view the school not only as something that
everybody has to go through, but also as a way of getting a few
qualifications which appeared to help their children to get 'tidy'
(good) working-class jobs. There were also some who believed
that the school offered an 'escape route' for their children,
although the number of parents seeing the school in this way was
probably very small. This characterization of the attitudes of
working-class parents in Middleport was not based on systematic
investigation and remains extremely tentative. What impact long-
term unemployment will have on parental attitudes to the educational system also remains unclear. What can be stated with greater
confidence, however, is that in Middleport there are important

social divisions and differences in working-class life styles (Bulmer 1975; Jenkins 1983). Such social divisions have usually been expressed by sociologists in terms of a continuum between the 'rough' and 'respectable'.

Therefore, working-class culture needs to be understood as a stock of commonly available cultural *resources* which people in the same class location use in different ways to order their social conduct and make sense of their changing life histories and social situations. It follows that the range of working-class responses to the school cannot be explained simply as the expression of working-class culture because pupil responses to the school will, at least in part, reflect a *selection* from that culture, unless we regress to a form of explanation relying on differences in working-class family 'types' or condemn the majority of Middleport children to the lowly status of ideological dupes as the price for celebrating Willis' lads as cultural heroes.

The reason for introducing the notion of pupil frames of reference is to enable a conceptual link to be made between pupil identity and wider meaning structures which are class specific. FORS are class specific because they represent the 'typical' ways in which working-class pupils from Middleport construct and assign meaning to different ways of being in school and becoming adult. Therefore, although the moral careers of pupils are lived by individuals they are at the same time the typical destinies of members of collectivities (Abrams 1982: p. 282). Thinking in terms of FORS therefore provides a conceptual link between pupil and social identity. It enables us to examine variations in working-class responses to school without losing sight of the fact that the way working-class pupils behave in school is the result of an interplay between the class cultural resources which are deployed in school, and internal school processes. It is also useful because it conveys the idea that FORS are not only constructed on the basis of past experience, but also include a projection into the future which provides the individual with a sense of continuity, predictability and meaning during a time of considerable uncertainty as they seek to make the transition from childhood to adulthood. During the final stages of schooling it is occupational identity which lies at the heart of the individual's life-line between childhood and adulthood. This is not to suggest that all school leavers have a clear idea of what job they want, but they are aware of the sort of jobs they would like and which they have a chance of getting. The existence of different FORS among working-class youth registers the fact that they are knowledgeable agents who have their own theories about life and their particular place in society. Pupil FORS are creatively constructed, reproduced, and transformed drawing upon the raw materials of class culture. This culture is the historical product of the past educational and labour market experiences of working-class people in Middleport. There-fore, the rapid increase in youth unemployment during the time these pupils were in the secondary school, has serious consequences for becoming adult and for the collective under-standing of what it means to be a working-class pupil in school.

It is because of an interest in the inter-connection between typical ways of being in school and becoming adult that the notion for FOR is used, rather than the concept of 'social identity', which I prefer to define more narrowly. For example, while male and female pupils have different social identities, they may share similar FORS when it comes to making sense of the school and transition into adult life. The FORS which actually exist among these working-class pupils is an empirical question which can only be answered by examining pupil orientations to school and employment, rather than being simply 'read off' from their class location. It is only when we have identified the character of working-class FORS that we can begin to evaluate the impact of the collapse of the transition from school to work for the individuals involved, for the school, and for the society of which they are a part.

During primary socialization in the family, children are *not* simply taught what they might expect to *become* in adult life, given an assessment of objective life chances. Rather, what is taught and externalized in action is a way of being in the world, which is implicitly communicated through the day-to-day social practices of significant others. Messages concerning who the child is and what the school is for will vary between (and sometimes within) households. Indeed the early experiences of the child in school may change the way parents think about the school. On entering the educational system these 'ways of being' in the world are externalized in *action*, which in the interactional process between teachers and pupils may lead pupils to actively limit their involve-ment and responsiveness to the day-to-day demands made by teachers. The school exposes the vast majority of children to alternative understandings of what it has to offer them and the sort of persons they might become. However, unless teachers can clearly show working-class pupils that there are 'real' opportunities to be gained from 'swotting' in school (see Chapter 4) in terms of social and educational advancement (which is usually seen to require access to O level study), it is extremely unlikely that they will orient themselves to the school in this way, although being offered such opportunities is no guarantee that working-class pupils will work for school success.

Teachers, for their part, are constantly engaged in a process of sifting and selection, which will frequently lead them to evaluate differences in pupil responses as representing actual and/or potential (in)educability. Therefore, pupil location in the academic order of the school cannot be explained solely in terms of the attitudes towards school exhibited by children, or as a result of the teacher's evaluation of the child's academic potential, which leads to the channelling of pupils into structurally different opportunities for academic success. It is the interplay between the pupils' collective understandings of being in the school and the school's own selection processes which provides the basis for understanding pupil FORS as they approach school-leaving age.

This approach offers a more fruitful basis for explaining why working-class pupils come to see the school in different ways. The study of working-class FORS also offers a way of overcoming the traditional, but spurious, division between the individual and society because the study of FORS must recognize that they are constructed through the meshing together of two types of historically organized time: the life history and the history of societies (Abrams 1982: p. 250), neither of which can be understood without understanding both. As Abrams has pointed out, the process of identity formation, or in this case of pupil FOR:

> and the process of social reproduction are one and the same. In so far as we can understand personal identity and social structure not as distinct states of being but as elements in a single process of becoming . . . the bases for such an understanding are to be found . . . in the empirical study of the 'becoming' of identities and societies. (p. 262)

There is no need to outline all that is entailed in Abrams' 'problematic of structuring' or, for that matter, Giddens' equally useful 'theory of structuration' (1986). Such approaches are important because they provide what Giddens calls 'sensitizing devices' (p. 326) for thinking about social life. The above quotation from Abrams should sensitize us to the fact that a study of the personal troubles confronting ordinary kids when opportunities for 'getting on' in working-class terms are collapsing around them, cannot be separated from the contemporary crisis in the educational system and British society, because the two events help to define each other (Erikson 1968).

There is a further compelling reason why the experiences of a relatively small number of pupils and school leavers from South Wales need to be theorized in the terms I have tried to outline in this chapter, namely that it holds out the promise of developing and enhancing 'the sociological imagination' in ways which have important implications for educational policy. According to Mills (1970), this imagination:

> enables its possessor to understand the larger historical scene in terms of its meaning for the inner life and the external career of a variety of individuals . . . .. It enables us to grasp history and biography and the relations between the two within society. (pp. 11–2)

The specific promise of this book is that it attempts to capture the relationship between the personal troubles of the ordinary kids and contemporary change in school and society. While it seems unlikely that a book about education and unemployment will be judged by its readers purely on the basis of the theoretical significance it is seen to have, the future direction of educational policy in fact depends crucially on the way the problem is cast. Mills makes the important distinction between 'private problems of milieu' and 'public issues of social structure'. Private problems concern the personal troubles confronting individuals or social groups of which they are directly and personally aware. 'A trouble is a private matter: values cherished by an individual are felt by him [or her] to be threatened' (p. 15). The personal troubles which threaten ordinary kids, stem from the fact that their FOR reflects past processes and practices rather than present circumstances.

It will be argued throughout this book that the personal troubles experienced by ordinary kids in Middleport are, in the main, a manifestation of public issues of social structure (Brown 1987a). A public issue, Mills tells us, is a public matter which often involves a crisis in institutional arrangements. The public issues which will be addressed concern the production and reproduction of educational and social inequalities. More specifically, they concern the way in which the state has defined the problem of youth unemployment and what it is doing about it. This is a public issue because as Mills tells us in a well-known passage from *The Sociological Imagination*:

> When, in a city of 100,000, only one man is unemployed, that is his

personal trouble, and for its relief we properly look to the character of the man, his skills, and his immediate opportunities. But when in a nation of 50 million employees, 15 million men are unemployed, that is an issue, and we may not hope to find its solution within the range of opportunities open to any one individual. The very structure of the problem and the range of possible solutions require us to consider the economic and political institutions of the society, and not merely the personal situation and character of a scatter of individuals. (p. 15)

The question of youth unemployment, therefore, is a public issue because the state has sought vocational solutions to youth unemployment which represent an attempt to maintain existing patterns of educational and social inequalities, at the expense of an alternative, and much needed, policy which is truly educational.

3 · Pupil orientations and youth unemployment

INTRODUCTION

The following two chapters will attempt to answer two specific questions. Firstly, who exactly are the ordinary kids and how do their attitudes to school and employment differ from other groups of pupils? Secondly, how have the ordinary kids responded to declining job opportunities for school leavers?

In Chapter 4 it will be shown that within the informal pupil culture (in all three schools) pupils identify three ways of 'being' in school, characterizable in terms of the *rems*, *swots*, and *ordinary kids*. The rems are usually non-examination pupils who are seen as unwilling to 'make an effort' in school both by other pupils and by teachers; their rejection of the school may or may not be manifest in the form of a conspicuous anti-school subculture. The swots are the academic pupils in the upper bands of the school, who are studying for O levels and intend to remain in full-time education beyond the age of 16. They are the pupils who are usually described by their peers as those pupils who always wear school uniform and 'suck up' to teachers. In schools such as Thomas High School and St Birinus, where the vast majority of pupils are from a working-class background, merely to study for O levels almost by definition invites labelling as a swot.

The ordinary kids stand somewhere between the rems and swots. They are not the high flyers but they do make an effort, yet without sucking up to teachers all the time. The ordinary kids are those pupils who are usually found in the middle bands, studying for CSEs rather than O levels. Most of them also intend to leave school at 16 years of age in the hope of finding a 'tidy' (good) working-class job.

In this chapter it will be shown that in schools where most pupils are from a working-class background, the rems, swots, and ordinary kid distinction reflects the adaptation of different orientations to the school. The rems have an alienated orientation, the swots a normative or normative instrumental orientation, and the ordinary kids an alienated instrumental orientation. [1]

For our initial purposes the questionnaire data collected while informants were still at school was divided into the *stayers* – those pupils who *intended* to continue their full-time education beyond the age of 16, most of whom were identified as the swots; and the *leavers* – those pupils who *intended* to leave school either before or after the CSE/O level examinations and look for work. The leaver category included most of the ordinary kids and rems. The distinction between stayers and leavers was based upon pupils' stated future intentions at the beginning of the Easter term in their fifth secondary year. These intentions and what pupils actually did when they attained school leaving age need to be clearly distinguished, as it will be shown in a later chapter that 40 per cent of the leavers eventually remained in full-time study in order to avoid the dole or Government schemes.

At least 80 per cent of the leavers were from manual working-class backgrounds, although this is an underestimation due to the problems associated with collecting accurate information from pupils about their parents' employment status.[2] Nevertheless, the leaver category represents a comparable group of pupils to those observed in other studies who have described working-class responses to school in terms of pupil acceptance or rejection (Hargreaves 1967; Willis 1977), and it will later be used to show why a bi-polar model of pupil acceptance or rejection is completely inadequate as a description and explanation of the ordinary kids' response to school.

The distinction between the stayers and leavers also raises the issue of gender differences in working-class responses. The problem is that, in line with other studies, female pupils were more willing to remain in full-time education at 16 years of age (58 per cent) than males (38 per cent). Whether this is also an indicator of gender differences in the way male and female pupils respond to the school will be considered in the following discussion. However, it is worth noting that later in this chapter the questionnaire data will be reorganized in terms of swots, rems, and ordinary kids; as a result, some of the female stayers are recategorized for reasons which will become apparent.

ARE THE ORDINARY KIDS CONFORMISTS?

The major task of this section is to examine whether the ordinary kids (who are mainly in the leaver category), can be categorized within a bi-polar model of pupil acceptance or rejection. If a bi-polar model of pupil acceptance or rejection provided an adequate description of working-class educational behaviour, we would have expected pupil attitudes to be either strongly pro- or anti-school. A comparison between the stayers and the leavers did reveal significant differences in attitudes to school. Twenty-eight per cent of stayers and only 9 per cent of leavers reported 'liking school a lot'; 4 per cent and 19 per cent respectively reported 'disliking school a lot'. What is particularly interesting about Table 3.1 is that over two-thirds of leavers reported no 'strongly' positive or negative attitude to school, therefore Table 3.1 provides little evidence for supposing that we can classify the leavers' attitudes to school in strongly positive or negative terms. It is also worth noting that despite the larger proportion of female

Table 3.1 *School leaver attitudes to school by future intentions and sex (%)*

	Stayers			Leavers		
	M	F	Total	M	F	Total
Like it a lot	23	32	28	12	5	9
Like it a bit	48	42	45	51	42	47
Not sure	8	5	7	9	6	8
Dislike it a bit	21	14	16	12	24	17
Dislike it a lot	—	7	4	16	22	19
Total (number)	83	132	215	138	95	233

pupils among the stayers, it was the girls, not the boys, in the leavers category who had the more negative attitudes to school life.

Writers advocating a bi-polar model of pupil acceptance or rejection have assumed that there is a critical period which leads to a polarization of pupil attitudes to school. An examination of how pupils perceived their former attitudes and whether they felt them to have changed may elicit the extent to which pupils are aware of such a process having taken place. An investigation of attitude change regarding school is of interest not because it tells us whether pupils' attitudes have *actually* changed but because it shows whether pupils are aware of a crucial shift in attitude during their time at secondary school. When pupils were asked whether they thought their attitude to school had changed, close to two-thirds stated that they had (60 per cent of boys and 70 per cent of girls). This finding conforms to previous studies although it has been less frequently recognized that it is the girls who most often record change in attitudes to school. The point at which attitudes were believed to have changed also varied between the sexes, the third secondary year being the most commonly stated time of change among the boys and the fourth secondary year among the girls. However, none of this information tells us anything about the direction of change. The direction of attitude change is shown in Table 3.2, and reveals that the proportion of

Table 3.2 *Nature of attitude change by future intention and sex (%)*

	Stayers			Leavers		
	M	F	Total	M	F	Total
Like/more involved	30	20	24	22	18	20
Dislike/less involved	18	31	26	45	43	44
Quals more important	24	7	12	8	2	5
Work getting harder	12	31	26	15	27	21
Other	15	12	12	10	11	10
Total (number)	38	82	110	60	56	116

leavers reporting attitude change, who state a growing dislike of, and less involvement in, school (44 per cent) is over double that of those stating an increased liking or involvement (20 per cent). A further 15 per cent of boys and 27 per cent of girls felt that school work had become more difficult or demanding. The response that school has become more difficult or demanding again does not tell us in which direction pupil attitudes have changed, but it does imply some level of involvement in school.

When the leavers are contrasted with the stayers, fewer of those wishing to continue their studies claimed to have come to dislike and be less involved in school life. The girls in both pupil categories were more likely than the boys to emphasize that work was 'getting harder' and less likely to emphasize the increasing importance of qualifications. Indeed it is worth noting that only 8 per cent of boys and 2 per cent of girls in the leavers category cited the increased importance of qualifications, as the main reason for a change in their attitude to school, compared with 24 per cent of boys and 7 per cent of girls who intended to continue full-time study, as the main reason for a change in their attitude to school. Despite problems of interpretation, Table 3.2 does not offer convincing evidence of a dichotomous division in pupil attitudes to school even among the leavers which previous studies have led us to expect.

The data presented so far suggest that although a majority of leavers are aware of attitude change to school, such attitudes show greater variation than that which would justify differentiating leavers' attitudes in terms of a bi-polar model of pupil acceptance or rejection. A large number of leavers neither exhibit nor develop 'strongly' positive or negative attitudes to school. In the attempt to describe what a more adequate typology of pupil orientations to school might look like, one might ask why pupils hold the attitudes that they do towards the school.

According to Hargreaves (1967) the development of a pro- or anti-school response resulted from pupils' perceived locations in the scholastic order. If this is true, one would expect to find more pupils taking O levels to exhibit a greater liking for school than those not taking O levels. This was indeed found to be the case although differences were not as large as one might have expected. However, further analysis also revealed important differences in attitudes among pupils taking CSE examinations. Table 3.3 shows that those pupils taking three or more CSEs had attitudes to school which were more like those taking O levels than the non-examination pupils (two or less CSEs).[3] Therefore, a difference in attitude to school occurs between those pupils taking

Table 3.3 *Attitudes to school according to qualifications being studied – all pupils regardless of future intentions (%)*

	Non-academic		Academic
	Non-exam	Exam	Exam
	Two or less CSEs	Three or more CSEs	O levels
Like it a lot	6	19	20
Like it a bit	28	47	49
Not sure	8	8	7
Dislike it a bit	11	15	19
Dislike it a lot	47	11	6
Total (number)	36	178	231

at least a few examinations, rather than between the academically successful and the rest.

This raises some doubts about Hargreaves' belief that attitudes to school will correspond to location in the academic pecking order, but it might be thought to lend some support to Willis' view that those who are taking qualifications are the conformists. However, the previous discussion already raises serious doubts about this claim, and further evidence of its inadequacy was apparent when the leavers were asked whether they thought school was a waste of time; only 5 per cent strongly agreed and 22 per cent stated the contrary. These figures again suggest that the vast majority of the leavers neither accept all of the perceived aims of the school, nor do they completely reject them. Therefore, the attitudes of a large proportion of the leavers cannot be explained away by simply *redescribing* them as the result of the ideological incorporation of working-class pupils into the middle-class culture of the school.

I do not wish to make any great claims about the data presented above in the ensuing discussion. It does not allow us to map pupil orientations to school, nor to begin explaining their existence. The channelling and selection of pupils for academic courses in the third, and early part of the fourth, year, is an important stage of the pupil's school 'career', and is perceived by pupils to be the time that their attitudes to school changed. But there was little evidence to suggest that such changes in attitude represented a great parting of the waves, dividing those who conform to school from those who do not. Despite the limitations of the above data it does lead to the suggestion that there is little support for the view that working-class responses to school can be understood in terms of either pupil acceptance or rejection, and that previous studies have incorporated what may in fact be a series of distinct working-class responses under the heading of 'conformist' or 'pro-school' pupil subcultures. It is these 'uncommitted' pupils who will be shown to be the ordinary kids. We therefore need to consider why these ordinary kids seem willing to make an effort in school whilst questioning its purpose and value.

WHY DO THE ORDINARY KIDS BOTHER TO MAKE AN EFFORT?

All pupils were asked what, if any, they thought were important subjects. Regardless of future intentions, mathematics was felt to be the most important subject by the boys (59 per cent), followed by English (29 per cent). The most important subjects reported by the girls were English (47 per cent) and mathematics (46 per cent). Pupils were then asked why they thought these subjects were important. Their responses were unequivocally *instrumental*. Over three-quarters of the leavers and 80 per cent of the stayers stated that these subjects were important in order to get a job. There was little difference between the sexes, with females recording the highest proportion of *instrumental* responses in each category. This finding challenges those of King (1971) that boys place a higher functional or instrumental value on school learning than girls, although it will be shown that this instrumentalism is directed towards different types of employment (Sharpe 1976; Byrne 1978).

It is evident that regardless of future intentions or sex a large number of pupils are *instrumental* about why they felt certain school subjects to be important. In an attempt to examine pupil attitudes to other school subjects, pupils were asked what subjects, if any, they liked. Table 3.4 shows that the most popular subjects among both male and female leavers were of a *practical* nature, although the subjects they liked were different. The most popular subjects for the boys were metalwork/woodwork. Approximately 41 per cent suggested that these were the subjects that they 'liked the most' (44 per cent Thomas High School, 37 per cent St Birinus, and 38 per cent Greenhill), compared with 2 per

Table 3.4 *Subjects reported as liked by those intending to continue their study and those intending to leave school (%)*

	Stayers			Leavers		
	M	F	Total	M	F	Total
English	5	24	17	12	19	15
Mathematics	18	8	12	7	11	9
Science	14	11	13	5	2	4
Humanities	18	21	20	14	13	13
Social/business/art	18	11	14	15	16	15
Wood/metalwork/T.D.	21	1	9	41	2	25
Domestic/office practice	2	20	13	1	33	14
Other	4	3	3	7	4	6
Total (number)	84	132	216	138	94	232

cent of the girls. One-third of the girls reported domestic and office practice subjects as the 'most liked' (35 per cent Thomas High School, 30 per cent St Birinus, two of the seven girls from Greenhill) compared with 1 per cent of the boys. Despite variations between schools and differences between the sexes in the subjects reported to be liked, what cannot be seen from the figures are the numbers of pupils from each sex taking a particular subject, as it seems unlikely that pupils will express a liking for a subject which they are not studying.

The channelling of pupils into subject areas viewed as most appropriate for each sex has been noted on numerous occasions (see Deem 1978; Spender and Sarah 1980; Delamont 1980). In Thomas High School there was certainly evidence that although teachers rarely overtly encouraged boys and girls to opt for sex stereotypical school subjects, the organization of subject choices in the fourth year made it extremely difficult for pupils to study a combination of subjects which did not conform to the division between woodwork, metalwork, motor mechanics, and technical drawing on the one hand, and childcare, home economics, and office practice on the other (Sutherland 1981: pp. 13–5). Indeed, boys were not permitted to take childcare, nor girls car mechanics in Thomas High School because they were told that there were not enough resources to cater for more than a small number of pupils, and therefore priority was given to girls and boys on the basis of the subject's perceived future relevance to individual pupils.[4]

There was also evidence that the subjects which pupils most enjoyed studying were also motivated by *instrumental* concerns. There was a clear link between the lessons pupils reported liking and occupational preferences. Among the male leavers who named a *practical* subject as the one they most liked, 78 per cent also had a desire to enter skilled engineering or building jobs. There was greater variation amongst the female leavers both in terms of the lessons they liked and the jobs they wanted (see below). However, almost two-thirds of girls who named domestic/ office practice as the subject they most liked, also mentioned personal services or clerical jobs as the ones they particularly wanted. If the subjects the leavers report as enjoyable are compared with the stayers, we find an important difference in the school subjects stated regardless of sex. Among the stayers there was a closer relationship between occupational preferences and *academic* (rather than practical) subjects, and over 60 per cent aspired to professional occupations.

The empirical findings of this study present a complex picture of pupil attitudes and involvement in school, and there are at least two conclusions which need to be noted from the foregoing information. First, it reveals that whilst there are important gender differences in educational experiences, *instrumental* attitudes based on the perceived relationship between school activity and future employment, dominated both male and female orientations to school. Thus, although boys and girls often studied different combinations of subjects, and preferred different jobs, a large proportion of the 'leavers' category were both primarily interested in the *practical* rather than *academic* content of school life. This should not be interpreted as the translation of a necessity into a virtue, given a probability of failure in academic subjects, but as a class cultural response which cross-cut gender divisions.[5] It is based on a cultural difference in the significance attached to *mental* and *manual* activity both in and outside school. Working-class girls and boys do not therefore inhabit different worlds within the school, and in the attempt to understand their educational behaviour, class and gender should not be understood as 'alternative or competing discrete modes of behaviour, but interactive – sometimes supporting, sometimes conflicting – pressures that are worked out on an individual basis' (Hogan 1982: p. 49).

Second, the combination of instrumental attitudes to school and an interest in practical rather than academic subjects helps us to understand why a large proportion of 'leavers' who have been identified as the ordinary kids are both willing to make an effort in school, yet reject much of what is taught as being boring and irrelevant. It would appear, therefore, that those who have advocated a bi-polar model of working-class responses to the school have failed to distinguish *behavioural* from *normative* conformity. In other words the fact that a large proportion of working-class pupils have appeared willing to make an effort in school, does *not* mean that we can assume that they accept the culture of the school and the values it seeks to transmit. The failure to recognize this distinction has been one of the reasons why Willis failed to acknowledge anything other than an anti-school response as a truly working-class response.

By posing the study of working-class responses to school in terms of pupil acceptance or rejection of the dominant (academic) value system operating in the school, a tendency inevitably develops to talk in either/or terms – either they accept the *normative* order of the school or reject it. However, an adequate understanding of working-class responses to school cannot be achieved in these terms. It is difficult to see why pupil responses should have to be defined dichotomously. May not pupils fall somewhere between total acceptance or rejection? Pupils may reject some aspects of the *normative* order of the school whilst accepting others. It may be more adequate to talk of the attitudes of such pupils in terms of *indifference* to the school. Endeavours to develop such formulations are an improvement. Ball (1981), for example, has tried to show that there are further subdivisions within the pro- and anti-school division, but such efforts must ultimately meet with limited success because pupil responses cannot be adequately described by adopting a linear model, let alone a dichotomy of acceptance or rejection. Bi-polar models have also been challenged by a number of symbolic interactionist writers who have emphasized the variability in pupil adaptations to school life. However, as I have already noted in the previous chapter, and as the evidence in this and the next chapter clearly shows, the exclusive focus on pupil adaptations in the classroom situation misses the significance of individual responses being part of the patterned reproduction of educational experiences which involves collective cultural interpretations of different ways of being a working-class pupil.

A TYPOLOGY OF PUPIL ORIENTATIONS

In order to develop these ideas more fully, we can suggest that the pupil orientations to school are understandable in terms of pupil FORS – which provide the necessary conceptual link between pupil and social identity. This is not to deny that pupils from different social class backgrounds can have the same orientation to school, but rather that orientations have different class cultural significance (see the next chapter). The ongoing interpretation of experience determines not only the sense of being in the school but also a sense of becoming adult which then acts as a reference-point for the evaluation of school activity. It is the interrelationship between being in school and becoming adult, which makes pupil interpretations of the link between school activities and occupational future such a powerful reason for making an effort among *instrumental* pupils, such as the ordinary kids. It also offers clear evidence that if we ignore the broader class cultural context within which pupils deploy cultural resources to make sense of their present and future life, we will fail to understand the significance of the institutional experiences of working-class pupils. Occupational preference is therefore assumed to be central in understanding pupil orientations to school in the later years of secondary education, but this does not preclude a consideration of other elements of school and non-school life, which further reinforce or work against the adaptation of a particular orientation.

Orientations should therefore be understood in the 'weak' sense, which is described by Blackburn and Mann (1979) as involving an 'orientation profile' which includes a set of expectations and relative priorities which moves away from the idea of a 'cost–benefit analysis' being conducted by the individual with respect to a particular concern. The importance of this point will be shown in the next chapter, which reveals that the ordinary kids' response to youth unemployment is not simply based on an equation involving effort in school and chances of getting 'tidy' working-class jobs, but that being in school provides them with a sense of social worth, dignity, and predictability even though they are not academically successful.

Figure 3.1 below is a simple analytical model which is useful in attempting to describe pupil orientations to the *formal* culture of the school. This typology does not show the careers of any individual pupil in the school, but attempts to identify the empirical range of pupil orientations, and is developed from the work of Etzioni (1961). This typology overcomes many of the problems associated with adaptational models of pupil sub-cultures derived from Merton (1957) and reworked by Harary (1966), Wakeford (1969), and Woods (1979; 1983). Merton was interested in the relationship between socialization into common goals and the opportunities of individuals and social groups

Figure 3.1 A typology of pupil orientations to school

Elements of formal school culture	Orientations to the formal culture of the school		
	Ends	Means	Conditions
Academic	Normative	Normative Instrumental	—
Practical	—	Alienated Instrumental	—
None	—	—	Alienated

differentially located within the social structure to achieve those goals by legitimate means. The problem with Merton's typology is, of course, that it assumes the successful inculcation of societal goals, for example, a common view of the value of academic success. This problem is also acute when attempts are made to adapt Merton's typology to the study of pupil adaptations. In the attempt to overcome problems of adapting Merton's formulation to the study of schooling, Woods offers a revised typology to account for personal goals *and* means which proves to be unsatisfactory given that one might ask how one can be indifferent or rebellious to one's own *goals*.

In the typology below we try to identify the differential commitments of actors to the school, and how these relate to different elements of the formal school culture. The ends/means/conditions classification in Figure 3.1 is needed because pupils may be oriented to the school as:

● An *end* in itself: they comply with the school because they are intrinsically interested and motivated to learn for its own sake.
● A *means*: will lead to a critical attitude involving the continual evaluation of what the school provides in terms of its *instrumental* value.
● A *condition* of existence (Parsons 1949): pupils attend school because attendance is compulsory, and therefore s/he must attend often enough to avoid prosecution.

It can also be shown that the elements of the formal school culture represented by the school curriculum are differentially evaluated by teachers (and employers). Of particular salience is the high status associated with the *academic* subjects – chemistry, physics, English literature, etc. – and the low status and priority given to *practical* subjects, which are usually CSE or non-examination subjects – childcare, metalwork, community studies, etc.

There is also a need to distinguish elements of the formal school culture because Table 3.4 above revealed that although the majority of both stayers and leavers are orientated to school as a *means*, they were interested in different aspects of school life. The *instrumental* attitudes of the stayers were geared towards the *academic* curriculum, while that of the leavers was geared towards *practical* school subjects. And of course there were some pupils who were not willing to make an effort regardless of whether school lessons were of an academic or practical nature.

It is now possible to specify four orientations to school which apply to all pupils irrespective of gender or social class. Pupils who are orientated to the academic elements of the formal culture of the school, we will describe as having a *normative* orientation. Here school work is seen as an *end* in itself, that is, the intrinsic value of 'education' is accepted for its own sake. There is a propensity for such pupils to accept what the school is seen to stand for. Figure 3.1 shows that a normative orientation to school only applies with respect to the academic curriculum given the bias towards such studies and the high status teachers attach to academic endeavour. At the time of this study it appeared that although it is logically possible for a pupil to be orientated to the *practical* elements of the formal school culture as an *end*, the low status, poor facilities, general organization of the curriculum, and structure of examinations makes it difficult for pupils to devote more than a small part of their schooling to these subjects. Such an orientation is empirically rare (virtually non-existent in this study), and arguably this was true for the majority of comprehensive schools in Britain. What is fascinating about recent innovations such as the Technical and Vocational Education Initiative (TVEI) is that they are attempting to augment the practical aspects of the school curriculum and increase their status in the scholastic order of things. It will be argued that the attempt to win a degree of normative commitment from the ordinary kids who have an alienated instrumental orientation has become part of the battle to win the compliance of large numbers of working-class pupils as the instrumental value of school continues to decline because of high rates of youth unemployment (see Chapter 5).

Opposed to a *normative* orientation is that characterized by those pupils who develop an anti-school subculture. Although it is important to recognize that the development of an *alienated* orientation is a *necessary* but not a *sufficient* condition for the development of an anti-school subculture as I will show in the next chapter. An alienated orientation is characteristically held by non-examination pupils who are neither orientated to the school as an intrinsically valuable learning experience, nor as a means to his or her individual ends, for what he or she can get out of it.

A normative or alienated orientation to the formal culture of the school can be understood in terms of pupil acceptance or rejection, but where an orientation is adopted to the school as a *means* (i.e. as an instrumental orientation), it cannot easily be located along the same continuum. *Instrumental* responses to school represent an analytically distinct dimension. These pupils' primary orientation to the school is explicable in terms of their perceptions of its ability to facilitate desired individual ends, most notably by qualifying them for entry into certain types of employment. It is possible to distinguish two instrumental orientations to the formal culture of the school: *normative instrumental* and *alienated instrumental*. From a normative instrumental orientation, despite the predominance of the pursuit of qualifications, there may also be elements of intrinsic interest in the academic aspects of the formal school culture. This orientation is associated with pupils of both types of class background who have found their way into the upper bands or streams of the school and aspire towards middle-class occupations. What is learnt at school, even if it does not directly relate to the occupational or other interests of the pupils, is viewed as a necessary prelude to the acquisition of 'required' and 'desired' knowledge. Those subjects in which these pupils have little interest are tolerated as necessary in order to gain additional qualifications, if access to particular occupations and institutions of higher education is to be gained. These pupils are more attuned to the formal culture of the school than pupils adopting an alienated instrumental orientation, since the *types of employment these pupils aspire to are perceived to be 'knowledge-based'*. It is this characteristic of their future employment which acts to bring these pupils closer to the normative aspects of the formal culture of the school.

The opposite of the normative instrumental is the alienated instrumental orientation. Here, individuals' identities are divorced from much of what is taught. Their involvement in the school, in terms of identification with its perceived aims, and what teachers 'stand for', is fairly limited. However, there are elements of interest and perceived 'relevance', centring upon the practical elements of the formal culture of the school, although much of what is taught is perceived as 'irrelevant', and undertaken with a minimum level of personal investment simply to get qualifications. For these pupils, compliance is maintained predominantly to the extent that they perceive that if they continue to 'do a bit', at least they will have something to 'show' for their years at school. The logic of this situation (as they define it) tends to lead them to maintain a degree of involvement in their schooling, if only for what they perceive they can 'get out of it'. This becomes increasingly important in the later years of schooling, given that pupils are exposed to an increasing number of activities and outside interests which may bring them into conflict with what is expected of them in school.

Although pupils from most schools can be distinguished in terms of the four orientations identified, the orientations may have different significance for their incumbents within the informal pupil culture depending upon the social class composition of the school. In this study of working-class educational behaviour both normative and normative instrumental orientations were identified with the swots because they were studying for O levels and intended to stay in full-time study beyond the age of 16. The dominant FOR of these pupils is characterized in terms of 'getting out' of the working class. An alienated orientation is associated with the Rems whose FOR is characterized in terms of 'getting in' to the working class by staking their claim to adult status at the earliest opportunity. The dominant working-class response to school in Middleport is however an alienated instrumental orientation which is associated with the ordinary kids, who exhibit a FOR in terms of 'getting on' in the working class (see Chapter 4).

If this interpretation of pupil responses to school is correct it not only raises serious objections to previous accounts of schooling the working class, and particularly those which view the vast majority of working-class pupils as conforming to the normative order of the school, whether these accounts are Marxist or non-Marxist or whether they emphasize the process of educational or cultural differentiation. The incorporation of the ordinary kids has depended upon particular historical circumstances which have made the pupils see that by making a limited commitment to school there were clear benefits to be accrued when it came to looking for a 'tidy' working-class job.

THE IMPACT OF YOUTH UNEMPLOYMENT

The rapid decline in job opportunities for school leavers in Middleport has fundamentally altered this situation. It can be hypothesized, therefore, that any perceived change in the labour market for school leavers will have an impact on pupils who adopt some form of *instrumental* orientation to school and this may threaten (if not undermine) pupil compliance. The compliance of pupils have a normative and alienated orientation is unlikely to shift in response to market conditions since, by definition, such pupils are pursuing 'education' for its own sake, or already view the school as a waste of time. The perceived contraction of job opportunities simply reinforces the view among alienated pupils (the rems) that school is irrelevant to future occupational destiny. However, this should not completely rule out the possibility that as occupational opportunities for unqualified school leavers continue to decline, the school is less likely to be seen as an obstacle to their gaining adult independence, since there are no jobs anyway.

Pupils adopting a normative instrumental orientation have been shown to be more closely involved in the formal cultural activities of the school and to have intrinsic interests in elements of academic study. Whether their interest in education for its own sake is sufficient to ensure the basis of compliance and commitment necessary to succeed in O level and A level study remains an open question. However, an interest in the academic aspects of the curriculum is likely to enable the school to maintain compliance more easily than among pupils where the form of instrumentalism is not accompanied by an interest in the academic curriculum. Indeed, this chapter will offer tentative evidence that the swots who have this orientation (which, in the main, will be pupils from a middle-class background), may be responding to rising youth unemployment by intensifying the competition for O levels and A levels in the realization that failure to achieve academic success may not only lead them to take jobs they feel are beneath them, but may force them to go on a Government scheme or the dole.

It is working-class ordinary kids who adopt an alienated instrumental orientation whose continuing compliance is most immediately threatened by perceptions of declining job prospects in apprentice training among the boys, and low-level clerical and personal service occupations among the girls. The reason for this is that an interest in *practical* elements in the school curriculum is not sufficient to sustain compliance if such endeavour is not linked to perceptions of real opportunities to get the working-class jobs they want. The remainder of this chapter will seek to substantiate and develop an analysis of pupil orientations to school and particularly that of the ordinary kids, and of the way their response to school may be affected by the rapid decline in job opportunities.

In order to do this we need to gain a better idea of the types of jobs these pupils want. Does the alienated instrumentalism of the ordinary kids reflect a similar orientation to employment – the maximizing of financial rewards with the minimum of commitment to the job – or do such pupils hope for something more from employment than they expect from school? Are occupational preferences an expression of something more fundamental than simply a way of making a living? In this regard it will be argued that obtaining certain types of employment is central to the achievement by pupils of culturally specified adult roles to which they aspire, and that certain types of certification are seen as necessary to obtain work in these occupations. Moreover, if we are to make sense of the impact of youth unemployment on pupil responses to school, we need to know how they perceive the job situation, and not simply assume that they know there are no jobs for them, and how aspirations relate to expectations. How aspirations relate to reality will be an issue reserved for a later chapter.

The first task is to specify the sorts of jobs the pupils want and in order to do this the data needs to be reclassified on the basis of pupil orientation rather than on the basis of stayers and leavers. Firstly, a group of forty-nine 'alienated' pupils were identified among the leavers.[6] In addition, for our initial purposes pupils intending to enter colleges of further education were included in the stayers category. Closer analysis of this category revealed that 40 per cent of boys and 60 per cent of girls intending to continue their studies in a college of further education had occupational preferences and interests in school subjects characteristic of the ordinary kids rather than the swots who have a normative instrumental or normative orientation, and were looking to enter vocational courses such as nursery nursing, secretarial courses, hotel and catering and car mechanics, rather than the further academic study customarily undertaken by pupils in the sixth form. These pupils were consequently categorized as having an alienated instrumental orientation to school. A further difficulty arose because although all three schools operated a 'traditional' sixth form, in St Birinus there was a popular secretarial course, which competed favourably with similar courses in colleges of further education. The girls intending to go on these courses are also included in the alienated instrumental category. There is no attempt to distinguish pupils adopting a normative orientation from those adopting a normative instrumental one, given a primary concern with the ordinary kids who are most likely to adopt an alienated instrumental orientation, and because both these orientations were identified with the swots.

As a result of re-grouping pupils on the basis of orientation to school we have three categories of pupils: 49 alienated, 225 alienated instrumental, and 177 with a normative instrumental/ normative orientation. For primarily presentational reasons the terms rems, swots and ordinary kids will be used to represent pupils having these different orientations to school – the rems have an alienated orientation, the swots a normative or normative instrumental orientation and the ordinary kids an alienated instrumental orientation.

The refinement of pupil categories allows us to examine the relationship between pupil orientations and occupational preferences and what these young people feel to be the most important aspects of the job they hope to enter. Table 3.5 confirms a major difference in occupational preferences on the basis of both orientation to school and sex, for example, 4 per cent of rems, 10 per cent of ordinary kids and 77 per cent of swots state occupational preferences for administrative, professional and executive occupations.

Rems and ordinary kids show a greater propensity to prefer personal service, clerical, commercial and skilled building and engineering jobs. Half the male rems state preferences for skilled jobs compared to 57 per cent of male ordinary kids. The difference between these groups of boys is that the former do not perceive the school as a *means* of getting an apprenticeship, which can be

Table 3.5 *Pupil occupational preferences by orientations and sex (%)*

Preferences:	Rems			Ordinary kids			Swots		
	M	F	Total	M	F	Total	M	F	Total
Skilled building engineering occupations	50	—	24	57	2	33	7	1	3
Hotel and catering occupations	5	8	6	4	6	5	5	—	2
Personal services	—	46	24	1	33	15	—	7	4
Transport/storage	14	—	7	5	2	4	—	2	1
Clerical	—	17	9	2	33	15	2	5	3
Commercial	5	25	15	6	16	10	3	7	6
Professional and administrative occupations	5	4	4	16	3	10	81	75	77
Unskilled	14	—	7	3	—	2	—	—	—
Armed forces	9	—	4	7	4	6	3	2	3
Total (number)	22	24	46	121	94	215	62	83	145

acquired by 'askin' a'round'. Moreover where day-release is expected by employers, discussion with the rems suggests that they are unlikely to fulfil training requirements. Discussion with the male rems also suggested that although they would like 'a trade' if they could find one, they are not committed to such a future to the same extent as the ordinary kids.

Among the ordinary kids there was virtually no difference in the percentage from each school stating a preference for skilled engineering or building occupations. However, differences in occupational preferences between schools were more prominent among girls displaying preferences for personal service and clerical occupations from Thomas High School and St Birinus. In Thomas High School 45 per cent compared with 16 per cent of the girls from St Birinus have a preference for personal service occupations (particularly childcare), and 20 per cent in Thomas High School and 50 per cent from St Birinus show a preference for clerical occupations. Differences in occupational preferences between these schools demonstrate the impact that school subjects which are perceived to be *relevant*, and which are taught in an interesting way, can have on the development of particular occupational preferences, if not the cultural horizons of preferences. In Thomas High School, childcare is a very popular course as is the secretarial course in St Birinus for the girls.

Pupil occupational preferences also present a clear dichotomy in terms of gender: 57 per cent of male ordinary kids had occupational preferences for skilled engineering and building occupations, compared with 2 per cent of the girls. Conversely, a third of the girls but only one male preferred occupations in the personal services; a third as opposed to two males preferred clerical occupations; and 16 per cent of the girls compared with 6 per cent of the boys preferred commercial occupations.

If occupational preferences are important for understanding what jobs pupils are likely to apply for and whether they will be satisfied with what jobs they do get (if any), it is also necessary to consider what it is they want from their employment. Among pupils having some form of *instrumental* orientation to school (ordinary kids and a large proportion of swots), the school is believed to provide a means of securing a certain type of life style of which employment is a central feature. However, the instru-mentalism identified here must be clearly distinguished from the way an instrumental orientation has been conceptualized within industrial sociology (Fox 1980). The study of *instrumentalism* amongst industrial workers has focused on the way employment is seen by these workers as a means of obtaining the greatest monetary returns for their efforts (Goldthorpe *et al.* 1969). The pre-eminence of financial considerations in the selection and expectations of what employment has to offer is not exclusive to 'older' workers; for example, Ginzberg *et al.* (1951), in their initial outline of a theory of occupational choice, wrote that for young people from low-income families 'money assumes so central a position in the scheme of values as to overshadow education' (p. 134).

In Britain a number of sociologists have suggested that monetary rewards from employment lie at the heart of working-class attitudes to employment (Lane 1972; Corrigan 1979). Of particular interest in this book is the question of whether there are recognizable differences between pupil categories in terms of what they want from future employment and whether paramount importance is placed on monetary rewards. This is important because we want to know whether there is more at stake if the ordinary kids do not get the jobs they want than simply not getting as much pay as they had hoped. Pupils were asked what they thought was the *most* important thing to have in the job they wanted. Table 3.6 clearly shows that there are important differences between groups of pupils depending upon their orientation to school. The most important aspect of future employment among the rems (38 per cent) and ordinary kids (31 per cent), was the desire to have good workmates and/or good working conditions.[7] The most important aspect of future

Table 3.6 *Most important thing to have in work (%)*

	Rems	Ordinary kids	Swots	Total
Socially/environmentally satisfactory	38	31	23	29
Life progress/qualifications	10	16	7	12
Opportunity to learn a skill	5	12	4	8
Interesting/enjoyable work	21	20	43	29
Money	17	8	11	10
Security	5	5	8	6
Other	5	8	4	6
Total (number)	42	201	160	403

employment among the swots was the desire for work that is interesting/enjoyable (43 per cent).

The rems report the most concern for monetary rewards from future employment (17 per cent) but even among these pupils 'interesting work' records a higher response rate. This finding should in no sense be taken to imply that monetary rewards are of little importance to these young people (regardless of orientation), because the need for money is something which is frequently taken for granted. However, these figures do suggest that at this phase in the life course, the nature of future employment is accompanied by other considerations besides money. Among the rems this may include good workmates, which tends to support Willis' view of the importance of 'having a laff' both at school as well as on the shop floor, although the environmental responses were more prominent among the girls than boys within this category of pupils.

The importance of getting a job which is intrinsically interesting/enjoyable far exceeds any other response among the swots. The ordinary kids' response to achieving qualifications to do with the job and the opportunity to learn a skill, once more suggests the desire of the ordinary kids to progress *within the job* (particularly the boys) rather than through further *academic* endeavour favoured by the swot. However, overall figures should not blind us to the importance of gender differences, particularly among the ordinary kids. Almost twice the percentage of girls emphasize the importance of the working environment and good workmates compared to boys who have the same orientation. It is probably true to say that this is partly due to the perceived lack of training opportunities and career structure (no matter how limited) confronting female ordinary kids in the labour market.

The conclusion from the foregoing discussion is that differences in the types of employment pupils hope to enter and in what they want from their work are related to pupil orientations to school, particularly between the swots and the rest. It has been argued that the ordinary kids who have an alienated instrumental orientation are characteristic of pupils hoping to 'get on' in working-class terms and to become a working-class adult in a respectable fashion. However, despite sharing an alienated instrumental orientation, male and female ordinary kids have different occupational preferences and show some variation concerning what they want from employment. 'Getting on' for the boys usually involves having an apprenticeship and eventually becoming a 'skilled man'. Traditional paths into employer-based training programmes and the formal designation of skilled status are less evident for ordinary working-class women. There is evidence to support the view that 'getting on' for these girls depends to a larger extent on finding jobs which give the appearance of respectability (McRobbie 1978; Gaskell 1983) in terms of the environment they work in and the people they work with.

The above discussion also highlights the need to distinguish clearly the instrumental evaluation of school as a means of gaining *preferred employment*, from the instrumental evaluation of work as a means of gaining *monetary returns* recorded by industrial sociologists. The existence of an *instrumental* orientation *to school* does not imply the existence of an instrumental orientation *to work*. The ordinary kids do not simply seek jobs which they believe to be 'well paid' but also select jobs on the basis of other considerations such as learning skills or doing a job which is interesting and that supports a particular sense of working-class identity. Hence the occupational preferences of ordinary kids need to be understood in terms of their attempt to find employment which will allow them to 'get on' in working-class terms. Therefore, if they do not get the jobs they want there is far more than money to lose.

The discussion so far also shows that ordinary kids do have occupational preferences which relate to their interests and to their understanding of school activities. However, their chances of realizing occupational preferences is another question. Table 3.6 shows that there is little concern about job security, but this probably results from an understanding that the immediate problem confronting school leavers is one of getting a job rather than keeping a job.

THE IMPACT OF UNEMPLOYMENT ON THE ORDINARY KIDS' ATTITUDES TO SCHOOL

Having attempted to outline the nature of the ordinary kids' orientation to employment it is now possible to evaluate the impact of youth unemployment on pupil *expectations* of future employment and the possible impact this is having on the ordinary kids' response to school. The spectacular decline in school leaver occupational opportunities makes it reasonable to assume that pupils confronted with such bleak occupational prospects will question the value of schooling, particularly the ordinary kids who have an alienated instrumental orientation, given that they may no longer believe that school certificates will help them to get the jobs they want and because their interest in the formal curriculum is insufficient to maintain their commitment to school. Without presupposing the extent to which pupils perceived occupational opportunities to be blocked, our informants were given the statement 'there are jobs if you make an effort to find one'. Nearly two-thirds of the sample *agree* (20 per cent 'strongly'). There was no statistically significant difference between categories of pupils or between the sexes (see Table 3.7).

Table 3.7 *If you make an effort you can find a job: by pupil orientations (%)*

	Rems	Ordinary kids	Swots	Total
Agree[1]	64	68	58	64
Not sure	21	24	26	24
Disagree[2]	16	9	16	12
Total (number)	44	217	176	435

[1] Includes those who 'strongly agree'.
[2] Includes those who 'strongly disagree'.

The importance of a widespread belief in the availability of employment for understanding the impact of perceptions of youth unemployment in the school has to be interpreted with care. For example, although some pupils believe that jobs are available it does not follow that they believe these are the types of employment they want.

What statements such as 'there are jobs if you make an effort to find one' cannot capture is the extent to which the ordinary kids are confident about their chances of entering the jobs they want, which may well have an important bearing on their response to school. When pupils were asked what job they expected as opposed to what job they wanted, the ordinary kids expressed considerable uncertainty, with a little over half expecting to enter the jobs they preferred. The ordinary kids preferring clerical and commercial occupations were more certain about their future prospects, with approximately 60 per cent expecting to enter the jobs they wanted. This compares with 54 per cent of those hoping for skilled building and engineering jobs and 44 per cent personal services. There is also considerable uncertainty about their chances of finding any job within six weeks of leaving school. Only 17 per cent of the ordinary kids thought they would find a job within six weeks of leaving school, and two-thirds stated that they did not know when they would get a job. Despite the degree of uncertainty expressed about finding jobs, and although the vast majority of ordinary kids stated a preference for jobs which they *realistically* have a chance of competing for, they were *unrealistic* in assessing their chances of entry into such a job (or perhaps any job).

What the ordinary kids' understanding of their chances of getting jobs reflects is an individualistic understanding of why some of these school leavers will get jobs and others will not. This represents a failure to translate private troubles into public issues and has been documented by a number of writers. The belief that there are still jobs available for the ordinary kids is, however, unsurprising for at least two further reasons. Firstly, research investigating the occupational knowledge of school leavers has found that information about what jobs are available is at best partial (Clarke 1980a; West and Newton 1983). Such research findings should warn us against assuming that young people have a complete or accurate knowledge of the 'job situation' especially at a time of rapid social and economic change. The data presented in this chapter revealed that despite the decline in occupational opportunities for school leavers nearly two-thirds of *all* pupils believed that jobs were still available if you were willing to 'make an effort to find one'.

Secondly, pupil perceptions of the (un)employment situation are not simply based on a rational calculation of their chances of finding particular types of employment. There is also a strong desire to believe that they can find 'suitable' employment, upon which their social identities and ways of making sense of their present and future lives are constructed. The need to construct one's future social identity in occupational terms reflects an 'inability' to perceive one's future life in any other way. To define oneself as 'unemployed' or 'unemployable' is to remove the basis for living a dignified life and maintaining a sense of social worth, unless he or she is capable either individually or collectively of constructing an alternative basis for future personal identity. A basis for understanding one's place in adult society other than in occupational terms is perhaps more clearly available for girls rather than boys (Gaskell and Lazerson 1980). Yet both sexes confront similar problems and share common anxieties about the future as they prepare to make the transition into the labour market. Therefore the psychological 'supports' for maintaining a belief in their eventual placement in full-time employment are extremely durable.

In the attempt to distinguish pupil perceptions of job availability and the value of working for qualifications, three categories of responses to the statement 'there are jobs if you make an effort to find one' were cross-tabulated against the three categories of response to another statement 'qualifications are a waste of time because there are no jobs for young people',[8] thus creating nine categories of pupil response. These categories are described in Table 3.8.

Table 3.8 presents the percentage falling into each category of response (e.g. +jobs/−quals). The evaluation of the worth of qualifications shows important variations on the basis of pupil orientations to school. The swots have the most positive attitude towards the value of qualifications even when future employment prospects are believed to be uncertain or blocked. When the perceived availability of employment is ignored only 7 per cent of swots thought that qualifications were a waste of time, compared with 14 per cent of ordinary kids and 37 per cent of the rems (Table 3.8, cols A–C). Figures for the swots do tend to support the idea that even when the job situation is believed to be unfavourable to those looking for jobs, such pupils will continue their pursuit for qualifications.

However, it should be remembered that orientations underlying the swots' approach to school – normative and normative instrumental orientations – have not been separated. The evidence suggests that the majority of these pupils adopt a normative instrumental rather than a normative orientation, and that 35 per cent of the swots who do question the availability of jobs maintain a belief in the value of qualifications for jobs (Table 3.8, cols H, I). What is important for the swots at this stage of the life course is that they obtain the basic scholastic require-ments for entry into institutions of higher education, or employer training schemes, leading to middle-class occupations. The fact that entry into the labour market is postponed well beyond the age of 16 for many of the swots also reduces the immediate impact of any belief they may have in the decline of job opportunities. Many of the swots were aware that the labour market *may* have changed by the time they will be competing for employment. Moreover,

Table 3.8 *The perceived availability of jobs and the value of qualifications (%)*

	Rems	Ordinary kids	Swots	Total
+ jobs − quals (A)	25	9	6	9
? jobs − quals (B)	5	4	1	3
− jobs − quals (C)	7	1	—	1
+ jobs ? quals (D)	16	7	2	6
? jobs ? quals (E)	7	8	5	7
− jobs ? quals (F)	2	2	2	2
+ jobs + quals (G)	23	53	50	49
? jobs + quals (H)	9	11	21	15
− jobs + quals (I)	7	5	14	9
Total (number)	44	214	176	434

+ indicates agreement with the availability of jobs or the belief that qualifications are worth working for, expressed by disagreement with the statement 'qualifications are a waste of time'.

− indicates disagreement with the statement that 'jobs are available if you make an effort', or with the belief that qualifications are not worth working for, expressed by an agreement with the statement that 'qualifications are a waste of time'.

? indicates uncertainty about the availability of jobs or the value of qualifications.

the geographical mobility associated with middle-class employment did not present these pupils with a defined local labour market to which assessments of future job prospects refer. The majority of swots are taking O levels and, therefore, as long as some jobs are perceived to be available, there will be a greater tendency to continue working for qualifications given the perceived exchange value of O levels as opposed to CSEs. Indeed, as job opportunities decline and access to higher education is reduced still further as a result of Government cuts, the swots are more likely to intensify their efforts to get good grades in examinations.

If the swots have the most positive attitude to the value of qualifications, the rems have the most negative view. Over 60 per cent are either unsure (25 per cent) or believe that qualifications are not worth working for (37 per cent) (Table 3.8, cols A–F). It was hypothesized that a belief in the declining job opportunities for school leavers would tend to *reinforce* the rems' alienated orientation to school. The relatively small sample size makes it difficult to draw any firm conclusions, but over three-fifths of the rems were not positively oriented to the value of qualifications. However, the 39 per cent of rems who did feel that qualifications were important can be understood from the way qualifications were viewed by the boys adopting an anti-school subculture (see Chapter 4), where it is argued that qualifications are important if you want to work in an office but they are not seen to be important for the sorts of jobs they intended to apply for. It may also reflect a belief that when occupational opportunities are scarce qualifications may help to produce a job, but despite this belief there would be little point in starting to work for qualifications for these pupils because it is too late.

Among pupils who previously made an effort in school, it was hypothesized that the ordinary kids who have an alienated instrumental orientation present the biggest threat to the social order of the school, because unless they perceive a clear relationship between the products of 'making an effort' in school and rewards in the labour market, these pupils will see little point in bothering to 'make an effort' because most school lessons have little intrinsic worth.

The evidence from Table 3.8 does suggest that it is the ordinary kids rather than the swots who are more likely to question the value of qualifications. On the basis of Table 3.8 it is possible to distinguish four categories of response among the ordinary kids concerning the perceived continuing value of qualifications, on which the ordinary kids' compliance to school has to a large extent depended.

1　A little over half the ordinary kids still believe there are jobs and that qualifications will help them to find one (Table 3.8, col. G). However it will be argued in later chapters that their understanding of why qualifications are important has shifted from one where qualifications are valued as a way of getting 'tidy' working-class jobs, to one where qualifications are valued as a way of getting 'any' job. As a consequence of this shift, there are increasing tensions and conflicts between the ordinary kids' class cultural understandings of 'being' in school and the realities of the labour market, and that these seriously threaten the continuing compliance to school of future groups of ordinary kids.

2 A further 16 per cent of ordinary kids compared with over a third of swots remain *optimistic* about the value of qualifications even when the availability of jobs is in doubt (Table 3.8, cols H, I). But it is the remaining 30 per cent of ordinary kids, compared with only 9 per cent of swots, who pose the most immediate threat to the school.

3 Sixteen per cent of the ordinary kids believe that there are jobs available if an effort is made to find one, but now believe it is 'who you know not what you know' which is going to get you a job (Table 3.8, cols A, D) – a belief which effectively withdraws the reason for bothering to 'make an effort' in school.

4 Equally, a further 15 per cent of ordinary kids (Table 3.8, cols B, C, E, F) show signs of becoming disillusioned with both school and society. They do not perceive much point in 'making an effort' in school, nor that they have much chance of finding employment.

The different responses to the job situation registered by the swots and ordinary kids provide tentative evidence of a social class difference, with the normative/normative instrumental orientations most commonly found among the middle classes and alienated/alienated instrumental orientations among the working class. It may well be that youth unemployment is generating a dual motivational system (see Chapter 7). As the decline in job opportunities increasingly becomes evident to younger pupils now coming through the primary and secondary schools, this class difference may become more pronounced.

Hence, although the majority of ordinary kids still believe qualifications to be worth working for, almost a third of ordinary kids question the value of qualifications, and many of those who continue to believe in the value of qualifications may view them as a way of getting 'any' job rather than helping the ordinary kids to get the jobs they want.

CONCLUSION

The major conclusion to be drawn from this chapter (which will be further substantiated in the next) is that the attempt to describe working-class responses to school in terms of pupil acceptance or rejection makes it impossible to explain why the majority of working-class pupils in this study have bothered to make an effort in school and the severe limits placed on this commitment. The chapter also highlights the fact that if an adequate understanding of working-class responses to the school is to be achieved it is necessary to theorize the interrelationship between class and gender (Griffin 1985). Despite important differences in the attitudes of ordinary girls and boys to school subjects and jobs, these differences are mediated and cross-cut in important ways by common class cultural understandings which lead both male and female ordinary kids to share the same orientation to school and the same understandings of what it is to be an ordinary working-class pupil in school.

The alienated instrumentalism of the ordinary kids has depended upon specific historical conditions which have permitted the ordinary kids to predict the likely outcomes of effort in school, thus making the effort worth while because it appeared to improve their chances of getting the jobs they wanted. For this reason the school has been able to define the large majority of the school population as failures (which seems to do little more than reinforce the irrelevance of academic study), without a major revolt from working-class pupils and parents. Yet as economic and social conditions outside the school have changed rapidly, so the inclusion of the ordinary kids becomes increasingly difficult to contain or justify.

Global statements about the impact of unemployment on the school must also be questioned on the basis of evidence presented in this chapter. There is evidence of a growing polarization among *instrumental* pupils depending on whether they adopted a normative instrumental (swots) or alienated instrumental (ordinary kids) orientation. While the swots are more likely to maintain a belief in the importance of qualifications and a commitment to the school, the ordinary kids are increasingly less likely to do so. The difference in response between the swots and ordinary kids provides tentative support for believing that there may be an important class difference in response to youth unemployment. Middle-class pupils and parents are intensifying the competition for certification, whilst large numbers of working-class pupils and parents are questioning the value and purpose of schooling more than ever before.

However, a majority of ordinary kids still believe that qualifications are worth pursuing, although this is more likely to be justified for getting 'any' job rather than the jobs they want. There appear to be a number of contributory factors as to why the majority of ordinary kids still see qualifications as a useful way of getting a job. Firstly, there is a 'learned incapacity' to conceptualize one's future other than in occupational terms, therefore there is a strong desire to maintain a sense of one's future in occupational terms. Secondly, the ordinary kids were in their final year of secondary school. The collapse in occupational opportunities was a recent event in the collective experience of the people of Middleport. It none the less seemed a bit pointless to give up the chance of a few qualifications when they had already completed so much of their 'fifteen thousand hours' (Rutter *et al.* 1979). Thirdly, an additional reason why there has not been a total collapse in the ordinary kids' compliance to school is that their understanding of the school and their place within it not only depends upon a rational calculation of what the school has to offer, but a moral evaluation of different ways of 'being' a working-class pupil in the school. There are certain ways of being which do not appeal to ordinary kids. Therefore, a full appreciation of working-class responses to school not only necessitates a study of pupil orientations to the formal culture of the school, but also of the collective class-cultural experiences and understandings which are manifest in the informal pupil culture. This is the focus of Chapter 4.

4 · Rems, swots, and ordinary kids

In this chapter we turn to an examination of the informal pupil culture, to show how the school is experienced as a collective process involving typical ways of being a working-class pupil. A study of the informal pupil culture is important because it represents the social and cultural context in which school is experienced on a daily basis, and the sociological context needed to bring the study of pupil orientations 'to life'. Orientations to school cannot be understood simply in terms of the school's socialization and selection processes because pupils are active agents in the schooling process. In terms of the theoretical discussion presented in Chapter 2 it is the interplay between the processes of cultural differentiation and educational differentiation which has to be grasped, and it is in terms of the informal pupil culture that we can begin to understand how pupils can collectively resist certain features of school life, and why working-class compliance to school may be historically variable. The school has its own cultural politics within which what it teaches and the demands made upon pupils are constantly open to question. A study of the informal pupil culture also shows the intended and unintended consequences of the ordinary kids' response to school and why the existing high rate of youth unemployment has personal and educational consequences for their future schooling.

Formal and informal cultures operating in the school have usually been regarded as standing in opposition to one another (i.e. adult/youth; middle/working-class) and this has led to studies of the extent to which young people have identified with *either* culture as the basis for understanding educational achievement (Coleman 1961; Downes, 1966) or how they seek to compensate for a lack of success in terms of the formal culture (Parsons 1961; Hargreaves 1967).

The way in which the informal pupil culture is understood in this book differs from the use cited above. The informal pupil culture is used here to refer to no more than a set of institutionally *located* resources which are available to pupils (individually or collectively) and are generated and reproduced in new and creative ways particularly at times of major educational or social change. In this sense of the term therefore *not some but all* pupils are involved in the informal pupil culture.[1] The extent to which the dominant themes of the pupil culture will be in tune with the attitudes and concerns of teachers and the type of social significance which is attached to different pupil subcultures, will depend upon the class cultural resources which pupils bring with them into the school.

As we have already noted, three subcultures can be detected in all three schools, characterized as the rems, swots, and ordinary kids. These are not the researcher's terms, they are part of the vocabulary of the informal pupil culture for making sense of and accounting for school experience. There was a general under-standing, regardless of the particular school, as to what a *swot* or *rem* looks like or does, but it is also specific to the social class composition of any given school. For example, in the middle-class school (Greenhill) a large proportion of *ordinary kids* were taking some O levels, whereas in a predominantly working-class school like Thomas High School (which will primarily concern us here), to be taking O levels was by definition to be a *swot*.

Swots are those pupils who are seen as conforming to the school, working hard, never getting into trouble with teachers, always wearing school uniform, etc. To a large extent those pupils adopt-ing a normative or normative instrumental orientation in Thomas High School were by definition swots. This categorization results from a belief that to be taking O levels means having worked hard and sucked up to teachers. However, the idea of a swot usually refers to a small group of pupils who are on the one hand 'really brainy' and are also seen to be docile and submissive.

The idea of the *rem* is taken from the term 'remedial'. It has strong moral overtones when applied by various groups of pupils in the school. The rem within the informal culture of the school (Thomas High School), is not used simply to refer to the pupils' perceived innate abilities, but to their failure or unwillingness to at least try to make something of themselves. In the main study school, the term rem was almost exclusively reserved for a group of boys adopting a male anti-school subculture. All the rems recognized in Thomas High School were classified as having an alienated orientation. The *ordinary kids* are somewhere between the swots and rems. They are defined with reference to what they are not (i.e. swots or rems) rather than to what they are (i.e. ordinary or average). The vast majority of these pupils adopted what has been described as an alienated instrumental orientation.

It is one of the major arguments of this book that an understanding of the working class in school cannot be achieved by focusing on the school's socialization and selection processes alone, neither can it be explained by adopting a unitary notion of working-class culture of the sort advanced by Willis. The school is involved in a sorting and selection process that does generate divisions between pupils. In the attempt to legitimate the processes of selection and allocation, which necessitates that only a few can 'succeed', teachers are constantly involved in the 'economy of respect'. In other words, although differences in educational attainment are held to be based on innate differences in ability and willingness to make an effort, levels of educational attainment are translated into differences in moral qualities, leading pupils who are academically successful to receive 'credit' for their achievements and those at the bottom to be 'discredited'. But if the school generates some of the raw materials for the development of *pupil subcultures*,[2] they are imbued with cultural and social significance originating in the material class culture of the neighbourhood from which pupils are drawn.

It was shown in the last chapter that the ordinary kids' response to the school was not only formed on the basis of their location in the academic order, but is also premised on a culturally prescribed understanding of what it means to be an ordinary kid in school. The informal pupil culture therefore provides the resources to resist the school's definition of the socially and morally worthy and unworthy, and to contest the school's definition of what knowledge is to be valued and worthy of study.

THE REMS

Within the informal pupil culture of Thomas High School rems are usually identified as those pupils who have an alienated orientation, and particularly those who have developed a conspicuous anti-school subculture. The reason for including a discussion of the anti-school subculture is not simply to duplicate what has gone before, but to reconsider the way it has been explained by Willis, and in particular to question the political significance which has been attached to the lads' resistance to school by Willis and others (Apple 1982a; Giroux 1981).

Most of those who developed an anti-school subculture in Thomas High School were male. Female pupils who adopted an alienated orientation tended to develop an individualistic rather than collective response to their alienation from school. These girls truanted more frequently than the boys, often so that they could look after younger children, do the domestic chores or, in a small number of cases, undertake part-time jobs. One of the reasons why the boys seemed more willing to attend school, albeit in an irregular fashion, was that it was a venue for meeting their friends, and to 'have a laugh'. Staying at home was often 'boring', the home was seen by boys as a place where there was nothing to do apart from lie in bed, or watch television, whereas for the girls being at home was regarded as an induction into a major part of their adult social lives. As one of the female ordinary kids noted:

> Kay: Most of the girls who used to mess around have left . . . but the boys for some strange reason have stayed on probably because they still like it 'ere [in school]. Maybe they're bored and they haven't got anythin' else to do.

Maybe. However, the absence of females engaged in conspicuously anti-school subcultures is certainly not universal. In Greenhill girls were well represented among a similar group of pupils, and the emphasis upon what has been called the 'cult of femininity' (McRobbie 1978) to explain the peripheral position of girls in the school generally, has perhaps been exaggerated (see Chapter 2). Although there was no distinct female anti-school subculture, I witnessed five fights in the school and three of these were between girls – albeit usually about boys!

Tidy lads

Pupils comprising the anti-school peer group recognized the label rem as pejorative. On the occasions when the word rem was used by these pupils its meaning was often inverted to denote conformity (i.e. an inability to act and think for yourself) and was directed at teachers as well as other groups of pupils (particularly the swots). The 'tidy lads' or the 'boys' were terms frequently used to distinguish themselves from other groups of pupils.

From retrospective accounts, the tidy lads' anti-school peer group was believed to have taken shape around the third year (as suggested by Willis). It may also be reasonable to suppose that entry into the anti-school peer group is partly fortuitous. What is not fortuitous is the pool of likely recruits. They are working-class males who are developing or had developed an alienated orientation to the school. A discussion with the head of the middle 'feeder' school, where most of the tidy lads came from, revealed that many of them had been identified and marked as 'potential' trouble-makers before stepping foot into Thomas High School. Indeed Dave, the leader of the tidy lads, was suggested by a teacher in the middle school to have been a compassionate case for euthanasia at the age of 12!

When the tidy lads talk about how and when their attitudes to school changed, their accounts were usually couched in terms of 'just getting bored' and 'started messing about'. There was virtually no reference to the difficulty of the work, but there was a sense that as they began to get bored and mess about, so school work was increasingly meaningless or difficult to understand:

> Dave: In the third year we used to do everythin' they [teachers] said, but now, we just don't take no notice of them.
> P.B.: Why do you think that is?
> Dave: It's gettin' older like, ent it.
> Den: You're gettin' bored like, just turn yourself off. . . .
> Tom: Teachers like, they don't do anythin' interesting, some do a little, half the time they just gives you a book and tell you [to] write it down.
> [This is then seen to spill over into their time out of school]
> Tom: At school like everyone gets bored and mucks about and all that and when you're out in the nights, you know, bored like, the boys go vandalizing then like, it's just the same.

School comes to be seen as little more than 'good for a laff like'. It's a place where you can meet your friends and 'find out what's happenin' in the nights, and everthin'. There is no regular attendance at school or lessons, indeed they are banned from many lessons, finding refuge in certain parts of the school where they are beyond regular staff supervision or find a teacher who is willing to take them into their class (which is why these pupils are so easy to gain access to for interviews in school).

The tidy lads' perceptions of their future possibilities, and their modest location in the scholastic hierarchy, lead them to view the school as engaged in unfair exchange. In part, this results from their seeing *their* future employment in terms of semi- and unskilled manual jobs and the school as a place to prepare people for office work.

> Alan: Like if you want to work in an office that's what you come to school for, to learn, you know, to work in an office, ent it. To write

and get used to it like. But if you don't want to work in an office, there's no point in comin' to school, you know, to learn about these things.

Larry: Right you does these maths; Pythagoras and all this stuff. You go to the employer, they just wants to know the basics whether you can add up and take away, stuff like that. Not all this stuff like Pythagoras, it's all stupid that is.

Tiny: It all depends what you wants to do really don't it (pause) you know, if you want a job in an office like, you're goin' to go for English and maths, if you can, but if you don't you know, you're not goin' to take much attention to 'em are you.

Larry: Like a wareho's assistant ent it, you're not goin' to go for English and maths.

Tiny: You're not goin' to go for any of the subjects really, are you, you know.

Alan: You know, it's only writin', ent it, English, and everybody knows how to write.

Den: . . . What you gonna do with history, you're not goin' to go out and be a knight or somethin' like that, are you?

If what is taught in school is viewed as irrelevant for the sort of work the tidy lads expect to enter, then the same can be said of studying for qualifications:

Larry: If you want to go digging the roads like, they ask you . . . say now there's a nice big chap now, really used to hard work, now and a little weed walks in with loads of brains, who's goin' to be the best in work like? The little weakling who can't lift the shovel, who's goin' to be best to do the job, you know, the big bloke. Well, he knows how to add up and take away and all this (pause) I mean, anyone can, yet they [teachers] say you need all the brains you can get to get a job, you know. I just can't see that, see, rubbish I think it is.

Den: Be fair, goin' to school for 10 years to be a postman, learnin' all this, gettin' all the qualifications just to stick a bit of fuckin' paper thro' a letter box.

Tom: You've got to learn sortin' and all that.

Den: But that's only goin' to take about a year to learn, same as any job.

Tom: What do you want ten CSEs, stuff like that for just sortin', you know . . . just learnin' things about the job.

Den: Just to learn to sign you name down the dole.

The tidy lads' perception of the school as little more than a condition of life (which they actively resist) leads the perception of unemployment to reinforce their view that qualifications are a waste of time even for the sort of jobs they want. The tidy lads believe that 'who you know' not 'what you know' becomes *more* important when employment opportunities for school leavers are scarce:

> *Larry*: It's who you know these days. You know, there's people who've got O levels, who don't know anyone, they don't get a job. You leave school, your old man and your mother knows someone, you goes up there [relation's place of employment] and they fix you up. It's who you know not what you know.
>
> *Dave*: It's not what you does these days, it's who you know, ent it.

Moreover, there is also an acknowledgement that the qualifications they could possibly obtain, would not greatly help them:

> *Dave*: I know I wouldn't pass 'em [qualifications]. It's not worth stayin' until June. I can leave at Easter. There's a better chance of getting a job. . . . If you're an employer and he has one A level or two A levels and I had loads of CSEs, they're goin' to take him. . . . CSEs are poxy.

Among working-class pupils adopting an alienated orientation the evaluation of the school in terms of their future occupational and adult lives represents a concern with 'getting into' the 'culture' proper: away from a world of 'school kids' and 'into' the world of working-class 'adults' at the earliest possible moment. An alienated orientation provides the basis for a *collective* understanding of the school manifest in the anti-school subculture of the tidy lads. In the attempt to translate what they expect to *become* beyond the school gates into reality the school is seen as having little bearing, other than that of a non-legitimated power, a power which stipulates that the tidy lads cannot seek full-time employment until the age of 16. Efforts to gain the compliance of the tidy lads increasingly lead the anti-school peer group to identify such attempts as deserving of ridicule or as simply repressive.

The development of an alienated orientation acts to free pupils from the basic exchanges commonly operating in the school (i.e. compliance to obtain interesting and/or useful knowledge). Where the demand for compliance is *collectively* understood as illegitimate, their resistance to the school finds expression in the attempt by the tidy lads to deploy the symbolic and stylistic elements of the working-class street-corner culture in the context of the school. It is the tidy lads' attempt to import the focal concerns of street-corner culture, involving the overt display of smoking, drinking and masculine prowess, which fuels the growing visible conflict between the tidy lads and other pupils and staff.

Group oppositions between pupils rarely led to direct physical confrontations, despite harassment and taunts from the tidy lads. On one occasion some of the tidy lads ran riot in the school, leading to the temporary exclusion of six of them for two weeks. Another incident between two of the tidy lads and one of the ordinary kids was recalled by Alan:

Alan: This bloke right [the ordinary kid] . . . he's a rem. We de-livers papers 'round here right. This bloke nicked a paper out of the doors. The next day he come up to Den and he goes 'oh I owes you 12p'. So Den says 'oh what for?' He goes 'oh I robbed a paper out of your door'. He told him like! He told him that he robbed it, so Den and Dave took him 'round the back and pissed all over him [laugh]. . . .

Larry: Anybody in their right mind would just forget about it. They wouldn't go back and tell him, you just robbed your paper . . . if a bloke robs a video you're not goin' to go back to the shop the next day and say 'oh here's £600 I just robbed a video'.

Confessions or 'grassing on your mates' (particularly to 'authority'), are seen by the tidy lads as the most self-demeaning acts which deserve an equally demeaning punishment – being urinated upon. Such incidents were not as common as is often supposed, but the tidy lads' disdain for the swots and some of the ordinary kids was frequently evident.

It is worth noting that the tidy lads' attitude towards the ordinary kids was ambivalent. Sometimes the idea of the swot referred to all pupils who bothered working in school, whether for CSEs or O levels. On other occasions the tidy lads recognized that there were ordinary kids who were 'okay' given some degree of 'street credibility' (i.e. that they could take care of themselves if necessary; were capable of 'pulling' the opposite sex; did not 'creep' or 'suck up' to teachers).

The tidy lads particularly perceived the swots taking O levels as attempting to distinguish themselves from other groups of pupils, as trying to act as if they were a 'class above the rest':

P.B.: How do you get on with pupils takin' O levels?

Den: Clifford, what a rem.

Tom: I don't both with 'em. . .they thinks they're higher class than you, all their swotty things. . . .

Pete: They don't want to talk to you.

Den: We don't want to talk to them, we just threatens them.

Tom: I know, but they thinks they're higher than you. The way they looks at you and all that, just smash them in the head. . . .

Chris: They loves it, people like Clifford up in the higher classes, he loves work he do . . ., 'cos they think they'll get a better job than us.

Tom: They might.

Chris: I don't care what they do.

The notion of a swot as understood by the tidy lads is double-edged. There is an acknowledgement that these pupils may get 'higher' jobs, but this is interpreted as requiring docile and effeminate behaviour. The claim to being superior to the tidy lads was also believed to be evident in teacher responses to members of the anti-school peer group:

Tom: They treats you like shit and how are you supposed to be nice in school when teachers are treatin' you like the scum of the earth . . . that you're second-class. All the swots come first.

Chris: They just don't want to know you as long as they gets to 'em [the swots].

Tom: That's why so many kids are turnin' 'round and hittin' teachers . . . you just get kind of frustrated don't you.

Dave: They just splits you up like brainy ones, like, Mrs Williams' class. She puts all the brainy ones one side. She teaches those three-quarters of the lesson, and gives about fuckin' two minutes to us then. I know we don't work fuckin' much, but she doesn't give any interest.

It is also believed that in employment you will be treated differently:

Den: [In a job you] feels as if you're someone, don't you? You feels important, feels they respect you.

P.B.: So do you think that's the problem with school?

Den: Yeah, they don't respect you.

Tom: They just looks down on you as another twat like.

Den: Somethin' out of a zoo.

To interpret the tidy lads' responses to the swots and teachers as a *reaction* to perceptions of personal failings, recognized by Hargreaves and others (i.e. to explain the anti-school subculture by relying on the process of *educational* differentiation) would be a mistake. The development of an alienated orientation, of which the tidy lads' anti-school subculture is a collective expression, is explicable given a class-specific FOR which does not value the school either intrinsically or extrinsically in the process of becoming a working-class adult. The tidy lads view the school as an induction into non-manual occupations, captured in the idea of 'office work', which holds little appeal:

> *Dave*: I don't want to be in an office or anythin' like that.
> *Skip*: No.
> *Dave*: I want to be outside, I don't mind where it is.
> *Skip*: Stores or somethin'. . . .
> *Alan*: We wouldn't like a job like that though, half of us see. So we wouldn't need all those O levels anyway.
> *Larry*: I want a job liftin' stuff on a buildin' site or somethin' like that, wareho's.
> *Alan*: Somethin' movin' 'round all the time, in a van.
> *Larry*: Goin' to work in different places. . . .
> *Larry*: They'll be clerks or somethin' like that, somethin' to do with a bank.
> *Alan*: Yeah, but that's what [they've] chosen to do ent it . . . who wants to work in an office?

If the tidy lads are *reacting* against anything in the school, it is the denial of dignity and respect which the term 'rem' epitomizes. The tidy lads believe that the school has not offered them the chance to show their 'strengths' or provide the basis for the evaluation of their social worth. They believe that they have been illegitimately tried before they have had time to commit the act to be judged. Even where 'practical' school subjects appear to offer the potential of being relevant and interesting, they believed that they are not taught properly. The true test of the tidy lads' abilities was seen as the ability to *do* the job, and 'if you can do it, it's not worth havin' the trainin' is it?'.

Being identified as one of the 'trouble-makers' and as a rem, however strongly contested, has consequences of which the tidy lads are well aware:

> *Dave*: They [managers] phone up the school . . . school's tellin' you to get out and find a job. They phones up the school after a reference for ya': 'oh, he's always mucking about'. He don't get the job then, school don't say anythin' good about you: 'oh he fools about'.
> *Alan*: They don't know what you're like outside . . . you know, how you can act really.
> *Dave*: They only see the part of you in school, what you act like in school.
> *Alan*: You could act the same outside, but on the other hand, you can be sensible when you want to.
> *Dave*: In the school oh . . . they goes oh . . . you're too thick, you're not sensible enough to get a job.

As an explanation of the tidy lads' anti-school subculture, much of what has been suggested supports a 'cultural' interpretation, but varies somewhat from that advanced by Willis.

First, those who are likely to enter an anti-school subculture will be recruited from among pupils developing an alienated orientation, which in turn must be explained in terms of the complex interplay between the process of educational and cultural differentiation. Second, considerable political significance has been attached to Willis' 'lads'' resistance to school and authority, which has been interpreted by Willis and others as a resistance to capitalism (Apple 1982b; Arnot and Whitty 1982). Capitalism's factory fodder (Bowles and Gintis 1976), who became its ideological dupes in order to maintain existing patterns of inequality (Althusser 1972; Bourdieu and Passeron 1977), now find themselves at the heart of a resistance movement offering the new 'royal road' to working-class liberation; they are as Willis tells us, 'far from walking corpses'. The lads' counter-school culture is 'actually bringing the system into crisis' (p. 1).

Although there is much to commend Willis' analysis of 'the lads' both Willis' research in the Midlands a decade ago and the present study in South Wales offer little support for the view that the actions of 'the lads' or tidy lads are directed towards the overthrow of any type of established order – although they do present a major problem for the day-to-day operation of classroom life.[3] The lads are trying to escape the educational system, not overthrow it. Therefore, these writers may have mistaken the 'regular army' of young workers for a 'resistance movement' offering the possibility of fundamental change.

Such a possibility is evident when Willis attempts to explain the fetishization of manual labour. In his view this takes on 'a significance and critical expression for its owner's social position and identity which is *no part of its own proper nature* (p. 146, my emphasis). His attempt to explain why 'the lads' become so hooked on the idea of entering heavy and unpleasant unskilled jobs is unconvincing. Because after demonstrating a clear ability to resist the authority of teachers, somehow and somewhat miraculously at the height of 'the lads' resistance to school, teachers and the media begin to have an impact on the way 'the lads' understand the world and their place within it. A process which contaminates 'the lads' class impulses' and condemns them to be effective agents of the reproduction of class relations as their energies are diverted away from exposing the unjust nature of a class society and towards the fetishization of manual labour and the development of sexist and racist attitudes.

The conclusion of the Middleport study is that an understanding of a future in semi- and unskilled jobs, masculine activity centring around doing 'real' work, is the *basis* for the development of the working-class anti-school subculture and *not* an unfortunate consequence of it. A further problem with Willis' account is that the significance attached to pupil resistance is not based upon the utterances and meanings it has for those doing the resisting, but depends upon the way in which the working class and the school are conceptualized within the social totality of capitalist societies, and an overriding concern among such writers to theorize educational practices in terms of a general theory of the functioning of capitalist societies or capitalist social relations (Culley and Demaine 1983: p. 16). Culley and Demaine have noted, following Tomlinson (1982), that inherent in Marxist accounts of the educational system is:

> a conception of interests as things inherent in a particular set of social relations *independent of any agency calculating these interests*. Due to their position in social relations, certain classes/groups are seen to have a *common essential interest* which exists as long as those social relations exist. (p. 162)

Therefore, any resistance by working-class pupils against the school (a capitalist state institution) is interpreted as a resistance to capitalism *per se*, without sufficient empirical evidence (A. Hargreaves 1982). Indeed, Fuller (1983) found that it was the girls who did not develop an anti-school subculture who displayed the greater awareness of contemporary political issues, rather than those pupils who openly resisted teacher authority.

The anti-school culture of the tidy lads does pose problems for the educational system in Britain, but does not necessarily, indeed may rarely, generate a threat to the reproduction of subordinate forms of labour power. The tidy lads' rejection of the school reproduces their location within the labour market, if qualifications are to be the primary means of entry for anything other than semi-skilled and unskilled employment. By doing nothing they are doing a great deal, excluding themselves from access to certification (Cousin 1984). This poses a threat to the educational order, but not to the wider social order, *unless* they reject the moral basis of the society in which they live – the work ethic, the mode of distribution of goods and services – which they do not appear to do. It has been argued that an understanding of a future in semi-skilled and unskilled jobs, and masculine activity centring around doing 'real' work, is the basis for the development, rather than the unfortunate consequence of the working-class counter-school subculture. Hence, at a time of declining occupational opportunities for school leavers, it is more likely to be those who have complied with the school, and who have developed expectations of having more than a series of 'shit' jobs, who threaten the existing social order when these aspirations remain unmet, rather than those who expect little else but unskilled employment (see Chapter 7).

The swots

In Thomas High School the swots are identified by other groups of pupils as adopting a pro-school subculture. In Thomas High School to be taking mainly O levels is almost by definition to be a swot, due to a belief that taking O levels is only possible if you are a certain 'type' of person (i.e. somebody who wants to work in an office or get a 'high' job). It is the personal characteristics of wearing school uniform, never being seen to be 'mucking about', and a perceived inability or unwillingness to 'have a laff' which are viewed as the trademark of the swot. Both boys and girls are identified as swots, but invariably swots are discussed in reference to the sex of the observer.

The notion of the swot, like that of the rem, is viewed by those it is applied to as pejorative. The swots recognize that they are different from other groups of pupils but deny the negative connotations associated with the term:

> *Paul*: Well . . . I can't really think of what you mean by a swot. I don't know anybody who goes home and swots, you know. I mean it's just a matter of getting your principles right and knowing you've got to do some work to get anywhere, you know it's just being sensible and realistic. You're not being a swot, you're just doing what you ought to be doing.

A distinction is made among the O level pupils between the act of swotting (i.e. working hard) and the personal characteristics of the archetypal swot (i.e. being docile and sucking up to teachers). There are only a few pupils among the O level pupils who are believed to qualify for the label 'swotty' – those who spend all their time working and never go out or have fun. The distinction between 'swots' and 'swotty swots' is captured in a discussion with Janet:

P.B.: How do you think you are seen by other groups of pupils?

Janet: Swots probably, you know, swotty . . . well they just think we're a bit stupid all the time working. You know, but it's stupid because I mean, I have just as much fun, and I work hard, but I go out at weekends, go to discos and things, but you know, I'm not a swot, I've got to, I just don't take any notice of them.

P.B.: So you don't see yourself as a swot?

Janet: Well I work hard, yeah, but have as much fun as well, I'm not sort of boring, or like somebody who works all the time – I couldn't.

P.B.: Are there many people who do work all the time?

Janet: Yeah, I suppose so, a couple of people not many. It's not very good for you to work all the time, you need a break.

There is a common understanding in all three schools of what a swot is. However, its significance between schools varies. In Greenhill it is possible to be working for some O levels without being identified as a swot, whereas in Thomas High School it is more difficult to work for O level qualifications without inviting such a categorization. Moreover, unlike middle-class 'swots' in Greenhill, similar pupils in Thomas High School are not necessarily encouraged to swot for examinations by parents, friends, and neighbours. On the contrary, the swots in Thomas High School are reminded of their differences from neighbours and other pupils, many of whom they grew up with. Parents of socially mobile working-class youth are frequently ambiguous about the fact that social mobility usually involves going away, i.e. becoming socially and geographically distant, although they recognize the financial and social benefits that would accrue to their children from such mobility. For the 'swots' in Greenhill, 'swotting' for qualifications is more likely to be viewed as a fact of life, as is evident in a conversation with Andrew:

Andrew: You don't look at it as something you're goin' to enjoy [working for examinations], you just look at it as something you've got to do. The situation is where you've got to get some sort of qualifications. . . . They're just something you've got to have. You can't get anywhere without them. So you've got to work for them . . . you need a good selection all 'round . . . I don't think that any subjects are more important than others. Only in certain fields, depending on what you're looking for, then it becomes important.

However, in Thomas High School swotting for qualifications is not simply a fact of life, or something that everyone has to endure; it is rather, something which has to be regularly accounted for or rationalized. An important rationale for 'swotting' is the sense of a 'calling', which is circularly reinforcing:

> *Alex*: If you can do it [school work] you owe it to yourself really, don't you? If you're able to do it and . . . em, because you want to get the best out of your life, but everyone does. Well . . . I do anyway. If you're capable to do it, you've got to work, you don't get anything without workin'. Some try and some people who aren't so bright would love it, to do O levels and they just haven't got the capacity to do it. We've got it so we might as well use it.

The perceived endowment of academic ability acts as a spur to further academic endeavour, which in turn reinforces this understanding of themselves as in some way different from other pupils. Entering the sixth form and going on to higher education was assumed to be the 'normal' thing to do among the swots in Greenhill, and is accompanied by an almost equally taken-for-granted belief that they will enter one of the professions. The swots in Thomas High School, however, were not so certain of the future. For example, Carol (regarded by teachers as one of the most promising pupils), was unclear about the purpose of pursuing additional 'learning' and particularly of going to university. This uncertainty was not reduced by the careers officer and teachers:

> [Talking about her careers interview]
> *Carol*: You've got to decide . . . when I went to the interview, you had to decide right away then, if we wanted to stay on or leave, and if you're going to university. They don't say what you could do after university. You're in just the same situation as if you leave school now. So I'd like them to tell you what sort of jobs you could do after university. . . . It was then [during the careers interview] I decided to do nursery nursing, 'cos I hadn't heard of the course before. As soon as I said I didn't want to stay on she didn't press the point, like, she just accepted that. You know, she could have questioned why I wanted to leave. She could have said more about the jobs I could have done after university.
> *P.B.*: If she had discussed jobs after university, would you have considered staying on?
> *Carol*: I think so, 'cos even the teachers are saying, 'oh yes stay on and go to university' but they're not saying what I could do, are they, when I leave.

As children from a working-class background move through the school, the school exposes the child to alternative understandings of what the school has to offer and what one might become on leaving. Such a re-evaluation by the child would involve an induction into the ideology of the school and particularly the notion of self-determination on the basis of innate abilities and personal effort. However, unless working-class pupils perceive a 'real' opportunity structure for educational advancement (i.e. usually viewed as access to O level study) and occupational advancement, it is extremely unlikely that they will identify with the school in this way. Pupils who find their way into the upper band or stream in the school are the most likely to develop a normative or normative instrumental orientation given that further academic endeavour could lead to O level qualifications, which provide the basis for further educational and occupational advancement. Yet access to O level examination routes may be a *necessary* but is not a *sufficient* condition for the development of such an orientation.

What is expected of them in school by teachers may clash with the attitudes of friends who may hold little regard for academic endeavour. In situations where the pupil cannot sustain the commitment necessary for relatively high levels of academic attainment – for example, where family members actively discourage or physically prevent the pupil from doing homework, or where the pupil cannot see the point of working hard if it is going to mean less contact with friends – the pupil may give up extraordinary activity in school and become one of the ordinary kids or rems. The problems confronting socially mobile working-class pupils have been noted in previous studies (Turner 1964; Jackson and Marsden 1966). In the case of Carol, although she had a normative instrumental orientation to school the range of occupational possibilities open beyond undergraduate study was not specified. There is an important sense in which she was asking, what sort of person can I *become* if I go to university. She did not receive a convincing answer and left school after O levels. The analysis of the rems showed that they perceived what is taught in school as a preparation for non-manual jobs. This is also true of the swot. What varies between these groups of pupils is the perceived relevance of school knowledge for *their* future lives.

It has been argued that the dominant orientation among working-class pupils taking O levels is normative instru-mentalism. From such an orientation (despite the predominance of the pursuit of qualifications) there are also elements of intrinsic interest in the academic aspects of the formal school culture:

> *Alison*: In history . . . you've got to look to the past to see the future and if you've got that in your head, then you look at history in a different way and it's more interesting for you, and it's the same in a lot of subjects.
>
> *Jane*: I was interested in biology, and I like to learn it. I was interested in how parts work and things and I thought it would be very interesting work, it wouldn't get boring . . . it would be interesting and well worth while.

What is taught in school, even if it does not directly relate to the occupational or other interests of the pupils, is viewed as a necessary prelude to the acquisition of 'required' and 'desired' knowledge:

> *Paul*: You have to get maths and English well, I did my maths [O level] last year and English. Those are important subjects because it gives you a sort of . . . I mean they're . . . important because you've got to have them. Other than that, I suppose the sciences you know . . . I mean they're indirectly what I want to do. The others are just subjects really, but I still enjoy what I do, well most of it anyway . . . a lot . . . well as far as I'm concerned they're just extra O levels . . . they're not going to actually help you – it's just a pass to get in, so that's why you do it.
>
> To stand any sort of chance of getting a job whether or not you're good at what you do you need qualifications before you can get a chance to do what you want to do . . . there are few subjects that help you in the end for what you want to do, but on the whole, you do the subjects just to say you're up to a certain standard, that's all they prove really.

Those subjects in which these pupils have little interest are tolerated as necessary in order to gain additional qualifications, if access to particular occupations and institutions of higher education is to be gained. These pupils are more attuned to the formal culture of the school than pupils having an alienated (rems) or alienated instrumental (ordinary kids) orientation, since as we have already seen, the *types of employment these pupils aspire to are perceived to be 'knowledge-based'*. It is this characteristic of their employment which acts to bring these pupils closer to the normative aspects of the formal culture of the school. The academic curriculum comprises subjects which may be not only interesting but also relevant to their future lives. The currency for translating 'ability' and 'effort' into desired jobs is seen to be paper qualifications:

> *Jane*: It's hard enough to get a job as it is, there's no point in not getting qualifications, because you think you're not goin' to get a job. You got to, em try hard . . . there's so much competition you've just got to do the best you can, you have got a chance then . . . to get a job or go to university.
>
> *Alan*: It's obvious really isn't it? If you haven't got nothing [no qualifications] you're going to be a 'messer-abouter' really. If you've never worked in school you're never goin' to work in a job. So if you've got qualifications, it shows you have attempted to work and things.

The quotation from Jane involves a recognition of the need for certification to meet the objective criterion for recruitment to certain jobs or institutions of higher education. Alan alternatively notes the acquisition of qualifications to be an index of 'social worth', in the sense that it represents a moral hierarchy on the basis both of innate ability but also effort. The swots also view themselves as having a different future from other pupils which finds expression in discussions of future employment:

> [Talking about pupils leaving without qualifications]
>
> *Rob*: It depends what they're goin' to do don't it? I think they should still take exams anyway just in case they lose their job, which is pretty likely, you know. Some of them . . . I know one who is going to work with his father in a sweet shop. I mean you're not going to get much out of that, money wise. You're goin' to get little out of it and it's pretty hard hours, particularly with newspapers, whereas in computing, you know, money is good.
>
> *Alison*: People think 'oh it's a factory, it's a doddle', you know, but people sitting there, you know, all day doing the same thing. It must be degrading for people, men of about forty, who are just sitting there doing the same thing. They must be very, well you've got to do that to take money home for the wife and kids, it must be really degrading. If I thought I had to do that, well if I'd end up like that I wouldn't want a job. I'd have to have a job where at the end of the day I could say well I've done something, I can see what I've done like. I'd have to have a challenge . . . otherwise I wouldn't enjoy it and if you don't enjoy your work what hope is there for you.

Whereas the rems' FOR can be seen in terms of 'getting in' to the working class, the swots in Thomas High School can be seen to have a FOR which usually involves 'getting out' of the working class. The importance of qualifications as a means to compete for middle-class occupations, also appears to underly the swots' understanding of declining occupational opportunities for all school leavers:

> *John*: Well, if you've got more qualifications you've got more chance of getting a job . . . well with such a large number of people out of work, they're [employers] goin' to take the ones with higher qualifications.
> *Peter*: It depends what you want to do really. I think if you work now, if you want to go to the sixth form or if you want to leave school, but if you want to leave school, there's not much chance of getting a job. There's no work about anyway, and if you want to do somethin' later in life, you've got to stay here [in school].
> *Linda*: Well there's so much unemployment now, ent there. There just aren't any jobs, especially for people who haven't got any qualifications. They can really afford to be choosy can't they and they'll employ people with qualifications. So people who haven't got any qualifications haven't got much chance really, so that's why we work, you know, so you'll have a better chance then.

Among the swots the perception of declining job opportunities reinforces the decision to work for qualifications and enter further study given a belief that there are few 'suitable' job opportunities for 16-year-old school leavers and for those who do not achieve 'good' grades. Therefore, the stakes involved in getting good qualifications are heightened rather than diminished among the swots.

Pupil divisions

Within the informal pupil culture of Thomas High School the stigma attached to being a swot is considerable, although this is true for both sexes, as one girl pointed out:

> *Mary*: The boys are more afraid of their friends calling them swots than girls are. . . . I don't know [why] it's just an image isn't it, you know. They just don't want to be seen as swotty.

In Thomas High School there is considerable pressure among the O level pupils to avoid the personal attributes of the swot and here the pro-school subculture acts to insulate these pupils from the hurtful personal consequences of the frequent barracking they are subjected to in school. They are the pupils most likely to identify with the formal culture of the school, but this is not to suggest that aspects of school life are not objected to and resisted (i.e. school uniform, the teaching of certain subjects). However, the development of a collective pro-school subculture acts to insulate the swots from the ridicule and social isolation which swotting for exams is perceived to involve among other groups of pupils, which provides a crucial source of present and future reference. The knowledge that it was they who were somehow out-of-the-ordinary in terms of other working-class people, as well as in terms of educational location, did lead to the overt expression of pupil oppositions as discussed in terms of the tidy lads.

In Thomas High School the sense of 'calling', i.e. of being academically able, was not only a way of rationalizing why they 'owe it to themselves' to continue studying, but was also a means of differentiating the swots from the ordinary kids and rems. Although this leads to a sense of innate superiority, it does not involve the same element of moral indignation associated with explaining differences in educational outcome in terms of the assertion of *effort*:

> *Julie*: If you don't get on with the teachers and you don't sort of like work, that's all they wants to do just get out [of school] as soon as they can. However, if you're going to leave school and you haven't got a job, it's pretty stupid . . . they'll only be sitting around the place, not doin' anything and no job in the end . . . they're stupid. They won't get a job anyway, so they end up on the dole. They've got the money, notin' to do, they just enjoy themselves.

It is the fecklessness of the rems which evokes the greatest animosity among the swots. Moreover, the tendency for the tidy lads to go around in a group and continually 'muck about' is viewed as part of an unwillingness (and to a lesser extent inability) to achieve their wants through personal effort and intellectual skills. In Greenhill where the majority of pupils were from a middle-class background, but where the boys and girls who were involved in the anti-school culture were from the working-class council estate which fell within the Greenhill catchment area, the division between the swots and rems was more pronounced:

> *Adrian*: Anyone below the Bs is called a 'rem' . . . it's a bit unfair I suppose, but a lot of them bring it on themselves, doing stupid things, causing trouble. . . . You walk 'round the school and you see hundreds of them. They bring it on themselves, they say 'oh I want to be different, I want to be different' and they'll all be different in exactly the same way, so they're not really different at all.
>
> *Julie*: In the Cs and Ds they don't do anything, and couldn't care less

. . . they just get put in a classroom, in the remedial classroom and they just get a teacher to sit with them and they play games and they go out and half of them don't come to school.

Jane: Well it's funny, I remember once I was in the pictures and I got followed 'round by this group of rems who were in the year below us and we were just tryin' to get rid of them, sitting there trying to watch this film, and they were bugging me, and they were saying 'oh you . . . swots, you're in the swots class . . . oh really' [middle-class accent]. They thought we were really snobbish, upper-class, but we're not really, at all. Well I don't think so, just normal. 'Cos they think sometimes 'oh yes she's a real bore, likes school'. I don't think they like me, because they feel I ought to cause trouble, and be like them and go against people who don't cause trouble. They don't like people sort of outside their group.

The attitude of the swots in both Thomas High School and Greenhill towards the ordinary kids was one of indifference. Although the ordinary kids were not taking O levels they were making an effort. One of the female swots characterized the difference between the rems and the ordinary kids as follows:

Steph: [The rems] . . . I mean they're the frightening lot, aren't they. Some of them are, some of them are the unintelligent ones, but some of them are nasty, as well as unintelligent, and I keep away from those. But the pupils who are doing CSEs they're just the same as us you know. You can't [blame them] just because they're not doing O levels, but the people who are not really bothered, they're a lot lazier anyway, they're a horrible group of people.

Adrian: I don't think anyone has any strongly held opinions [about the ordinary kids] . . . just because they're doing CSEs, they're just normal.

Ordinary kids

So far an attempt has been made to outline the attitudes and nature of the social divisions within the informal pupil culture of the school from the point of view of the rems and swots. We now turn to a consideration of the ordinary kids within the informal pupil culture and extend the analysis of unemployment on the ordinary kids' response to school. The ordinary kids in Thomas High School clearly distinguish between school subjects that they believed to be relevant and the rest. They also believed that certain subjects contained knowledge which is worth knowing, while other things taught under the same subject heading were a waste of time:

> *P.B.*: What subjects do you think are the most important?
> *Jane*: Well, I suppose maths in some ways, but all this Pythagoras and all that jazz, I don't think that's worth it, you know. I used to be alright in maths when I used to work. I used to do loads of things then, count loads of votes up, but all the rest then, I think it's dull. As long as you can count and take away and divide and times, you know. It's stupid doing all these . . . what do you call it? . . . all this complicated stuff.
> *Pat*: Well I can't see how maths is important to be honest, as long as you can count. I used to work in a shop right, in a fruit shop and the orders we had, a lot of money was involved, and I never used to give the wrong change, and then I failed my maths exam.
> *Martin*: We got maths lessons, they're puttin in like, all different things, like algebra, cross-sections and trigonometry and all that, but like me, I want to be a welder, won't need none of it. Might have somethin' like adding up, to measure a piece of metal to which you're goin' to weld to it. But you don't need nothin' like statistics like, things like that . . . like science, you don't want to know all the different things.
> *Spike*: I can write a letter, you know, anybody can write a letter, but ah you know, what do you call them now? What do they call the bits of the words like mar-ma-lade?
> *P.B.* Syllables.
> *Spike*: What's the point in teachin' you that, you know. You're not going to go for a job and say, 'oh I like mar-ma-lade. Those are syl-la-bles [laugh], you know, it's absolutely stupid like.

The ordinary kids evaluate school subjects on the basis of what knowledge they believe to be necessary for future employment and, to a more limited extent, for everyday life. Despite a recognition that English and mathematics are important subjects, there is a pragmatic evaluation of those aspects of the subject which will be useful. This acts to limit pupil involvement in the subject beyond that of obtaining an understanding of the 'basics'. Beyond the basics much of the school curriculum is viewed as irrelevant. If this is true of English and mathematics, the value of other school subjects is more hotly disputed. Attitudes to history provide a good example:

> *Mark*: History, with history now, say somebody wants to be a motor mechanic say, I can't see where history comes into it, you know, I can't really see what history has got to do with school, you know . . . with learnin', 'cos history is . . . it . . . just deals with the past.

Anne: They teach you things like history. What's history goin' to do when you leave school, ent it? I like taking it, but what's it goin' to do when you leave school? Typin', yeah that's alright. Cookery's alright, needlework, but stuff like history, English, what are they goin' to do when you leave school, ent it, really. It's not goin' to help you, help you workin', can't do something with history.

The perceptions of much of what is taught in school as irrelevant or unimportant, even in Alison's case where she likes history, suggest that these pupils' *instrumental* orientation to the school curriculum prevents the development of any intrinsic interest in what is taught. Gaining the compliance of the ordinary kids is not achieved as a result of developing an intrinsic interest in school subjects but as a consequence of the perceived relationship between qualifications and future employment.

The limited involvement exhibited by the ordinary kids in the formal culture of the school is also evident from observations of classroom interaction. The ordinary kids do what is minimally required to placate the teacher and to pass examinations, particularly where the subject is viewed as a waste of time or boring due to the way it is taught or to its assumed future irrelevance. By the time these pupils reach the fourth year what the teacher expects from certain groups of pupils and what the pupils expect from teachers and are prepared to invest in lessons (i.e. what they offer of themselves and expect from school on a day-to-day basis) has largely become routinized. This is not to suggest that there is not a process of negotiation in each lesson, which may on occasions break down. Classroom life is punctuated to various extents with surreptitious or open conversations and the 'learning' process is commonly engaged in with a minimum of commitment:

Martin: In science not many people do work. In science we do writing. Like in commerce, again it's not workin' really, writin' down on a piece of paper and it's forgotten then, in the next lesson. Writin' down on a piece of paper we've forgotten what we write down . . . we're not taking it in.

[Group discussion of work in class]
Pete: We just write all the time, if he's got to dictate, he just gives us a book, and we've got to write a passage out like, you don't take it in, you just writes it.
Martin: Just writes it down.
P.B.: Why do you do it then? I mean . . . em, why do it if it's just dictation or writing from a book?
Ray: Got to do it to pass the test, ent you.

> *P.B.*: So you write it out and when you get near to the exams you re-read it?
>
> *All*: Yeah.
>
> *Pete*: That's what you do to get the exams.
>
> *Brigid*: If a teacher, you know, right . . . tried to encourage us right, 'don't do this don't do that', perhaps it would help, but they just let us do what we want to. Not that that bothers us, because we love it sometimes don't we, 'oh it's great not workin', but when it comes to the exams you're sorry.

'Having a laff' is important to the ordinary kids, but this often comes into conflict with ensuring that you have something to show for your years at school and gaining qualifications. There is a belief that most of the entry qualifications for skilled manual jobs (boys) and low-level non-manual occupations (girls) can be achieved through 'doing a bit'.

The difference between the ordinary kids and the rems is *not* that the ordinary kids are not exposed to an increasing number of activities and 'outside interests' which may bring them into conflict with the school (although there may be important qualitative differences in the nature and frequency of exposure in and between groups of pupils). It is not the case that ordinary kids will not engage in generational and class youth subcultures, but rather, that these rarely become full-blown, which would bring them into direct opposition to school.

It is the overt forms of 'adulthood' that the authorities within the school perceive most sensitively as a threat to that 'authority'. The level of 'tolerance' exercised by teachers concerning the wearing of school uniform and behavioural standards will obviously vary from school to school. It will also depend upon the teacher's evaluation of the 'potential' threat to school authority. In other words, behaviour which, when performed by the rems, is regarded as a serious breach of school discipline, is regarded as only a meaningless prank when performed by the swots. However, wearing school uniform and behaviour in and around the school are issues of potential and actual conflict and negotiation in which the ordinary kids are frequently involved. An example of this is Jane talking about why she was constantly reprimanded about her appearance by the head of pastoral care:

> *Jane*: I think that if we're not allowed to wear earrings, they're not [teachers], because you see Miss Jones, come to school, earring down here, look at the way Mrs Walker dresses, you know. Stupid, they should set an example, you know. Some things they ban is stupid,

like boys wearing white socks, you know, the Cromby overcoats, they banned them, it's stupid – and leg warmers! I think they've gone too far banning things like that, or surf beads, you know them surf beads.

P.B.: Yeah.

Jane: Banned them.

P.B.: Why do you think they ban them?

Jane: I got told off for the colour of my hair the other day. She [head of pastoral care] gave me a row over the colour of my hair [it was blonde but nothing out of the ordinary].

P.B.: Why, what did she say about it?

Jane: She stopped me in the middle of the corridor because she was in a bad mood, she thought she'd take it out on me, she pulled me 'round, she said, 'where's your tie Miss Davies? I'm always wearing my tie, I'm never without it, 'cos you know, it's natural, put it on first thing in the morning. Where it went to I don't know. I lost it. I couldn't find it and I was late getting up and havin' murders gettin' out of the ho's' and gettin' to registration and the only time I forgets it now, she sees me. She goes 'oh, I bet you remember to do your hair'. I goes no, I got up late, I brushed it back and I just came to school. She said 'yeah you can see that, the colour is disgusting and the shape of it! Not the right style for school, get your fringe cut.' So she says it in front of everyone like, I was shamed.

P.B.: Did you get it cut?

Jane: Yeah [laugh], she says she's goin' to do it herself. The only reason I did have it cut was that I was going to the hairdressers the next night anyway, to have my hair cut. But otherwise I wouldn't have, you know, why should I 'cos she has her hair the way she wants it, short like a boy.

A number of points could be made about Jane's remarks, but what is of importance here, is that the teacher's reaction to Jane, who was no different in her appearance from the other female ordinary kids, suggests that there was a constant monitoring of appearance of all pupils, by some of the senior members of staff. Although Jane felt unfairly reprimanded, she did not enter into open conflict with the teacher. A similar confrontation with Dave, one of the tidy lads, ultimately led to his expulsion.

Despite a desire among the ordinary kids to engage in youth subcultural styles, which usually preclude the wearing of school uniform (associated with the swots), careful negotiation is attempted to avoid overt hostility and conflict with teachers, since this may have serious consequences for further academic study and chance of achieving reasonable grades in the 16+ examinations. The ordinary kids also attempt to avoid conflict and hostility with 'authority' lest they are defined as beyond the boundary of 'ordinary' (i.e. as rems).

The ordinary kids will rarely enter into *direct* opposition, or develop a high level of involvement in or identification with the school. Working-class pupils who are similarly located in the school appear to share a similar subcultural understanding of being and acting in the school. There are therefore considerable peer-group pressures towards conformity with the norms of behaviour about how to act in school. It becomes increasingly difficult for a small minority of ordinary kids to pull their socks up even if they wanted to. This is evident in a discussion about teachers' attitudes to one of the ordinary kids:

> *Pat*: They said . . .[I'm] not showing much interest in hard work and told me to improve and I did for a while. Then everybody else didn't. I told them to shut their mouth . . . . If you're put in a class like, with em, people who don't work you tend to go like them, rather talk to them, 'cos everyone I know in my class like, talks, you know.

Even when an attempt is made to sustain a commitment to work harder, there is a constant pressure towards attuning your school work to those of your classmates. At the same time, peer-group pressure works against pupils moving into direct opposition to teachers which would also involve a departure from the subcultural understanding of what it is to be an ordinary kid, in this case in the direction of the rems.

The ordinary kids' stratification of pupils

In the informal pupil culture of the school, group oppositions between the ordinary kids and other groups of pupils appear to exist and to be acknowledged. Pupils who adopt a conspicuously anti-school subcultural style are characterized as the rems and are believed to be *below* them in some respects. However, in Thomas High School this rarely takes the form of an all-embracing castigation; neither are they in *awe* of those perceived to be 'above' them: they exhibit no overriding desire to join the swots. A swot is *primarily* something other than they are, as indeed is a rem. The attitudes of the ordinary kids to the rems and swots are expressed by reference to different types of futures, characterized by a FOR which can be defined as 'getting on' in working-class terms. For example, few of the rems are seen to stay on to take qualifications, and all ordinary kids describe them, with varying degrees of intensity, as lazy, feckless, and stupid. The rems are seen as having a future in unskilled employment and as most likely to experience long periods of unemployment.

The withdrawal of any commitment to the school, and the decision to leave before taking the final exams, is attributed by the ordinary kids to a manifest lack of moral fibre and in some cases to innate intellectual deficiencies. The ordinary kids see the decisions to get out of school at the earliest possible moment or not bothering to sit the final exams as 'giving up'. It is this decision which is important for understanding the attitudes of the ordinary kids to the distribution of employment opportunities. The distinction between the ordinary kids and the rems reproduces within the school a division, within the working class, between the deserving and undeserving, the respectable and the rough. The idea of the rem is not simply an educational by-product of pupil stratification (indeed pupils perceived to have 'real' learning difficulties receive a limited degree of sympathy and it is felt that they should be helped). However, the rems as characterized by the ordinary kids are the 'undeserving rough element' who 'drop out' of school because they 'can't be bothered'. Hence, bound up in the cultural understanding of different types of *futures* between the rems and ordinary kids is a *moral* assessment of *social worth*.

Here are examples of ordinary kids talking about pupils not bothering to take exams:

Amanda: I think that's a waste of time, I think it's stupid, 'cos they spent all these years at school haven't they, you know. They could have tried, if they had CSEs at least it's somethin . . . at least they're tryin' ent they.

Mark: Oh yeah, if you wants to be somebody, if you don't, I don't really have no disrespect for 'em, but if you want to be a lay-about, job creation and all that, what's the future in that, digging a garden. . . . What security for your family is that, you know. What prospects have you got for the future, right 'I'll be famous' [imitating some of the rems], you see 'em out of school now doing all this heavy stuff. 'Oh I've got a job, I've got forty quid a week in Burgerland', what's the point in that?

Anna: Like my friends, they don't see the use of 'em [qualifications] they think I'm stupid because I'm staying on for exams, but I don't think I'm stupid; they're the stupid ones, they're the ones who are goin' to be sitting on the dole for the next three or four years. They're the ones who don't even want to get a job, just sponge from their parents . . . I don't want to spend my life like that.

[Group discussion]

Pete: Well they're all dull like, you're not getting nothin' out of school, you come to school for all those years like, ten years, is it?

Ray: What about Dave and Den – they come to school?

Martin: But what do they come to school for?

Pete: They come to school for ten years and don't get anything out of it at the end. Don't get no exams or nothin'.

Martin: Dave and Den and all them, they comes to school just for a laff.

Pete: They didn't waste their time 'cos they learnt to read and write and add-up like, but they've got nothin' to show for what they've done.

Ray: You can have a good time without doin' what they're doin'.

Martin: Yeah.

[Martin also talks about himself and his two friends in an individual interview. Here he is suggesting why he was not doing so well at school as before.]

Martin: I don't know, stayin' with my mates it is . . . they're just the same as Dave and Den, they hang 'round, they don't do no work, but they're not like those lot . . . we're on different tracks, don't do work, if we wants to we could, but we don't.

P.B.: Yet you say you're on different tracks . . . what do you mean by that?

Martin: Well we *can* work, we can work, you know. If we put our minds to it, we could work but they don't know much, they're dull them lot are.

P.B.: Why do you think that is?

Martin: They haven't bothered, they're stupid, messin' around all the time.

P.B.: So why do you bother takin' exams?

Martin: Got to, well them lot, I have a better chance of gettin' a job, than them lot. If I passes my exams. They 'aint got nothin' but ah . . . it's up to them.

The ordinary kids recognize working for qualifications as symbolic of social and moral worth, largely independent of elevated scholastic attainment. To leave school without qualifications is believed by the ordinary kids to be a waste of one's years at school for 'that's what you're in school for really, qualifications and a job when you leave'. It is this view which underpins the ordinary kids' instrumental attitude to school and makes the everyday interactions of school life possible.

Equally, if 'making an effort' by working for qualifications stands as a symbol of social and moral worth, largely independent of the level of educational attainment, it is not surprising that the attitude of the ordinary kids towards the swots is often ambiguous:

[Talking about pupils taking O levels]

Jacky: Swots, don't bother with them.

Sal: The ones that sits 'round with their little sandwich boxes, talkin' about colours of beds.

Jacky: The kinds of things they talk about is really stupid.

Diane: I wouldn't like to go 'round with 'em as friends.

P.B.: Why not?

Diane: They just sits there and talk.

[After describing how they get on with two of the O level kids I then asked them what they thought about the rest of the O level pupils]

Diane: Say 'hello' now an' again, but they don't seem to mix in with us, like all us come in [to school].

Barbara: Brains on one side, thickies on the other.

P.B.: Do you think they see themselves as brainier?

Diane: Yeah, they do some of them . . . they usually keep to themselves really don't they? . . . all keep to themselves.

P.B.: Why do you think that is?

Diane: 'Cos they all eat sandwiches and all sit 'round in a circle (laugh) [in the youth wing at lunch time] they don't have dinners or pasties.

Pete: Oh I talk to 'em, but they're just like swots, way above me . . . I talk to 'em, chats with 'em but not a lot of lessons . . . most of 'em will become computer operators or somethin', tech' drawing designers.

P.B.: What do you think they feel about kids who are takin' CSEs, people like you?

Martin: I don't know, they don't think much, they keep on with their work like, they're all serious like, stayin' in . . . they must be in almost every night, swottin' for the exams.

[Group discussion about O level pupils]

P.B.: Do you think they have much of a laugh?

Ray: No.

Pete: No not the brainy people.

Ray: Have you seen Mathews . . . have you ever seen Mathews smile. I've never seen him smile. . . .

Adrian: Some are alright, half these girls I haven't got much time for . . . they treat you as if you're lower than them, as if they were much older than you . . . they treat you as if they're the ones with the knowledge and you're the kid.

P.B.: What about ah . . . the kids in this school takin' O levels.

All: Swots.

Pete: Ah . . . they're not swots like.

Ray: They are!

Pete: They're just clever.

Ray: Mathews!

Pete: He's takin' degrees he is [laugh].

Martin: He must have an I.Q. of about three million.

P.B.: Do you have much to do with them?

Pete: No, I hangs 'round with Mick Jones.

Martin: How much did Mathews get, he had about 98 for physics this year just gone.

Pete: Yeah 98 and 96 for chemistry. I don't hang around with him see, if I met him in an alley I'd hit the shit out of him [laugh].

Martin: Who'd want a life like that? He never goes out in the nights, every single night, he's in the house . . . Jones and Francis they're alright.

Ray: That's not a life is it, stupid.

Martin: Not all the time anyway, that's stupid.

The attitude of the ordinary kids to the swots is consistent with the typical working-class understandings of what is involved in 'getting on'. The vocabulary used to describe groups of pupils may be specific to the school, but this expresses an understanding which is derived from class-cultural elements. The ordinary kids have little interest in the formal culture of the school. The value of academic endeavour for its own sake and the exchange value of academic credentials for the types of employment preferred by the ordinary kids mean that their social identities and sense of social worth are not strictly tied to achieved levels of academic attainment. Consequently the acquisition of O levels, and the possibility of continuing at school for A levels, is viewed as a preparation for a different type of employment appropriate for different types of people. The commitment to the school exhibited by the swots is felt to be unnecessary, given the desirability of employment to which modest levels of scholastic attainment have (at least until recently) given access.

The ideology of meritocracy evident in the attitudes of teachers in their attempt to legitimate the process of selection and their everyday social practices might have been expected to lead the ordinary kids to see themselves as failures when compared with the swots. But this has not been found to be the case. It is not being suggested that the ordinary kids do not have an idea of merit as a basis for evaluating social worth. They do. However, merit as understood by the ordinary kids does not place paramount importance on the academic hierarchy. The ordinary kids will evaluate themselves and other groups of pupils on the basis of 'effort' rather than achievement. The idea of making an effort is complicated by the fact that it is derived from a collective understanding of what is ordinarily expected within the informal subculture of the ordinary kids. It is because ordinary kids judge social worth on the basis of a positive evaluation of 'making an effort' that they have an ambiguous attitude towards the swots.

Typically, the swots are believed to be morally deviant. Their deviance results from 'swotting' which involves doing more than 'making an effort'. Having apparent ability and the ambition to 'get out' are not in themselves deviant. Rather it is the resort to *excessive* work as a means of achieving success which attracts moral condemnation. The amount of work a person does is thought to be within their control. To opt to work more than others is therefore to separate oneself from and reject identification with other pupils, a rejection which attracts efforts at social control. Therefore, the swots are seen to achieve academic success at the expense of other pupils, by working excessively long hours, 'never going out in the nights', and creeping to teachers. Similarly the voluntary projection of self beyond group norms is also evident in the attitudes of the ordinary kids to the rems, given the rems' unwillingness to 'make an effort'. Both excessive work and the refusal to work offend against 'ordinariness'. Both are taken as rejection of the moral order built out of a desire for social solidarity and a recognition of the pragmatic value of work as a demand of the school environment. Swots reject the requirement for solidarity, rems claim an alternative solidarity built on a refusal to accept the necessity of school work. The ordinary kids therefore feel threatened in two ways. The existence of the swots offers the alternative of making it on one's own through sheer dedication to the task of 'getting out'. The rems offer the alternative of freedom from the demands, frustrations, and boredom of school discipline and school work which they sometimes see as irrelevant and illegitimate. The ordinary kids will almost certainly entertain fantasies about being either a swot or a rem – each has its attractions. However, ordinariness is secured by a constant attention to the different kinds of costs which will be incurred if it is given up: swots have to surrender the world of the present of youthful enjoyment, rems have that already, but at the price of a future on the dole or in dead-end jobs.

Ordinary kids and the perception of unemployment

It has been argued that the school compliance of pupils who exhibit an alienated instrumentalism is particularly volatile, since the basis of their compliance with the school rests on a view of schooling as a 'means' of obtaining credentials to compete for certain types of employment. The range of occupational possibilities seen to be available does not preclude the ordinary kids from feeling that they may ultimately have to settle for a semi- or unskilled job, or, as a last resort, a Government scheme. The perceptions of the job situation among the ordinary kids are not uniform, and we have seen that most of the school leavers in the study believe that jobs are available if an effort is made to find one. The perceptions of restricted job opportunities (or perceptions of increasing competition for those 'good' jobs which are available), have not led to a wholesale rejection of the importance of qualifications among the ordinary kids (see Chapter 6):

> Liz: When you leave school with no qualifications and the unemployment is as it is now, you won't be able to get a job, they're looking for school leavers with, you know, qualifications.
>
> Mark: Well the job situation . . . well it's worse now and there's not much chance of you gettin' jobs because of the situation, but if you've got qualifications behind you, the employer will take somebody who's got qualifications before someone who hasn't got qualifications. . . .
>
> [If four people go for a job, two with qualifications and two without], he's bound to pick one of the two that have got qualifications, and the two that haven't got qualifications are stupid. The ones that have tried their best are the ones most suitable for the job. I think qualifications can help you quite a lot for jobs.
>
> Jane: Oh yeah, now I do; when you're young you don't realize, you know. When I'm this age you start to realize like, how hard it is to get a job and things like that. . . . You need the qualifications these days 'cos if there's going to be a job they're going to take the one with qualifications, and that's the end of it.

However, faith in the value of qualifications as a means of securing employment was not always so certainly expressed among the ordinary kids. The ordinary kids are in a double bind, for not only do they confront the possibility of not finding a 'tidy' job, but a growing doubt about their chances of getting 'any' job. As can be seen from the following quotations, it is possible to recognize a growing uncertainty and ambiguity in their reasons for working for qualifications:

> [Group discussion]
> Amy: All the teachers are the same, they say 'oh you should get this, you could pass in this', but they're no good to you, when you're

leavin'. I don't see the point in havin' 'em . . . people these days have got qualifications but they still haven't got jobs.

Sue: It all depends what job you want.

Amy: But, you know, they don't get you anywhere. It's good to have them though.

P.B.: Why do you think it's good to 'ave 'em then?

Amy: Well like, you know, if someone went for a job and they didn't have qualifications, it's obvious the other one . . . they'd go for the one with qualifications. But half the time they just don't bother about them, they ask for them mind ya. . . .

P.B.: Do you think qualifications are worth working for?

Neal: Ah . . . I don't know, I suppose so. They don't seem to know do they, because you can't get a job, but ah . . . maybe things will improve later on and you'll need them. I wouldn't leave school without qualifications.

P.B.: Why not?

Neal: Because you wouldn't be able to get a job without them. If you wants a good job. If you just wants to leave school and go on the YOPs scheme or the . . . you know, they just take a lot of people who haven't got qualifications on a YOP scheme. I wouldn't leave school without them. If you want a good job, you know, without going on a YOP, you've got to have qualifications. . . .

Adrian: Well I don't know, well yeah, I think so because if you've got them [qualifications], then . . . well I don't know really. I think half the time it just depends what type of person you are really, but it's good to have them behind you.

Among the ordinary kids we can suggest that even where a high degree of uncertainty may exist concerning their chances of securing a 'tidy' job, qualifications are seen, sometimes ambiguously, as the best way of securing *any* job. To 'give up', and to leave school without attempting examinations, is also to 'give up' your legitimate claim to those occupational opportunities which are available. As we have seen the ordinary kids do appear to have some notion of a moral hierarchy of social worth, premised upon their *efforts* and, in a more limited way, their achievements in school:

Pete: If you see a load of people unemployed, you can't laugh at 'em, it's not really their fault is it really. It's their fault if they haven't got any education like, but you can't do much about it anyway like.

Here we can detect the idea of the deserving and the undeserving, (i.e. those who have tried to work at school, and look for employment without success; and those who could not be bothered in school, and consequently don't deserve a job – at least not before those who had made an effort have had the first option). This is also evident in a group discussion with some of the 'ordinary' girls:

> *Jane*: Mary H. . . she's as thick as shit.
> *Pat*: She's in Jones's for English [remedial class].
> *Elaine*: Yeah, look at her now, right, she . . . she's useless. She's in the bottom class of all and if there was a lower one, she'd be in that. Then there's people then, like us, you know, alright, CSEs behind us, but there's her, she's got a job, there's us.
> *Jane*: On the dole.
> *P.B.*: Do you think that's fair?
> *Lynn*: I certainly don't. My brother right, my brother's got nine O levels and he's up the warehouse right. He's workin' with the same boys who don't have no CSEs at all and they're all crappy jobs. Don't do nothin' all day and he's had nine O levels. So you can't . . . if you've got CSEs you can't, you know, sometimes you can't be guaranteed a job.

Here we find the idea that those with the best qualifications – those who have made an effort – should have the best jobs. Yet with only CSEs to one's name there is a realization that there are others competing for the same jobs:

> *Martin*: There's not many jobs around and it's not easy to get a job but you've got to keep on tryin'. . . . If there was jobs 'round, you know, if I got certain CSEs or O level passes, I can get that job like that [clicks fingers], but you can't be that sure any more . . . right now we're takin' CSEs and we think that ah . . . we haven't got a chance of gettin' a job because we're takin' CSEs and they'll be people goin' for it with O levels, so that puts us down. We haven't got a chance, 'cos there's goin' to be somebody else with O levels. They're goin' to have more chance than us and that's putting us down a lot.

Access to 'good' jobs may increasingly be perceived to be blocked. The ordinary kids pursue paper qualifications in the knowledge that these will at least give them something to show for their years at school, providing a legitimate claim to what occupational opportunities do exist. It is seen to separate the ordinary kids from the rems who have not made an effort, as scholastic qualifications become seen as important for increasing numbers of semi- and unskilled jobs. However, there is an intuitive understanding that for semi- and unskilled jobs it is often a question of 'who you know, not what you know', and that they will always be competing with other school leavers with better qualifications: 'he might have ten O levels and still be sweeping the roads'. The use of qualifications as the criterion of employability is also greeted with an element of scepticism. The use of certification as the basis for job selection is frequently questioned, given a belief that being able to do the job cannot be determined simply by your qualifications:

> *Anne*: I'd like to do somethin' with children, with children you have to get four O levels to do it. I could do it, I mind my niece now all day when I'm off school. I could do it easy but you have to have four O levels for it.
>
> *P.B.*: What do you think about that?
>
> *Anne*: It's stupid . . . some people haven't got any qualifications have they. They should take you in, some people are quite good with children, some people I think, aren't.
>
> *P.B.*: So you don't think you should have to have the qualifications?
>
> *Anne*: No, not really no. It might be hard now but they learn you what to do, they teach you. They got to show you everythin' when you go for a job really, haven't they really. Like workin' in a bank, they got to show you what to do, once you know what to do then you can do it. I think it's silly havin' qualifications for jobs.
>
> The people with O levels would have it, you know, 'cos they're ranked you know, I've done the same work as them. I does child care but they got the O level and I haven't . . . I could do it better than some other people, 'cos I've been brought up with a little child.

In this instance, school qualifications are not viewed as a legitimate basis for securing a job, in competition with proven ability to be able to 'do' the work. Indeed, pupil perceptions of unemployment are often anecdotal and localized. It would be incorrect, however, to suggest that these perceptions and interpretations of the (un)employment situation are simply based on a rational calculation of their chances of finding particular types of employment. One of the conclusions of this study is that the ordinary kids, although *realistic* about the type of jobs they *could* enter, are none the less *unrealistic* in their expectations of actually finding such jobs (see Chapter 3). The decline in job opportunities for the ordinary kids is not solely a problem of finding a 'suitable' job once they have left school.

The current levels of youth unemployment also generate problems for *being* in school. The problem of declining employment opportunities for the ordinary kids while they are at school stems from the way they understand the relationship between school activity and the reward structure operating in the labour market. Previously 'making an effort' was seen as a way of gaining certification which offered the real possibility of getting the jobs they wanted, consistent with the desire to 'get on' in working-class terms. Yet the projected future employment of the ordinary kids is not only an important basis for their compliance in school; it is also a basis for maintaining their respect and dignity in an institution engaged in the sorting and selection of 'talent' which rewards people who are 'not like us' (i.e. the swots). The ordinary kids are respectable because they can point to their chances of getting the sorts of jobs which are highly esteemed in the working-class neighbourhoods of Middleport. So although they are not 'successes' as defined by the school (and which the ordinary kids have little desire to be), they are not rems – they do 'make an effort' in school, which allows them to distinguish themselves from both the swots and the rems.

The uncertainty about future occupational roles evident among the ordinary kids is coupled with a knowledge that the swots may increasingly be competing for 'their' jobs. Conversely, the ordinary kids recognize that they may have to take any job they can find, yet the view that qualifications are important for 'any' job is contradicted by the knowledge that the acquisition of many semi- and unskilled jobs depends on 'who you know' not 'what you know'. The rems who have not bothered to make an effort in school are seen to leave school before taking examinations to snap up the few occupational opportunities which are available. The fact that the ordinary kids are being forced to bring into question the relationship between 'making an effort' in school and their occupational future presents a personal crisis. This crisis is caused by growing doubts about the value of making an effort in school and their position within it, and their place in adult society. The school's attempt to maintain the compliance of the ordinary kids will be the topic of the next chapter.

CONCLUSION: GETTING IN, GETTING ON, OR GETTING OUT

In this and the previous chapter we have examined the basis of working-class orientations to school and how these different ways of being in school are collectively experienced within the informal pupil culture. These different ways of being a working-class pupil in Thomas High School correspond with three different FORS. These can be typified in terms of 'getting in', 'getting on' or 'getting out' of the working class. Figure 4.1 shows how these FORS relate to pupil orientations to school and the informal pupil

Figure 4.1 Working-class pupils in school

Orientation to school	Alienated	Alienated instrumental	Normative/ normative instrumental
Location in pupil culture	Rems	Ordinary kids	Swots
Frame of reference (FOR)	Getting in	Getting on	Getting out

culture. In conclusion I will provide a brief description of each FOR, ending with that held by the ordinary kids.

Getting in

This FOR is adopted by those pupils who have an alienated orientation to school. The school holds little interest or meaning for these pupils both in terms of what the school attempts to teach, and in terms of their perceived futures. Their future reference is the world of working-class adults rather than a world of 'school kids', and they will attempt to leave school and find employment at the first opportunity in order to have money in their pockets and claim adult independence. Unemployment has not altered their attitude to school, but reinforces the view that making an effort is irrelevant because there are fewer job opportunities. Unemployment does however make it increasingly difficult for the rems (including the tidy lads) to 'get in'. Their rejection of the school and unwillingness to make an effort ensures that the rems are a regular target for moral indignation which acts as a powerful source of social division among the working-class youth of Middleport.

Getting out

This FOR is held by those working-class pupils who view their future as educationally, occupationally, and socially distinct from the majority of working-class parents, neighbours, and peers who live in the working-class neighbourhoods of Middleport. Such a FOR involves pupils adopting a normative or normative instrumental orientation to the school because academic success is crucial if 'getting out' is to be achieved. It also often requires the pupil to change his or her educational and social identity in important ways, and the school is a means to that transformation.

Youth unemployment has intensified the struggle for certification, but whether future groups of working-class pupils will risk
the social and moral consequences of being labelled a swot, when
they may still be unemployed even if they make it into higher
education remains to be seen. Meanwhile the close identification
of the swots with teachers is condemned by the ordinary kids and
rems as demeaning and a projection of the self beyond what is
ordinarily expected of working-class kids in school.

Getting on

This is the FOR of the ordinary kids. Their alienated instrumental
orientation to school has served both to ensure their incorporation
given that they regarded what the school had to offer as a means to
their social advancement within the working class, and as a source
of collective resistance to the school's definition of success and
moral worth, and which severely limits the amount of effort they
are prepared to make. Making an effort by working for
qualifications stands as a symbol of social and moral worth which
the ordinary kids recognize to be largely independent of the level
of academic attainment. The ordinary kids adopt a thoroughly
practical strategy for living a dignified life over which they feel to
be in command. But in so doing they are reproducing a social and
moral division within the working class. These divisions are
predicated on future performance in the market for jobs and
ultimately translate into divisions among working adults.
However, youth unemployment and economic restructuring has
thrown the ordinary kids' understanding of the school and social
life into disarray. This has not only generated private troubles for
ordinary kids but professional troubles for teachers as the crisis in
the classroom intensifies, as the whole *raison d'être* for teaching
and learning for the majority of teachers and pupils in working-
class schools has been seriously brought into question (see
Chapter 5). The crisis in the classroom has *not* been directly caused
by unemployment, but rather it has brought the underlying
contradictions in the schooling of ordinary kids to a head. In
subsequent chapters the contradictions underlying the schooling
of the ordinary kids are explored in greater detail; the next chapter
is specifically concerned with the political and classroom context
of the new vocationalism as a way of maintaining the compliance
of the ordinary kids and overcoming the problem of youth
unemployment.

5 · Ordinary kids and the new vocationalism

The problems which the ordinary kids are experiencing as they prepare to enter the labour market have been 'officially' blamed on the school's failure to prepare pupils for economic realities. In response to these apparent failings, the Thatcher Government is increasing the vocational emphasis and technical content of the curriculum in an effort to tighten the bond between school and local industry. The ordinary kids in this study left school before the new vocationalism had begun to alter classroom practices, and there is already evidence of considerable variations in the way programmes such as the TVEI will be organized in different schools (Dale 1986). However, the purpose of this chapter is to consider the political and classroom context of the new vocationalism which was defined in Chapter 1 as 'making the preparation for a place in the occupational structure the *raison d'être* of public education' (Grubb and Lazerson 1982).

There are at least three reasons why this discussion is required. Firstly, the rationale for the new vocationalism pays no attention to the ways working-class pupils have historically experienced the school and labour market. Second, the new vocationalism cannot solve the contradictions in the educational experiences of the ordinary kids, or the professional troubles of teachers. Third, the new vocationalism is a recipe for inequality. It represents an attempt to preserve the privileged education of the middle class at the expense of a broad-based comprehensive education for *all* pupils which would offer some hope for both school and society. This final point will be more fully considered in Chapter 7. Here, the political context of the new vocationalism is considered as a necessary backdrop for understanding its classroom context.

THE POLITICAL CONTEXT OF THE NEW VOCATIONALISM

In the era of the welfare state and continuous economic growth, there was little disagreement among politicians that secondary education should be expanded and opportunities increased.

Although the Conservative and Labour Parties were responding to somewhat different tunes they were both dancing to the beat of the post-industrial society. This society was seen to demand greater investment in 'human capital' to meet the growing need for skilled and highly educated workers. Moreover, for investment in education to yield its potential economic returns, it was argued, particularly by liberal reformers, that the educational system must be restructured in order to improve opportunities for pupils from a working-class background and thereby to draw upon a hitherto untapped 'pool of ability'. The pursuit of the dual objectives of increasing social justice and economic efficiency culminated in the transition to comprehensive education and various compensatory educational programmes were introduced in the hope that talented children from socially disadvantaged backgrounds would be able to respond to new educational opportunities and fuel the British economy.

However, whilst Britain's economic prosperity was seen to depend on the schools' ability to tap the 'pool of ability' in the 1960s, by the late 1970s such efforts had been identified as a source of social and economic liability. The parliamentary political consensus was dead. Kogan (1978) has noted that by the end of 1977 it was only the daring or the self-interested who were willing to call for more educational growth as a certain way to economic and social salvation (p. 4). Educational reform had not only failed to produce a more equitable society, it had also failed to prevent economic recession and unemployment. Vociferous members of the Conservative right such as Rhodes Boyson (1975) asserted that the attempt to use the educational system as an instrument for orchestrating social reform had gone too far, too fast, and was now a contributory factor in Britain's social and economic malaise. There was also a growing consensus among employers that the educational system was failing to produce the suitably qualified and willing workers needed if British industry was to flourish. In short the schools were believed to be producing too many consumers and not enough producers of wealth. John Methuen, then Director of the CBI, argued that:

> after one of the longest periods of compulsory education in Europe, many young people seem ill-equipped for almost any kind of employment and woefully ignorant about the basic economic facts.
> [in Hopkins 1978: p. 129]

This apparent gulf between the products of the educational

system and the needs of industry was not a new criticism to be levelled at the school (Reeder 1981; Watts 1983; Dale 1985). None the less it was something which the Labour Government of the day believed it could not ignore. In October 1976 James Callaghan launched the much publicized 'great debate' on education, at Ruskin College, Oxford. A number of topics were outlined for regional debate of which the relationship between the school and local industry was identified as an important issue.

The launch of the great debate and the regional conferences which followed did little to quell the growing concern and criticism being levelled against comprehensive education from employers and the right. Indeed, it set the stage for a further and more penetrating attack on post-war educational reforms. The important point to note for our purposes, is that the Conservative critique of comprehensive education did not question the educational system's potential for providing solutions to Britain's economic and social problems. It was the way this potential was conceived and executed by liberal reformers which provided the focus for criticism. The right's critique denies the existence of any *simple* relationship between economic efficiency and investment in education. Instead it was claimed that a disproportionate number of school leavers are unemployed and unprepared for the world of work.

Consistent with this idea that Britain's economic ills (including youth unemployment) are rooted in the educational system is a belief that the occupational aspirations of school leavers are hopelessly out of tune with economic circumstances, and if left intact may lead to social unrest. As one senior official at the Department of Education and Science put it:

> We are in a period of considerable social change. There may be social unrest, but we can cope with the Toxteths. But, if we have a highly educated and idle population we may possibly anticipate more serious social conflict. *People must be educated once more to know their place.*
>
> (Ranson 1984, emphasis added)

As a result of this diagnosis the Thatcher Government (partly under the guise of falling rolls) has used major surgery on the educational budget.

There have also been efforts to remedy the apparent mismatch between the needs of industry and the products of the school by restructuring the secondary school curriculum. The Manpower

Services Commission (rather than the Department of Education and Science) has been provided with funds to introduce new forms of technical and vocational education. The Technical and Vocational Educational Initiative began during September 1983 in fourteen areas in England and Wales. The current total is over 100. According to the MSC the main purpose of TVEI is to make the school curriculum more relevant to the world of work, and it is intended to be available for all pupils who want to take part regardless of sex or educational attainment (MSC 1985b). However, it is evident from speeches by leading conservative reformers such as Lord Young and Norman Tebbit, that they are particularly interested in developing new forms of technical education for non-academic pupils such as the ordinary kids, or, as Norman Tebbit put it, 'for those who do not fancy the rich and academic diet, we are providing them with a rather more nourishing technical diet' (see McCulloch 1986: p. 44).

What such a policy ignores is the way the ordinary kids have actually experienced the school and labour market prior to the collapse of 'tidy' jobs for ordinary kids. For example, the apparent mismatch between education and industry is often measured in terms of attitudinal differences between teachers and employers (Bridges 1981; Watts 1983). As a result it is assumed that teachers are constantly feeding their pupils with negative images and attitudes about business, industry, and technology, which influence their pupils' occupational ambitions (Anderson *et al.* 1982). The belief that the educational system is playing a key role in perpetuating an unhealthy disregard for technology and industry has also been popularized since the publication of Wiener's *English Culture and the Decline of the Industrial Spirit* (1981). His work reveals a pervasive middle- and upper-class frame of mind which has long been hostile to industrialism and economic growth. He correctly believes that this cultural tradition has dominated the education system, but the obvious flaw with using his argument as proof that school leavers have inappropriate attitudes for economic survival, is his assumption that members of modern societies share a common culture and to infer therefore that anti-business and anti-industrial attitudes are endemic throughout British society.

What this study of ordinary kids reveals, however, is that the vast majority of working-class pupils do not develop educational and occupational aspirations commonly found among the middle class. It has been shown that the ordinary kids' FOR sets limits on their educational ambitions and range of occupational preferences in terms of 'getting on' in working-class terms. These are exactly the jobs the Government seems to think school leavers do not want! All the evidence leads to the conclusion that if the ordinary kids' occupational preferences and expectations are out of tune with economic realities it is not because the school has implanted unrealistic expectations or anti-industrial sentiments but that the school has failed to dampen the expectations of gaining first of all 'tidy' and then 'any' job. To understand why this is the case requires us to take account, not only of the structure and content of the educational system but the actual process of schooling. There-fore, in order to understand why ordinary kids come to view the world in the way that they do we must take account of their working-class FOR. It is precisely because of the limited impact of the school on the cultural practices and understanding of the ordinary kids that the transition from school into manual and low-grade white-collar jobs has remained unproblematic until there were no longer enough of these jobs to allow ordinary kids the chance of 'getting on'.

This conclusion generates considerable scepticism about the recent Government attempts to tighten the bond between school and employment. Youth unemployment is not an 'educational problem', but as Watts (1978) has noted it is a problem *for* education. The mismatch between educational and occupational opportunities which has existed in the post-war period, has successfully been accommodated due to the production of social identities among working-class youth which has limited their demand for education. Youth unemployment is a problem for education because it severs the connection between the reward structures of the school and the labour market, which led the ordinary kids to see that there was a point in making an effort. Economic restructuring in South Wales, as elsewhere, has presented the school with the problem of maintaining the co-operation of the ordinary kids, and preparing them for an uncertain economic future.

Understanding this classroom context is therefore vital for understanding why the new vocationalism will do little to improve the ordinary kids' chances of employment, and hence will not solve the crisis in education. It is the purpose of this chapter to further that understanding. We begin with the ordinary kids' response to the more traditional way of preparing and fitting school leavers into appropriate forms of employment; their attitudes to careers education; and then consider their response to Government schemes.

CAREERS FOR ORDINARY KIDS

In recent years careers education has been 'officially' identified as one of the ways young people can be taught about industrial and economic life in Britain in the hope that this will lead to an appreciation of the importance of industry to Britain's future prosperity. It has been suggested that an effective careers education and guidance programme will help young people to appraise their qualities and preferences on the basis of a realistic appreciation of the opportunities which are available. Such an appraisal would be preparing young people to take full advantage of available training programmes and allow them to settle, without difficulty, into the requirements of the job (Central Policy Review Staff 1980: p. 34). A more modest responsibility which careers education[1] has been asked to assume, is to improve the flow of labour market information to school leavers, which has in the past been found to be inadequate (Clarke 1980a).

Careers teachers and officers, on the other hand, have been engaged in an on-going debate about the ultimate responsibilities of the practitioners: i.e. should they primarily be concerned with preparing school leavers for unemployment or boring low-paid jobs or should careers education place the predilections and interests of pupils before manpower requirements?[2]

Kirton (1983) has argued that the decline in job opportunities for school leavers has exacerbated the tension between the often contradictory philosophies of the careers movement, which prides itself on the virtues of being 'client-centred'. When few job opportunities are available for school leavers, he suggests that careers teachers and officers will emphasize the 'positive' role of providing their pupils with the best possible chance of finding a job.

Concern among practitioners about how the careers movement should respond to youth unemployment comes at a time when the careers movement is under pressure to overcome the mismatch between education and industry, and perhaps at a time when its clients may view the careers service as being irrelevant because it offers little hope as an avenue to 'proper' jobs.

Careers education in Thomas High School

When the clouds of political dialogue and philosophical debate about the aims of careers education are dispersed (at least temporarily) to expose the day-to-day practices of careers education in Middleport's comprehensive schools it appears far removed from the crossfire of rhetoric. In the three schools visited in this study, two fall far behind the Department of Education and Science (1980) recommendations that:

> systematic careers education should begin no later than the third secondary year, and it is normally desirable that it should occupy a specific place in the timetable. Periods of work experience and work observation can be useful for pupils of all levels of ability. (p. 8)

In Thomas High School the careers teacher was a senior member of staff who was expected to fit in careers guidance with other teaching and supervisory responsibilities. Work experience was permitted but its organization was left to the discretion of pupils. The fact that such extra-curricular activities were not time-tabled ensured that only 'non-examination' pupils could spare the time from study for CSEs and O levels. Only 5 per cent of pupils in Thomas High School had been on work experience programmes while at school, but almost half of the fifth-formers had engaged in part-time employment.

Like other aspects of school life, attitudes to careers education depend upon pupil orientations to school and the labour market. Willis (1977) has shown how at least one group of working-class pupils (the lads), do not simply *receive* the lessons teachers and careers officers have to teach, but interpret careers education in terms of the cultural understandings and meanings which the anti-school subculture engenders.

Unfortunately, Willis was unwilling to concede that other working-class pupils who do not adopt an anti-school subculture may also develop collective cultural interpretations which lead them to assimilate careers information in ways which have relevance to *them*. We would therefore expect the ordinary kids to interpret careers education in terms of its significance to helping them to find out about 'good' working-class jobs, and as a source of information about where potential opportunities exist, rather than having much impact on the framing of occupational preference. It is only for those working-class pupils in the top band of the school (swots) that we would expect careers education to have an impact on the framing of the pupil's occupational and social future in terms of 'getting out' of the working class.

Moreover, whether careers education can have an influence on gender differences in occupational preferences remains uncertain. But careers education will tend to reinforce rather than offer a basis for the reassessment of pupils' occupational preferences unless three criteria are met. First, greater emphasis should be placed on careers teachers/officers to encourage consideration of the whole range of employment to *all* pupils regardless of sex. Second, more effort should be put into devising compensatory measures which ensure that both sexes have equal opportunity to undertake the full range of school subjects, and third, employers' recruitment practices should be changed so as to allow pupils to perceive occupational opportunities as not being gender-specific (Equal Opportunities Commission 1985).

Despite the limited brief with which the ordinary kids evaluate the usefulness of careers provision, the vast majority of ordinary kids (90 per cent) who had been interviewed by the careers officer believed that their careers interview was of some help. One of the reasons why the ordinary kids seem to be reasonably satisfied with their careers interview is that the careers service is able to provide occupational information about the sorts of jobs which the ordinary kids were applying for. For example, a list of employers recruiting apprentices is compiled and distributed annually, and information about courses at local colleges of further education is readily available to the careers adviser if the ordinary kids want to know about what options are available if they cannot find appropriate employment (Watts 1981).

Where *informal* rather than *formal* recruitment practices are adopted by employers the careers service is unlikely to be aware of vacancies let alone be capable of helping school leavers to take them up. It is the rems who are the most likely to seek employment when no formal qualifications are required. Few of the tidy lads had bothered attending the careers interview, some were even unaware that such an interview could be arranged at school. Amongst the tidy lads there was a standing joke that if you were male and not taking examinations you were going to go on the dole, go on a Government scheme, or work in a warehouse. However, for those rems (including the tidy lads) who did attend a careers interview most found it of some help. Somewhat surprisingly it was the swots who found their careers information of least help. Many of the swots complained about a lack of guidance

and information about job opportunities and university and poly-
technic courses, as one of the female swots commented about the
career officer: 'I suppose she was prepared for the normal run of
the mill, but I think a careers advisor should be prepared for
everything.'

It is also worth noting that a larger proportion of girls than boys
found their careers interview of help. The finding that the female
ordinary kids are more favourable in their assessment of careers
provision may reflect differences in the parents' ability or interest
in providing labour market information to their children. Among
the ordinary kids this was indeed found to be the case. Fifty-five
per cent of both boys and girls felt their mothers were a very
helpful source of information about jobs, but it was the perceived
helpfulness of the fathers which varied between the sexes. Over 60
per cent of boys compared with a little over a third of the ordinary
girls stated their father to be 'very helpful' on this matter.

The belief that careers officers and careers teachers may have
more influence on the particular jobs the ordinary kids apply for
rather than upon the perceived limits on the range of jobs which
the ordinary kids view as appropriate and desirable is difficult to
substantiate quantitatively from the data available in this study.
The question – which asked pupils to evaluate how helpful
various people had been in providing them with information
about jobs – was difficult to interpret, because the question did
not permit the respondent to distinguish between those persons
who had provided occupational information about what jobs
were available, and those who had influenced the structuring of
occupational preferences. This problem is evident in much of the
existing literature which has attempted to evaluate the relative
importance of *informal* (parents, relatives, and peers) and *formal*
(teachers, careers officers etc.) influences on occupational decision
making (Veness 1962; West and Newton 1983). Despite these
difficulties much of the literature shows that *informal* influences
are the most important factor affecting occupational decision
making (Clarke 1980a).

In this study over half of the ordinary kids stated that careers
teachers and/or careers officers had been very helpful – about the
same as the proportion who found parents helpful. A similar
pattern of response was evident among the rems. However, only
40 per cent of swots felt that careers teachers/officers had been
'very helpful' and the parents of swots were not felt to be of much
more help. Obviously from pupil responses to this question it is

not possible to determine whether careers provision in school is being evaluated in the same way as occupational information received from parents. But in an area of high unemployment such as Middleport the ability of working-class parents to provide labour market information and to be able to 'put a good word in with the boss' in order to fix-up their children with a job may be declining. When the ordinary kids were asked to evaluate how helpful parents had been in providing information and the influence they had had on occupational decision making, pupils whose fathers and mothers were unemployed were reported to be *less* helpful than those with parents in full-time jobs.

The possible declining influence of working-class parents as a traditional source of labour market information and contacts was evident when the ordinary kids were asked how they would go about finding a job. Less than 10 per cent placed their faith in getting a job through personal contacts, whereas over half the ordinary kids thought that the best way of getting a job was through their own efforts by applying directly to firms. What this suggests is that the ordinary kids still think that jobs are available but that to get them it is necessary to 'make an effort' and not rely on family and friends, or the careers service, which was mentioned as the first method of finding a job by under one-quarter of the ordinary kids.

If personal contacts were seen to be of little help in finding jobs due to unemployment and the constant threat of redundancy which meant that many of the firms offering access to 'tidy' working-class jobs were no longer recruiting school leavers, it is also the case that the value of the careers service was also questioned as a route to 'proper' jobs, because it was increasingly identified as a placement agency for Government schemes. The general message the careers service was conveying to the ordinary kids was that if they could not find a job, there were always Government schemes available which could improve their employability, if not ensure their employment.

The conclusion to be reached from the discussion of careers and ordinary kids is that any attempt to use careers education to tighten the bond between school and the local labour market will meet with limited success. More careers education and guidance will fail to 'cool out' the ordinary kids' desire to 'get on' and their preference for jobs which will allow them to do so. Such attempts will meet with considerable resistance because it is not simply a job, but a way of being in the world which is at stake. The identification of unskilled work with the rems acts to negate any suggestion from careers teachers that 'blind alley' jobs may be a more realistic prospect for their qualities given the opportunities which are available (Central Policy Review Staff 1980).

Although the ordinary kids were positive in their evaluation of the occupational information supplied by the careers service, the information provided was often patchy and provided on an *ad hoc* basis. If the careers officer is able to supply the ordinary kids with more information about real jobs rather than Government schemes, present services for ordinary kids could be improved. Moreover, they *do* feel there is a need for careers education about how to write a letter of application, and present themselves at an interview. But even here there is a feeling that any ordinary kid *can* write a letter, which will tend to lead ordinary kids to identify careers education as suitable for the rem. Government schemes are another part of the institution provision aimed at improving school leavers' chances of employment which the ordinary kids identify as being suitable only for rems.[3]

ORDINARY KIDS AND GOVERNMENT SCHEMES

The Youth Opportunities Programme developed out of growing concern to ensure that:

> all young people of 16 to 18 years of age who have no job or who are not engaged in further or higher education should have the opportunity of training, or participating in a job creation programme, or of work experience.
>
> (MSC 1977: p. 3)

The bleak occupational prospects which confronted the ordinary kids made them aware that they might not find a suitable job when they leave school and face the option of going on the dole or going on a Government scheme. From what we already know about the ordinary kids, their willingness to go on a scheme will depend upon whether they believe a scheme would allow access to a good working-class job. Hence, the success of the Youth Opportunities Programme (YOP) and its sequel, the Youth Training Scheme (YTS), will depend upon the perceived relevance the scheme has in the attempt to fulfil future occupational preferences. State provision for unemployed school leavers has changed rapidly as employment prospects have continued to decline. A number of writers have suggested that Government schemes are not simply part of a move towards a comprehensive manpower policy (MSC 1977; Holland 1986) which is the rationale offered by the MSC, but rather a political response born out of a fear of social unrest in the cities and an attempt to reduce labour costs (Rees and Atkinson 1982; Gleeson 1983).

In the following discussion we examine the ordinary kids' attitude towards Government schemes while they were still at school. At the time they expressed these attitudes the YOP was being phased out in preferences to a 'twelve-month' scheme, as the ordinary kids saw it. In order to avoid any unnecessary confusion, questions about Government schemes were phrased to monitor pupils' attitudes to YOP rather than YTS. However, there seems to be little ground for believing that pupils had a firm idea about how the new provision would be different from the YOP. Indeed when the ordinary kids were aware that changes in the structure of Government schemes were being planned, the two issues which were raised concerned the possible reduction in payment if the schemes were to improve the amount of training offered, and whether schemes should be made compulsory for unemployed school leavers.

Pupils were asked whether they would rather earn £25 in a factory or £15 a week in a workshop or college if more training were provided. A little under half of the ordinary kids were willing to take a reduction in money if more training were offered. This was double the number of ordinary kids stating a preference for more money rather than more training, which supports the view that if the ordinary kids cannot find jobs, it is quality training for 'tidy' working-class jobs they want and are prepared to make financial sacrifices to get it. This was more than twice the proportion of rems who were willing to take a drop in money for more training (20 per cent). The swots, however, were more concerned that training should come before financial consideration, although a large proportion of the swots came from families in a better position to support their children materially as they move towards adult independence. On the issue of compulsory schemes for the young unemployed, approximately one-third of ordinary kids 'disagreed' and a slightly larger proportion were undecided about whether or not Government schemes should be made compulsory. However, the response to compulsion recorded a significant difference between groups of pupils. The swots – who were the least likely to have to go on a scheme – were the most strongly opposed to compulsion and rems were most favourable to the idea of *compulsion*.

The ordinary kids were generally more willing to place 'quality' training before money during the initial transition from school, but remain divided about whether it was desirable to make schemes compulsory for unemployed school leavers. There was little difference between ordinary boys and girls on the issue of 'quality' training, but 40 per cent of the ordinary boys disagreed with the idea of making schemes compulsory for unemployed school leavers as opposed to a quarter of the girls.

More importantly, gender differences were also in evidence when pupils were asked if they would be willing to go on a Government scheme. Once again it was the female ordinary kids

Table 5.1 *Whether pupils would be willing to go on a Government scheme (%)*

	Rems	Ordinary kids	Swots	Total
Yes	54	50	33	44
No	15	20	38	27
Don't Know	31	29	29	29
Total (number)	48	221	170	439

who showed the more favourable response to official provision for school leavers. Almost 60 per cent of female ordinary kids said they would go on a scheme and a little over 40 per cent of the boys, and approximately a third of each sex remained undecided. There were also differences in the reported willingness of categories of pupils to go on a scheme regardless of sex.

Table 5.1 shows half the ordinary kids stating a willingness to go on a scheme compared with one-third of swots. The proportion of swots stating a refusal to go on a scheme (38 per cent) was almost double the proportion of ordinary kids (20 per cent). The rems stated the greatest willingness to participate in a scheme and although they also stated the greatest uncertainty about whether they would participate in a scheme only 15 per cent of these pupils categorically stated that they would not be willing to participate.

We would expect such differences in the willingness of groups of pupils to go on a YOP/YTS to reflect variations in what pupils believe schemes to be providing. In the attempt to capture the range of pupil attitudes about schemes a variety of questions were

Table 5.2 *Pupil attitudes to Government schemes: % 'agreeing' with each statement*

	Rems	Ordinary kids	Swots	Total
Positive statements				
Teaches you the skill to get a job	71	81	80	80
Gives you the experience to get a job	82	74	76	76
If you do well you will be offered a permanent job	44	26	16	24
Negative statements				
Government schemes are a waste of time because there are no jobs	29	16	15	17
Government schemes are a way of keeping young people off the streets	50	51	43	48
Government schemes in industry are cheap labour for employers	69	64	64	64

asked which required pupils to express their level of agreement/disagreement. Table 5.2 shows that despite the rems being the most likely to view schemes as 'cheap labour' they also show the highest proportion of pupils believing that schemes provide the experience necessary to get a job and thought that doing well on a scheme would lead to the offer of full-time employment. The swots were the least likely to believe that a scheme is a way to obtaining permanent employment, and also the least likely to believe that a YOP/YTS is a way of keeping young people off the streets.

A large proportion of ordinary kids felt (like other groups of pupils) that Government schemes are cheap labour, but were divided on the question of whether the YOP/YTS was a way of keeping young people off the streets (51 per cent agreed). Only one-quarter of ordinary kids felt that a YOP/YTS would lead to the offer of a permanent job. Despite a belief that the YOP/YTS exploits young people, the ordinary kids remain convinced that schemes *do* provide the opportunity to learn occupational skills and offer work experience necessary to gain permanent employment.

The response of the ordinary kids to particular aspects of Government schemes should not distort the general sense in which the ordinary kids have not accepted the assignment of a

Government scheme as a 'normal' part of the transition from school. Schemes are a last resort and one which some of the ordinary kids are clearly not prepared to entertain. If schemes are seen as tolerable in circumstances where there are no jobs, their future as a credible bridge between school and work nonetheless depends upon their ability to provide 'real' training for 'proper' jobs.

There is an uneasy tension between the view that schemes are cheap labour and unlikely to directly lead to a 'proper' job (i.e. 'kept on'), with a belief that the schemes may actually provide the skills and training which will enhance job prospects. What is evident is that the legitimacy of the schemes does *not* depend upon the promise of a job on completion of a scheme (see the next chapter). Working for qualifications was seen by the ordinary kids as a means to getting good working-class jobs and gradually came to be seen as a way of getting *any* job as employment prospects further declined. In the same way, compliance with Government schemes in periods of low unemployment may be viewed by potential trainees to depend upon the promise of employment on completion of a scheme (Stafford 1981), but as occupational opportunities further decline they may come to be perceived as a way of equipping the ordinary kids with the skills and experience necessary to *compete* for the few jobs which remain.

An alternative to going on a scheme is the attempt to gain employment while on the dole but one of the problems with being unemployed is that it presents the ordinary kids with the problem of exhibiting their 'ordinariness'. The defining feature of ordinariness in Thomas High School involved being seen to be 'making an effort' or to be 'doing something' rather than ''anging around the 'ouse' or 'doing nothin'' – a distinction which operated so powerfully as to constitute the moral basis for the separation of the ordinary kids from the rems. Consequently, even for the ordinary kids who believe that Government schemes are 'not for them', considerable pressure may be brought to bear by peers and parents to make every effort to avoid the dole:

P.B.: Paul, you mentioned that Government schemes keep you off the streets; do you think that it's important to be kept off the streets?

Paul: Ah well, not kept off the streets I suppose but havin' you somethin' to do. When you've got nothin' to do that leads to trouble on the streets and, you know, and all that business. Like people hiding behind the thing that you can riot because there's no jobs, but if they were on some sort of thing . . . a lot of them don't go on these work experience things 'cos they're cheap labour, but at least you're off the streets, you're workin' and it's better to have money in your pocket than a brick in your hand throwing at somebody really. So [schemes] are a very good idea really, 'cos it gives you a chance to work and a chance that you might get a job as well then, see.

Despite uncertainty about the value of Government schemes and their identification with the rems, Government schemes may paradoxically offer some of the ordinary kids a way of maintaining respectability while they are on the lookout for employment. However, the degree of uncertainty and those refusing to go on a scheme shows that there remains considerable resistance to Government schemes from ordinary kids because they are no substitute for 'proper' jobs.

Moreover, the discussion of the ordinary kids' attitudes towards careers education and Government schemes over-whelmingly demonstrates that what the ordinary kids want are genuine opportunities to 'get on' with, and in, their lives as culturally defined within the working-class neighbourhoods of Middleport. Such a conclusion raises important questions about the rationale and consequences of attempting to tighten the bond between the school and the local labour market. Although the ordinary kids in this study had left school before the launching of the TVEI, consideration of the classroom context (as well as the political context of TVEI) in which such innovations must operate in practice, raises important and uncomfortable questions for the teaching profession.

It also illustrates how the political response to the problem of unemployment which lies behind TVEI connects with the professional problems confronting teachers. A failure to recognize this connection results in the inability to translate the professional troubles confronting teaches into public issues about the relationship between education and society, which the school must prepare pupils to enter.

Finn (1983) has argued that the new vocationalism amounts to a:

crude experiment in social engineering, the needs and aspirations of the young working class in particular are being manipulated and their expectation systematically reduced. This is the political project of the Thatcher government, and it is in this light that we need to assess the various programmes that they have initiated. (p. 45)

Although I share much of Finn's concern about the new vocationalism his somewhat deterministic account of the consequences and changes in the schooling of working-class pupils ignores the practices and cultural understandings of pupils. It also ignores the unintended consequences of teachers attempting to overcome their own professional troubles. As Walker and Barton (1986) have noted:

> The danger is that a real consequence of the pressure on teachers, which arise from the stress of stage-managing contradictions deepened by mass youth unemployment, is that they may be coerced, seduced or recruited into courses of action that isolated them from their fellows, increasing their powerlessness and threaten their own interests and ambitions. (p. 8)

The remainder of this chapter will attempt to show the nature of the problems confronting teachers in schools such as Thomas High School, how TVEI may be used to overcome them, and the consequences of such actions for schooling ordinary kids.

THE CLASSROOM CONTEXT OF THE NEW VOCATIONALISM

In this book I have argued that the school compliance of the ordinary kids has depended upon certain historical conditions in which the reward structure of the school and labour market corresponded sufficiently to allow pupils to predict the likely outcome of efforts in school. The teachers I spoke to in Middleport also acknowledged that most of what is taught in comprehensive schools has always been irrelevant to the future lives of working-class school leavers. However, despite considerable bouts of boredom, low levels of academic endeavour and attainment exhibited by the ordinary kids, and a sense of futility among many of the school staff, teachers were able and willing to justify what they were doing on the grounds that modest levels of academic achievement appeared to provide access to the sorts of jobs their pupils wanted. This rationale for a far from satisfactory situation can no longer be sustained, and the realization of this fact is seriously affecting teachers' morale, and forcing teachers to find new ways of justifying their day-to-day practices both to themselves and to their pupils. The decline in the opportunities for ordinary kids has therefore presented the teaching profession with a dual problem. First, how to ensure the compliance of the ordinary kids without which day-to-day institutional practices would be impossible. Second, even if order can be maintained, teachers confront a crisis in *morale*, given that maintaining social order becomes an end in itself rather than a means of imparting school knowledge.

Evidence from Thomas High School suggests that teachers, given a lack of alternative resources, will continue to bolster the unstable foundations on which the compliance of the ordinary kids is grounded. However, teachers are well aware that the effort–qualifications–jobs motivational sequence is losing its hold:

> *Janet*: When I first started here . . . um . . . I used to be able to say if you get this qualification in typin' or office practice or whatever, it's going to stand you in good stead for a job. I mean I can't say that now, they'd just laugh if I said that. They know different . . . em . . . I think employment was a big motivator.
>
> *Mary*: There isn't the incentive now to get the CSEs to go and get a job. Ah, talking to my third year options I was saying 'okay, if you want a certain job, bear that in mind and make sure you get the right sort of general subjects to do that anyway. But don't just go and look for CSEs for a job, do what you enjoy. Do something you're likely to get something out of, and an interest in, even if it doesn't get you a job.' Because for lots of them – as things stand at the moment – they're not going to have jobs. Half their fathers are redundant.
>
> *Mat*: I consciously don't say anything about their chances of getting a job. I don't know what I'd replace it with . . . it will be difficult to replace that, because that's their whole life to them when they leave school. They want a job – they want the money and the satisfaction which goes with it. I think it will be very difficult to replace that.

One of the people most acutely aware of this problem and its consequences was the head teacher:

> *Peter*: Without doubt we can no longer . . . ah . . . bribe pupils by saying you be good, we'll give you a good reference and that will be a meal ticket . . . the necessary way to a job. I think that has gone. I think it's less important now to stress the career importance of a particular subject or, you know, geography will help you getting a job in local government, surveying or teaching or whatever it might be. I think this sort of approach has to disappear. I don't think we can any longer say that a particular subject is appropriate entirely to a particular sphere of employment. I think we have got to get back to the idea that education has value in itself. That the study of the subject area has value in itself and we've got to make the subject relevant as far as the youngsters are concerned in order to maintain their interest . . . a great number of pupils are disillusioned by the whole business of the relevance of education to unemployment

now. A lot of them realize that they are going to be unemployed . . . we have got to put in a lot of spade work as far as the relevance of the school to, ah, such things as leisure, preparation for being unemployed and so on . . . for long periods. Educating to the work sharing idea, it will come in too late for a generation, and I'm very sad to have to say that we've lost a generation . . . these children come to school, ah . . . they go home in the evening, perhaps mum and dad might have lost their jobs. Perhaps dad has been out of work for some time and mum's still working. So the whole balance has changed . . . as far as this is concerned, a certain tradition . . . approaches and so on are no longer there.

One of the changes is that the teaching profession can no longer quietly suffer with the knowledge that much of what they are teaching to ordinary working-class pupils in the later years of secondary education is boring and irrelevant. The growth in youth unemployment has highlighted the problem of what to teach pupils who are not believed to be benefiting from an academic curriculum, certainly not after the age of 14.

These problems coupled with the prevailing climate of Government cutbacks and falling school rolls along with the financial incentives offered to local education authorities and schools makes TVEI an all-too-inviting innovation (Watts 1983; Bates 1984). The TVEI offers teachers the opportunity of bolstering their own sense of purpose and pupil compliance by placing less emphasis on the value of qualifications which can be traded in the market for jobs, and more upon the *direct* relevance of school learning to employment. This emphasis upon the extrinsic value of school *learning*, rather than school certificates, is seen as providing the opportunity for making the move to increase the *practical* content of the curriculum more *intrinsically* meaningful and interesting.

But if more involvement in practical endeavour is the carrot dangled in front of the ordinary kids, there is also a stick. The more sinister aspect of recent attempts to reform the educational system involves a shift from relatively impersonal and objective (although academic) systems of educational assessment, to one where the school increasingly emphasizes the personality package (Fromm 1962) where pupils' subjective attributes are assessed on a highly subjective basis. It is the whole person which is now on show and at stake in the market for jobs. It is the personality package which must be sold in the market place. This trend, epitomized by the growing popularity of 'pupil profiles', emphasizes – as the kids do themselves – that it is not only 'what you know' which gets one a job. The school's attempt to maintain the compliance of large numbers of working-class pupils has therefore involved an attempt to *formalize* the informal elements of recruitment practices into the school's brief.

However, such changes continue to tie the teacher's authority closely to the exchange value of school learning for jobs, and to set limits upon that authority consistent with the ordinary kids' previous orientation to the school. It also serves to highlight serious contradictions in the school's attempt to win the compliance of large numbers of working-class pupils. The success of some of the ordinary kids' social inferiors in the school (i.e. rems) in getting jobs on the basis of 'who you know' provides them with evidence that if it is a question of getting 'any' job, then it is not who you *are* or *what* you know, but *who* you know, which is of crucial importance. So long as the school does not have control of the social networks of working-class people, it will *fail* to formalize the extensive use of informal recruitment practice on the basis of 'who you know'. What this conclusion also highlights is the contradiction between the criteria which the school assumes will be used when young people are selected for employment, and the characteristics actually required by employers. They are frequently not those positively valued within the school (Lavercombe and Fleming 1981; Ashton and Maguire 1986).

Moreover, the more teachers are forced to emphasize the personality package of pupils as a factor in job acquisition, the more pupils are likely to believe that the only reason for compliance is because the teacher has the power to define the pupils. Compliance is a matter of doing what you are told under threat of not getting the good school reference necessary to help find employment. A further threat to the ordinary kids' compliance results from the ambivalence evident among these pupils about whether occupational opportunities should be based upon the possession of appropriate formal qualifications, or on proven ability to do the job.

Moves to make the school curriculum more vocationally relevant, by teaching pupils more of what they need to know to *do* the job, may both heighten their desire to enter 'appropriate' employment and cause them to view the discrepancy between an ability to *do* the job, and the need for increasing numbers of academic qualifications to *get* the job, as manifestly unjust. For example, some of the swots have been forced to 'trade down' and apply for jobs once the preserve of the ordinary kids. This is not only sensed by the ordinary kids as an illegitimate use of qualifications achieved by extraordinary activity at school, but one which leads them to think that 'making an effort' to achieve some qualifications is futile, because they know that there will always be someone better qualified who is likely to get the job, irrespective of ability to *do* the job.

I am not suggesting that the vast majority of teachers have got involved in the TVEI because they see their role as agents of social control. There is a genuine concern that the educational system has been failing many of its pupils in more ways than one for far too long, and that TVEI does hold the potential for progressive educational reform such as a new pedagogy of experiential learning and problem solving against traditional or academic learning (Ranson *et al.* 1986; Blackman 1987). There is also a genuine belief that greater involvement in technical and vocational education may be in the best interests of *their* pupils, in the hope that it is they who will get a job. Yet a consequence of teachers having to work within the constraints of the 'chalk face' and attempting to resolve their personal and professional troubles, is that the question of school leaver 'employability' is not defined as it should be, as relative to the *demand* for labour, but as a personal trouble which can only be overcome at the expense of other teachers' equally deserving (or undeserving) pupils. In the short term the TVEI may help to maintain some degree of interest in school life, at least among the ordinary kids, due to an interest in 'practical' school subjects. However, the contradictions between what the ordinary kids want from school and labour market realities cannot be resolved on a diet of technical studies, despite its being more palatable.

The wisdom of spending more time and effort in school preparing pupils for jobs which do not exist was again clearly recognized by the head teacher of Thomas High School:

> *Peter*: We have to prepare the children through school, through subjects in school . . . to live in a world rather than just thinking it's about work . . . somehow or another we have to provide them with the necessary skills to be self-sufficient to work on their own and earn money in a very different world situation . . . I think we have to encourage them to keep fit – physically and mentally – so developing aesthetic values and an outlook which will mean that they are no longer pigeon-holed, in the sense that we pigeon-hole people. 'What are you?' 'Oh I'm a retired surgeon' or 'retired labourer' or whatever.

'Oh I'm a redundant steel worker' or whatever. We tend to pigeon-hole people and I think we have to get away from this.

Although this vision of the future is at least superficially appealing, the idea of educating for leisure or unemployment is rarely regarded as a universal educational strategy but one appropriate for those pupils who are unlikely to get jobs. Of course the pigeon-holing of the ordinary kid may be restricting and fail to do justice to the 'whole person' but as we have seen it is an important basis for providing a sense of dignity and social identity. However superficially appealing the head teacher's view of the future may sound, it neglects the realities of the world which the ordinary kids will enter. It also neglects the fact that the majority of the population between the ages of 16 and 60 are *in* jobs and so long as personal identity, social status, and material prosperity largely depends on employment, calls to restructure the educational system in order to prepare the ordinary kids for leisure or unemployment will be resisted and rejected.

However, such a debate is far removed from current trends in secondary education, which is increasingly being geared to prepare working-class pupils for employment. It has been shown that if the school can be accused of teaching an unnecessarily academic curriculum which pays little regard to technology, business, and industry it has failed to have much impact on the attitudes and outlook of the ordinary kids. It would appear that if Weiner's account of Britain's economic decline has any purchase it is in regard to middle-class pupils in public and private education where attention needs to be focused. Despite this conclusion, the new vocationalism has been directed at the more expendable part of the school population – ordinary working-class pupils. The existing structure of power, privilege, and inequality remains untouched. Indeed it may be reinforced because what we are witnessing with the expansion of the TVEI is more far-reaching than the mere introduction of more technical studies, it is the *vocationalization of working-class education* (Brown 1987b). It is a policy which attempts to legitimate the provision of a socially appropriate training, rather than a socially 'just' education for large numbers of working-class pupils, as part of the inescapable duty of the Government to ensure that the work of the school matches national needs (DES 1980). Exactly which national needs are being served by the new vocationalism is considered in the concluding chapter, along with the teachers' response to the new vocationalism.

One of the main conclusions of this chapter is that as the ordinary kids are bringing the purpose of the school and their willingness to make an effort into question, so teachers have been forced to supplement the existing structure of social control, previously based on a relatively objective assessment of the child's *academic* profile. They have done this by enlarging the area for assessment, by emphasizing the child's *social* profile (attitudes, motivation, disposition) as an increasingly important factor for job acquisition. 'Badges of ability' (qualifications) are therefore being supplemented with the need for 'badges of *acceptability*' (having the right attitudes to authority, and the right 'personality package'). Although the student's social profile may be legitimated in terms of employers' needs to evaluate their future employees as persons and not just certificate holders, it is also a way of policing pupils and offering the *potential* for constant surveillance. Moreover, the reinforcement of objective forms of assessment with more subjective evaluations involves the public recognition of the difference between working-class and middle-class FORS, which lies behind the hitherto relatively privatized social and cultural content of being an ordinary kid in school. This is not only likely to extend class bias in educational assessment, as Bernstein (1977) perceptively showed in the shift from visible to invisible pedagogy in the primary school, it also makes it likely that, with their backs against the wall, teachers will become less tolerant of working-class indifference and resistance to definitions of school knowledge and school success, which will intensify classroom conflict.

Hence, the failure to convert the professional troubles of teachers into public issues concerning the future direction of educational and social priorities, implicitly accepts that there is a need to tighten the bond between school and industry, and that the problem of youth unemployment is partly the fault of the school. This has left the school defenceless against political initiatives such as the new vocationalism, which will not only lead to greater educational inequality, it will also do little to alleviate the longer-term crisis in the classroom.

6 · Ordinary kids in the labour market

In earlier chapters it was argued that the ordinary kids' FOR not only represented a way of 'making a living' but a way of 'making a life'. The purpose of this chapter is to assess the ordinary kids' performance in the labour market and whether they have reconciled their ambition to 'get on' in working-class terms to the labour market realities of the 1980s. Writers have generally recognized the importance of a person gaining employment in order to participate fully in the society in which he or she lives (Jahoda 1982; Hayes and Nutman 1981), and to successfully make the transition into adulthood (Sofer 1974; Kelvin 1981). Eggleston (1982) has suggested that:

> Work experience provides the basic contexts for 'normal' life. These include the use of time, the achievement of social 'standing' with its rights and duties and many of the attitudes and values that underpin participation in all the other human contexts offered by society. We may express the situation in two ways. One is that vocational identity is the key to social identity. The other is that work is the central instrument of social control in modern society. Without the experience of work, how can the individual develop an adequate social identity and how can the society exercise the social control over its members necessary to achieve stability and continuity? (p. 4)

The labour market realities of the 1980s are such that the vast majority of ordinary kids are either unemployed, not in the jobs they want, or have postponed their transition into the labour market. How have the ordinary kids responded to this situation 18 months after reaching school leaving age? Have they developed disaffected attitudes when they compare their lot with the one which has been held out to them as their legitimate condition (Kornhauser 1960: p. 160) by teachers and parents? Has the FOR characteristic of the ordinary kids substantially changed? And if so, do such changes relate to differences in experiences since completing compulsory schooling? The ordinary kids' response to their experiences since leaving school is also of sociological interest, because differences in educational performance and pupil divisions within school have usually been identified as a major determinant of variations in working-class life styles and intra-class divisions (Willis 1977; Jenkins 1983). The suggestion that it is becoming increasingly difficult to predict the labour market biography of early school leavers on the basis of educational performance also raises the question of what consequences changes in labour market conditions are having on the social and moral divisions as understood by the ordinary kids. These are the main questions to be examined in this chapter.

THE DESTINATIONS OF THE ORDINARY KIDS

At 16+ we have information for 163 of the 225 ordinary kids in the original sample. [1] Table 6.1 shows what happened to the ordinary kids in October of the year they intended to leave school and a little over a year later. The table shows that less than 60 per cent of ordinary kids entered the labour market at the time they intended to. The large proportion of ordinary kids opting to stay in full-time study rather than enter the labour market was unexpected because virtually all of them had intended to leave full-time study at 16 years of age, and stated that they were looking forward to having a job. The primary motivation for the ordinary kids' retreat from the labour market was the bleak prospect of finding a job if they left school at the age of 16, and for this significant minority of ordinary kids full-time study was judged to be preferable to a Government scheme or the dole queue. [2] The extension of full-time education for these ordinary kids signals a failure in the attempt to find suitable employment at the time they had intended to leave school.

Table 6.1 *The destinations of ordinary kids 3 and 18 months after attaining school-leaving age (%)*

	3 months			18 months		
	M	F	Total	M	F	Total
Full-time job	19	16	18	42	34	38
Unemployed	13	5	9	17	22	19
Government scheme	30	28	29	8	10	9
School or college	39	48	43	32	32	32
Other	—	3	1	2	3	3
Total (number)	88	75	163	89	73	162

Table 6.1 also shows that only 18 per cent of ordinary kids entered employment soon after leaving school and the proportion becoming unemployed was under 10 per cent rather than almost 40 per cent because 29 per cent were on Government schemes. Over a year later the proportion of ordinary kids in employment had more than doubled, but still stood at under 40 per cent. The proportion unemployed had also more than doubled to almost 20 per cent, but the percentage of ordinary kids on schemes had declined by two-thirds to under 10 per cent. Although not shown in Table 6.1 over 40 per cent of ordinary kids with labour market experience have not had a full-time job of any kind. Approximately the same proportion had experienced a period of unemployment between 1 and 6 months, and a further 15 per cent had been unemployed for over 6 months.[3] Almost one-third of the ordinary kids remained for a second year of additional study.

The conclusion to be drawn from this introductory discussion is that over 60 per cent of the ordinary kids are not doing what they wanted a year and a half after attaining school leaving age – that is, being in employment. However, even among those who found jobs many are not in the jobs they wanted. Twenty per cent of ordinary kids confront an eighteenth birthday celebration on the dole and the only reason this proportion is not considerably higher is because a significant minority have postponed their departure from full-time education or have gone onto a Government scheme.

Table 6.1 also reveals differences in the destination of ordinary girls and boys. Over twice the proportion of boys were unemployed after 3 months in the labour market. Such differences were not, however, due to a larger proportion of girls finding jobs, but due to the greater willingness of the girls to stay out of the labour market by remaining in full-time study. A year later the same proportion of female ordinary kids had entered the labour market, but remain less likely to be in jobs and more likely to be unemployed or on a Government scheme.

These gender differences are particularly surprising because in Middleport there has been a shift away from traditional forms of 'male' employment in heavy manufacturing, coal, and steel, and a growth in the proportion of jobs in service industries, which have tended to be undertaken by females. This raises the question of whether male ordinary kids are taking jobs which were preferred by the girls at school. There is tentative evidence to suggest that a larger proportion of boys hoping for clerical and commercial occupations actually entered such jobs. However, this was due to male swots 'trading downwards' into clerical jobs when they were unable to find professional and adminstrative jobs rather than the manifestation of a shift in applications from male ordinary kids from manual to non-manual occupations, although it was male ordinary kids rather than male swots who entered commercial jobs. Whether there will be an increasing tendency for boys and girls to seek 'non-traditional' forms of gender-specific employment remains to be seen, but as Keil and Newton (1980) have noted:

> It is only in times of relatively high unemployment that the transition from full-time education to full-time employment proves difficult; and even then it is because jobs have to be taken which are considered below the appropriate skill level or status level rather than crossing sex lines. (p. 109)

Differences in the proportion of male and female ordinary kids in employment can only partly be explained as the result of sexist recruitment practices adopted by employers (Equal Opportunities Commission 1985), because boys and girls continue to prefer and apply for different types of jobs.[4] Ashton and Maguire (1980b) have found that female school leavers face stiff competition from married women who have recently entered the labour market in greater numbers and who are willing to work part-time and whom employers may prefer because they are believed to be more stable and reliable as employees.

The reason why the girls have been less likely to find jobs than the boys lies beyond the scope of this study. What *can* be examined, however, is whether the differences in labour market performance has led to an increasing sense of conflict between the sexes. While the ordinary kids were at school the boys were more likely than girls to feel that boys should have preference over available jobs and apprenticeships. This seems to be what is happening in the labour market: not only were boys more likely to be in jobs than girls, but of those in jobs providing some form of apprentice training (30 per cent) over three-quarters were obtained by boys (Keil and Newton 1980).

The proportion of ordinary girls who disagreed with the statement that men should be given jobs before women declined from 86 per cent when in school to a little under three-quarters. Among the boys there was a sizeable increase from 61 per cent in school to 89 per cent in the labour market who *disagreed* with the view that men should be given priority over females in the labour market. It may well be that as a larger proportion of male ordinary kids had found jobs they no longer viewed girls as a threat. But given the substantial proportions of boys and girls still looking for employment, this does appear to represent a change in attitude – particularly among the boys, who seem to have become more egalitarian. There is also a small change in the attitude of girls, which led 12 per cent to state that they *agreed* that it was more important to let boys have jobs before girls. It is also possible that, confronted with bleak occupational prospects, some of the girls may be considering marriage and/or 'having a family' at an earlier age than might otherwise have been the case if jobs were available. Moreover, among those currently looking for jobs nearly a quarter of girls in contrast with 8 per cent of boys did not think they had as much chance of getting a job as someone of the same age but of the opposite sex. The poor job opportunities for female ordinary kids may be forcing them to retreat into the home (Bloxham 1983; Cohen 1982), but few revel in their enforced domesticity (Donovan and Oddy 1982).

It is extremely difficult to identify the reasons why some of the ordinary kids have found jobs while others have become unemployed. Gender is obviously important, because male and female school leavers will have different labour market locations with respect to different types of jobs, and will also tend to apply for different types of employment. But this does not help to explain differences between ordinary kids of the same sex. Having a parent who can put in a good word for you, being in the right place at the right time, and the extent to which he or she may be willing to take 'any' job, will all play a part.

Ninety per cent of the unemployed ordinary kids had been to see the careers officer since leaving school, compared with a little under two-thirds of those currently in employment. As one might expect, it was the ordinary kids in jobs who were more likely to have perceived their discussion(s) with careers officers as 'very helpful' (57 per cent), compared with 42 per cent of the ordinary kids who were unemployed. The same proportion, approximately one-third of those who found jobs, did so through personal contacts or the careers service. Approaching firms directly, which was reported by over half the ordinary kids while in school as the most promising way of finding a job, was mentioned by under 10 per cent of the ordinary kids in jobs as the major contributory factor in finding employment. Approaching firms directly was also reported by under 10 per cent of the unemployed ordinary kids as their best chance of finding a job. This is probably because of the large numbers of school leavers chasing so few jobs that they know it to be hopeless trying for jobs unless they have contacts. They may be personal contacts, reported by 37 per cent of unemployed ordinary kids as offering the best chance of finding a job; or more formal contacts with employers arranged through the careers service (39 per cent). Thus depite the possibility that parent and friends, particularly those parents and friends who are unemployed, may be less successful in finding jobs for their children by 'asking around' or 'putting in a good word', the proportion of unemployed ordinary kids believing this to be the best way of finding jobs doubled since leaving school.

The main purpose of this chapter is to consider the consequences of the collapse of job opportunities for ordinary kids, rather than attempting to provide an explanation of why the ordinary kids have experienced the labour market in different ways. However, recent work on the fate of redundant steel workers with which I have been associated in South Wales (Harris *et al.* 1987) shows that in a local labour market where few job opportunities exist, the reliance on standard variables such as qualifications are by themselves weak predictors of successful subsequent labour market careers. Ashton and Maguire (1980a) have also argued that a large proportion of jobs which are open to school leavers do not depend upon educational attainment. In earlier chapters it was argued that the compliance of the ordinary kids depended to a large extent upon the assumption that by making an effort in school, they would improve their chances of 'getting on' in working-class terms. In a situation where there are few job opportunities for school leavers, the acquisition of school certificates was believed by some of the ordinary kids to be a means of getting any job, even if it was not the one they would prefer. This raises the question to what extent the efforts of the ordinary kids in school have helped them in the labour market compared with other categories of school leavers.

Such an analysis presents a number of problems, chief of which is the small number of rems and swots with labour market experience which makes it difficult to draw clear conclusions about these groups in comparison with the ordinary kids. Moreover, the rems and swots who have labour market experience may not be representative of each category. The relatively low response

Table 6.2 *The shape of labour market biographies among groups of school leavers irrespective of additional study (%)*

	Rems	Ordinary kids	Swots	Total
Have had a permanent job	65	59	61	60
Proportion having one job	63	91	79	84
Experience of a Government scheme	77	62	72	66
Number of Government schemes				
One	45	67	67	64
Two	55	23	25	29
Three or more	—	10	8	8
Length of unemployment				
Up to one month	39	48	44	46
Between 1 and 6 months	46	38	44	40
Over 6 months	15	15	13	14

rate among the rems may reflect a greater willingness among those who have had greater success in the labour market to fill in and return the questionnaire. The swot with labour market experience may also not be truly representative of that category, because the existence of such an orientation usually involves the continuation of full-time study beyond the age of 16. Therefore they do not have the same location in the labour market – because of their relatively poor qualifications – as those who have stayed in full-time study despite sharing the same orientations at school.

In spite of the problem of sample size and representativeness, it remains an important part of this study to consider whether there are any differences in labour market biography between the rems, swots, and ordinary kids. A comparison of the absolute rates of employment shows little variation in the proportions of school leavers having had a permanent job (see Table 6.2). What differences in employment histories do exist are small and show no clear pattern. The ordinary kids with labour market experience were the least likely to have had a job, but those ordinary kids who did get jobs represented the largest proportion obtaining employment within 6 months of leaving school, and were the most likely to have stayed in their first job.

On the basis of these findings, if the ordinary kids continued to make an effort in school in order to get any job, they have failed. This belief is supported by Lavercombe and Fleming (1981) who were interested in the relationship between pupil attitudes to school and the experience of unemployment immediately after leaving school. They found that the duration of unemployment was not significantly related to pupil attitudes to school, employment, or teacher authority. Neither did pupils who passed a greater number of CSEs get jobs significantly more quickly than other pupils.

A problem with examining absolute rates of employment and unemployment is that they represent no more than 'snapshots' in a dynamic process (Roberts 1984; Harris *et al.* 1987). Moreover, the short time that these school leavers have been in the labour market makes it impossible to accurately predict the shape of their labour market biographies. What we do know is that the tendency for some young workers to shift from job to job (Carter 1966; Cherry 1976) has been abruptly curtailed for all school leavers (Raffe 1983). Job changing was rare in the Middleport study. Over 80 per cent of those in jobs remained in their first job and only two young workers had entered more than two jobs. It would appear that those school leavers finding jobs are staying put, given a lack of perceived occupational opportunities elsewhere.

Roberts *et al.* (1981) suggested that the main consequence of youth unemployment is that the stretches of unemployment between jobs are longer. Therefore, young people affected by unemployment are:

> sentenced to sub-employment, not long-term idleness, and many of these young people are from neighbourhoods where, in the full-employment era, the majority of school leavers spent their early careers moving between unskilled jobs. In these localities, sub-employment is not a novel career pattern.
>
> (Roberts 1983: p. 137)

This interpretation of the working class in the labour market not only underestimates the experience of long-term unemployment among qualified school leavers, which Roberts now believes is generating a new 'under-class' (Roberts *et al.* 1987), but it also ignores the cultural significance attached to different types of employment by different groups of working-class youth. The argument that declining job opportunties are less of a problem for qualified school leavers because they can trade down obviously has some truth, but it is not as straightforward as Roberts believes (Roberts 1983). Firstly, the variations in employer recruitment practices (Lavercombe and Fleming 1981; Ashton *et al.* 1982; Jenkins 1983) may not necessarily make more qualified leavers attractive to employers for jobs with which employers believe an ambitious school leaver would quickly become bored and dissatisfied (Willis 1977). Secondly, some of the ordinary kids may be unwilling to take a 'shit' job since it is not simply an occupational label which may be at stake but the basis for personal dignity, respect, and advancement within the working class. Therefore, although the ordinary kids are no more likely to have had a job since leaving school they may be selective in the types of jobs they are applying for and entering.

Table 6.3 shows the social class of preferred job at school and that entered (where applicable). The table not only shows that the vast majority of these beginning workers have taken jobs which by preference they would not enter, it also shows that there are important differences in the type of jobs the rems, swots and ordinary kids are entering. Nearly three-quarters of the rems are in semi-skilled or unskilled jobs, compared to approximately one-quarter of ordinary kids. The ordinary kids are not proving able to obtain apprenticeships in engineering, hairdressing, building, and childcare, which are all represented in the Registrar General's III manual category. Many of the girls are opting for clerical and shop work; which explains much of the 20 per cent increase in the number of ordinary kids entering skilled non-manual jobs as defined by the Registrar General. Gender differences in employment among the ordinary kids will be considered in more detail below, but one point which can be made here is that the large percentage increase in skilled non-manual jobs in the swot category results from a failure to obtain professional and administrative jobs; and this includes boys obtaining skilled non-manual jobs which involve clerical rather than shop work. Over 60 per cent of swots leaving school failed to enter professional and administrative jobs, and over half the rems failed to enter skilled manual and non-manual employment.

Table 6.3 also shows that the rems, swots, and ordinary kids are not only entering different sorts of jobs but are applying for different jobs. Some of the ordinary kids and swots may well be 'hanging on' in the hope of getting the job they want rather than snatching the first job that becomes available. While at school 7 per cent of ordinary kids who eventually became unemployed or went on a Government scheme disagreed with the statement 'any jobs better than none'. The proportion of these ordinary kids disagreeing that any job is better than none increased to almost one-third. The increase in the proportion of ordinary kids

Table 6.3 Orientations at school and the social class of occupation (%) where applicable

Social class	Rems			Ordinary kids			Swots			Totals		
	occ asp	act occ	% diff	occ asp	act occ	% diff	occ asp	act occ	% diff	occ asp	act occ	% diff
I	—	—	0	3	—	−3	10	—	−10	4	—	−4
II	—	—	0	4	2	−2	58	4	−54	15	2	−13
IIIA	20	7	−13	23	43	+20	20	52	+32	22	40	+18
IIIB	60	20	−40	57	30	−27	8	28	+20	46	28	−18
IV	4	47	+43	7	19	+12	—	8	+8	5	20	+15
V	12	27	+15	—	6	+6	—	—	0	2	8	+6
ARM F	4	—	−4	7	—	−7	5	8	+3	6	2	−4
Total (number)	25	15		111	63		40	25		176	103	

reporting that they are not prepared to apply for 'any' job does lend support to the belief that some of the ordinary kids have withstood the pressure to apply for whatever jobs are known to be available. Some of the unemployed ordinary kids may not be prepared (at least in their early labour market career) to compromise what they see as the legitimate claim to make a particular type of future.

The willingness of most of the ordinary kids to continue to make an effort in school, was probably as much, if not more, important as a way of maintaining their sense of dignity and identity than as a means of entering 'tidy' working-class jobs. This has important sociological implications because to understand the transition from school, we need to be aware of the range of occupational opportunties which are available in the local labour market, and the different ways in which these school leavers will be orientated to such opportunities. The ordinary kids are predisposed towards the construction of a certain type of labour market biography. The transition to (un)employment is an interactive process. Things do not simply happen to people in the market for jobs, it requires and involves *agency* (i.e. they have to apply for a job before they can be accepted or rejected by employers). It is in this sense that the ordinary kids are creating their own labour market biographies. This remains true regardless of the *resources* (i.e. qualifications, school reports, etc.), which may improve market capacity or power to secure a specific type of employment. Moreover, the FORS identified among working-class youth and manifest in pupil occupational preferences represent more than an expression of different ways of 'making a living': they reflect different ways of 'making a life'. It is this way of life which looks like eluding all but a small minority of ordinary kids. How the ordinary kids have responded to their labour market experiences, and in particular whether they have adapted their FOR to labour market realities is our next concern.

THE ORDINARY KIDS ON GOVERNMENT SCHEMES

A large proportion of ordinary kids had been on a six-month YOP or twelve-month YTS (62 per cent) despite the fact that while they were at school there was little doubt among the ordinary kids (and swots) that schemes were only suitable for the rems who had not been bothered to make an effort, and did not deserve anything better. The large number of ordinary kids entering schemes once again testifies to how bleak the ordinary kids' occupational prospects are given that they have been forced to bridge the gap between school and an uncertain economic future with at least one programme. One-third of ordinary kids with labour market experience have been on more than one scheme.

In the previous chapter it was shown that while at school the ordinary kids believed that YOP/YTS did provide occupational skills and work experience, as well as providing a source of cheap labour for employers. Given that half of the ordinary kids who went on a scheme left before its completion, and under 30 per cent of those who remained to the end of the programme were 'kept on' by employers, we would anticipate a significant shift in the ordinary kids' attitudes to schemes. Table 6.4 shows that this has *not* happened. The ordinary kids continue to believe that schemes are a useful way of acquiring employment-related skills and experience when prop : jobs are not available. The favourable responses to the training elements of schemes is supported by most of the available research evidence (Roberts 1984).

They also continue to see the schemes as exploitative and to a lesser extent a way of keeping young people off the streets. However, the view that Government schemes are a waste of time because there are no jobs met with little support. The belief that YOP/YTS is politically motivated (a way of keeping young people off the street), and exploitative (cheap labour for employers) is not sufficient to negate the positive characteristics for those ordinary kids who entered a scheme. The attitudes to Government schemes considered in Table 6.4 are not of equal importance for understanding whether they will maintain compliance with formal provisions for unemployed school leavers.

On the basis of our data it would appear that the volatile nature of compliance with schemes has been mistakenly understood to rest on the promise of employment on completion of the scheme (Stafford 1981). Youthaid (1981b) have argued that as the numbers completing YOP were increasingly unable to find employment, so there was an increasing danger that the schemes will lose credibility. This view now appears to be the result of studying a relatively buoyant labour market. The present study of ordinary kids in less favourable labour market conditions suggests that the viability of YOP/YTS does not depend upon the promise of a permanent job on the completion of a scheme. Rather. it crucially depends on the belief that jobs are available for *some* school leavers, and schemes provide a way of improving one's employ-

Table 6.4 Attitudes to Government schemes before and after entering a programme – (%) agreeing with each statement

	Rems		Ordinary kids		Swots		Total	
	Before	After	Before	After	Before	After	Before	After
Positive statements								
Teaches you the skills to get a job	71	89	81	87	80	83	80	86
Gives you the experience to get a job	82	94	74	82	76	81	76	84
Do well on a scheme and you will be kept on	44	33	26	27	16	31	24	29
Negative statements								
Schemes are a waste of time as there are no jobs	29	17	16	16	15	11	17	15
Way of keeping people off the streets	50	56	51	49	43	40	48	48
Schemes are simply cheap labour for employers	69	67	64	67	64	69	64	68

ment *chances*. Such an idea is reinforced by the view that having the 'right attitude' to the job is the most important criterion adopted by employers for recruiting young people.[5] An important part of having the 'right attitude' is a willingness to make an effort, being 'seen to be doing something', which is demonstrated by entry onto a YOP/YTS. This appropriation of schemes by the ordinary kids inadvertently reinforces the 'official' view that unemployment is a private trouble. Young people may not be held responsible for unemployment in general, but the reason why any particular individual is unemployed rather than another is assumed to relate to the personal characteristics of the individuals compared. The ordinary kids appear to be unable to see beyond the logic of the Government's approaches to youth unemployment, which emphasizes a need to equip unemployed young people:

> to adapt successfully to the demands of employment; to have a fuller appreciation of the world of industry, business and technology in which they will be working; and to develop basic and recognized skills which employers will require in the future.
>
> (Department of Employment 1981: p. 7)

Yet if Government schemes are intended to regulate or systematically reduce the ambitions of working-class youth (Finn 1983) they have failed (see below). The ordinary kids who have gone onto schemes have done so in order to make the most of no job – as a way of staying in circulation (Roberts 1983) and as a means of 'moral rescue' (Lee *et al.* 1987). Government schemes have therefore been used by the ordinary kids as a way of *maintaining* their existing FOR; their use is not evidence of a willingness to abandon it.

The YTS is now regarded in official circles as the creation of a permanent bridge between school and employment (Department of Employment 1981) and as part of a comprehensive economic strategy rather than as a response to school leaver unemployment. The YOP has been superseded by the one-year YTS which in turn has been extended into a two-year programme. Regardless of these changes YTS is no substitute for 'proper' jobs, irrespective of the training they might provide. The ordinary kids will continue to evaluate the programmes in terms of their utility as a way of getting the jobs they want, and as a way of mantaining their social and occupational identities which are framed in terms of 'getting on' in the working class. It should also be remembered that a large minority of ordinary kids opted to stay in full-time study in order to avoid schemes as well as the dole, and some elected to seek employment while on the dole.

THE ORDINARY KIDS IN EMPLOYMENT

The ordinary kids who found employment may be regarded as the 'lucky' ones, although many did not enter the jobs they wanted (see Table 6.5). The largest discrepancy between occupational preferences at school and occupations actually entered by the female ordinary kids was to be found in personal service (e.g. hairdressing, nursery nursing) occupations. In contrast, a substantially higher proportion of girls than had hoped, actually found work in shops (+20 per cent) and offices (+14 per cent). The proportion of *boys*, hoping for skilled building and engineering occupations, showed a 19 per cent deficit when compared with those actually in such jobs. If these figures are adjusted to include all ordinary kids who stated a preference for skilled manual occupations at school, in the region of three-quarters of the boys with a preference for skilled engineering and building occupations have not realized their preference, as is the case with all but one of the girls stating a preference for personal service

Table 6.5 *Occupation preferences of male and female ordinary kids at school and the employment achieved by the ordinary kids who found jobs (%)*

	Occupational preferences at school			Occupations achieved		
	M	F	Total	M	F	Total
Skilled engin/building occupations	57	—	31	38	8	25
Hotel catering	3	6	4	8	12	10
Personal service	—	39	18	5	4	5
Clerical	2	25	13	5	39	19
Commercial	6	15	10	19	35	25
Admin/prof/exec	15	4	10	3	—	2
Misc. manufacture/ semi/unskilled	9	3	6	22	4	14
Armed forces	6	6	6	—	—	—
Don't know	2	3	3	—	—	—
Total (number)	88	72	160	37	26	63

jobs. How have these ordinary kids responded to their mixed fortunes in the labour market? Have they reconciled their school ambitions to labour market conditions in the knowledge that they have at least found a job, or do they remain hopeful of getting the jobs they wanted when they were at school?

If we are to substantiate the claim that the ordinary kids' FOR is an important factor in explaining how the ordinary kids *experience* the labour market, the question of job satisfaction becomes an important issue. A traditional question asked of young workers is the degree of their satisfaction with existing employment. The vast majority of this literature has found a surprisingly high level of job satisfaction with what may appear to the researcher as boring and mundane work (Clarke 1980b: p.7). It has also been taken to support the argument that even where stated occupational preferences are not met after leaving school, reported rates of job satisfaction remain high. This finding has led to the conclusion that prior orientations to the labour market are largely irrelevant; i.e. jobs are not entered into on the basis of ambitions, but ambitions are adapted to the occupations that young people find themselves able to enter (Roberts 1974: p. 147). What I want to question here is the adequacy of taking responses to job satisfaction as a basis for arguing that prior orientations to employment have little impact on labour market experiences, and therefore the assumption that if school leavers report being satisfied with their employment, we can conclude that these young workers are successfully accommodating their ambitions to labour market conditions with little psychological dissonance.

Over 90 per cent of the ordinary kids in employment *did* state that they were either 'very satisfied' (41 per cent) or 'satisfied' (51 per cent) with their current employment. Yet as Stewart and Blackburn (1975) have noted, statements of satisfaction appear to be made within the 'context of necessary external constraints'. In a situation where many of their fellow school leavers cannot find employment, it is hardly surprising that they report some degree of satisfaction with actually having a job, regardless of its content. While satisfaction may be expressed in terms of what is possible at this particular time, Stewart and Blackburn note that *liking* is expressed within a framework of what is thought to be desirable. In the attempt to place responses to job satisfaction within a wider context, the ordinary kids in employment were asked what job they would most like. Only 17 per cent of the ordinary kids in employment – constituting just 6 per cent of all ordinary kids –

reported their present job as the one they would *now* like and therefore can be said to be *truly* content with their current employment. The ordinary kids in employment are not accom-modating prior orientations to labour market conditions, as the prime-facie evidence based on responses to job satisfaction would appear to suggest; and although the ordinary kids who find employment may well be 'fortunate' when compared with their unemployed peers, they may be as dissatisfied as some of the ordinary kids on schemes or on the dole.

What the ordinary kids want from their employment

The study of the ordinary kids' response to labour market conditions also requires us to reconsider what the ordinary kids want from their employment. In Chapter 3 it was shown that the ordinary kids hoped that their employment would offer more than simply a way of earning a living. Table 6.6 shows the responses to what the ordinary kids thought to be the most important thing for them to gain from their employment, regardless of whether they are currently in jobs. This table once again highlights the importance of rewards from employment other than money. At this stage of the life-cycle, 'getting on' in working-class terms does not involve a form of instrumentalism as understood by industrial sociologists – i.e. minimum commitment for maximum material rewards (Goldthorpe *et al.* 1969; Blackburn and Mann 1979). Again, this raises serious doubts about the characterization of the labour market experiences of this group of school leavers as unproblematically adjusting their FOR to labour market and employment conditions. Table 6.6 also shows an increasing proportion of the ordinary kids stating job security as *most* important, its rank order moving from seventh to third place. There was also a change in the rank order with 'good work mates and/or working environment' giving way to 'interesting' work as the *most* popular response.

The emphasis placed upon job security is particularly evident among those in employment. The differences in response to job security among the (un)employed suggest that job security only becomes 'truly' important once someone has a job, even if it is not the job he or she wanted. Yet the increasing emphasis on job security does suggest that some of the ordinary kids welcome greater stability once employment is found. The reason why the proportion stating job security to be 'most important' has

Table 6.6 *The most important thing to be gained from a job: ordinary kids (%)*

	At school		All ordinary kids	
	%	Rank order	%	Rank change
Environment (social/clean)	31	1	17	−1
Life progress	16	3	13	−1
Opportunity to learn a skill	12	4	7	−2
Interesting/enjoyable work	20	2	36	+1
Money	8	5	9	0
Security	5	7	14	+4
Other	8	6	5	−1
Total (number)	201		152	

increased since leaving school is likely to be a result of the perception of difficulties involved in finding a job, and an awareness that, if present employment is lost, the chances of finding alternative employment is unlikely.

Among ordinary kids with labour market experience, responses to what is believed to be the most important thing to have in employment varied little apart from the question of job security. However, there was a significant difference between those with labour market experience and those remaining in full-time study (although not shown in Table 6.6). The variations between these categories of ordinary kids is largely due to the fact that over 60 per cent of those remaning in full-time study reported an interest in the job as being the most important aspect of working life. This shift in 'interest' brings the ordinary kids in full-time study much closer to the pattern of responses among the swots at school (about which more will be said below).[6]

Concluding the discussion of the ordinary kids in employment, it is evident that money has *not* become increasingly important when considered along with other aspects of working life. What is clear is that a growing proportion of ordinary kids want work that is interesting, secure, and helps them to 'get on'. A declining number of ordinary kids appear to be settling for good workmates or working environment as a compensation for uninteresting, uncreative, and boring jobs. At least with the first flutter of wings, there is little attempt to ground their wants concerning employment in the reality that only a few are likely to gain it, let alone to gain the jobs they actually want.

Table 6.7 *Occupational preference and expectations among the ordinary kids not in employment (%)*

Occupational categories	At school		Unemployed		In full-time study		All not in employment	
	Occ pref	Occ expectn	Occ pref	Occ expectn	Occ pref	Occ expectn	Occ pref	Occ expectn
Skilled building/engineering	31	20	26	4	—	—	14	2
Hotel and catering	4	3	6	2	10	7	7	4
Personal services	18	7	11	4	10	7	10	5
Clerical	13	9	13	12	14	17	13	14
Commercial	10	12	4	18	5	5	4	12
Administrative/professional	10	4	20	8	48	39	32	22
Miscellaneous	6	8	7	24	—	2	4	14
Armed forces	6	2	2	—	2	2	2	1
Don't know	3	37	13	29	12	20	12	25
Total (number)	160	148	55	51	42	41	97	92

THE ORDINARY KIDS NOT IN EMPLOYMENT

Having suggested that there is little difference among the ordinary kids with labour market experience as to what they would like from their employment, we can now consider whether there has been a significant change in the occupational preferences and expectations among those *not* in employment. Table 6.7 shows the occupational preferences and expectations reported by the ordinary kids currently unemployed or on a Government scheme, and those in their second year of full-time study. A comparison of the occupational preferences among ordinary kids at school who are now unemployed (including those on Government schemes) shows a slight *decrease* in the proportion aspiring to skilled building, engineering, and personal service occupations, and a more significant *increase* both in the proportion now not knowing what job they would most like, and among those aspiring to professional and administrative jobs. Despite such changes it is evident that even among the unemployed ordinary kids, their orientation to the sorts of jobs they hope to obtain have not radically changed. The largest shift in occupational preferences was found, not amongst those with labour market experience, but those who remained in full-time study, almost one-half of whom now aspire to professional and administrative jobs compared to one-tenth of the ordinary kids at school.

When current occupational preferences are compared to occupational expectations we find that the unemployed ordinary kids do *not* expect to enter the jobs they wanted. This discrepancy between occupational preferences and expectations is most dramatically illustrated in the case of skilled building and engineering occupations (preferred by 26 per cent but expected by only 4 per cent), while expectations outstrip preferences in the case of misc./unskilled jobs (three-fold), shop work (four-fold). The proportion who did not know what to expect was more than double the proportion expressing no preference. There was also considerable uncertainty among the unemployed about whether they would get a job; over two-thirds did not know when they would get a job and one-fifth thought it would take at least six months. However, despite the differences in occupational preferences and expectations identified among the unemployed ordinary kids they have not abandoned the desire, even if they are not hopeful of getting the jobs they want. This provides further evidence that if the purpose of Government schemes was intended to 'cool out' the ordinary kids' ambition to 'get on' they have failed, because the culturally prescribed form of becoming adult in a respectable fashion remains even when the means to its achievement no longer exists for more than a small minority.

The ordinary kids in full-time study were more optimistic about their chances of getting the jobs they hoped to enter: sixteen of the twenty aspiring to professional and administrative jobs expected to enter them. The experience of approximately half the ordinary kids in full-time study since the completion of compulsory schooling has succeeded, where five years of secondary education failed, to transform an understanding of their occupational futures from one of 'getting on' to that of 'getting out' of their class of origin.

However, despite the ordinary kids in full-time study being better qualified than other ordinary kids, the competition for middle-class jobs brings them into competition with middle-class youth, many of whom were identified as having a normative or normative instrumental orientation at school. Unfortunately the time span of the present study makes it impossible to study the transition of the ordinary kids who currently remain in full-time study, but it can be argued that the gap between aspirations and objective chances in the labour market may make their transition from full-time study particularly 'out of the ordinary'.

In attempting to summarize the findings of these data and their implications for understanding the ordinary kids' transition into working-class adulthood, we can usefully distinguish variations in the positions ordinary kids occupy in relation to the market for jobs:

1 There are an extremely small proportion (6 per cent) of ordinary kids who appear to make the transition from school into the types of employment they want.
2 There are others who are in employment but not in the jobs they prefer, although they hope, if not expect, to enter preferred occupations.
3 An alternative to applying for a job you do not really want or going on a Government scheme or becoming unemployed has been to remain in full-time education, in the attempt to gain additional qualifications to ensure 'suitable' employment. Where study has been pursued into a second year, what may be regarded as 'suitable' employment at 16 may have shifted 'upwards'. In other words additional study may lead to a reconstitution of what one might

become which, given the present labour market situation and their likely labour market capacity, may have the result that the ordinary kids remaining in full-time study will confront major problems of adjustment as they eventually move into the labour market.

4 A large proportion of ordinary kids who eventually found a job or became unemployed had been on a Government scheme. The proportion of ordinary kids leaving a scheme before its completion suggests that it was perceived as a stop-gap while looking for a permanent job. It was also seen to give a 'competitive edge' in the attempt to equip themselves with skills and experience, and represent the 'right' attitude to employers, despite a belief that the schemes exploited school leavers. The basis of their compliance with the schemes is not that they are a direct means to employment (i.e. being 'kept on'), but a 'means of making the most of no job'. The majority of ordinary kids, although hoping that a scheme will improve their chances of getting the sort of job they want, now view the schemes as a way of remaining in circulation, and maintaining their sense of dignity and identity.

5 Finally there are those ordinary kids who are unemployed. Over a quarter of the ordinary kids with labour market experience have been unemployed for more than three months, and almost half of these for more than six months (not including time spent on Government schemes). Responses to unemployment obviously depend upon its duration. If it is short-term it is unlikely to threaten social identity. However, despite the relatively short time the ordinary kids have been in the labour market it is the group of long-term unemployed whose social identity may be particularly out of tune with their understanding of what they *could* have become, or could now be becoming. The experience of long-term unemployment not only threatens the chances of the ordinary kids 'getting on', but also of gaining the status of working-class adult, previously arranged through the transition to employment, and eventually, marriage (Leonard 1980; Jenkins 1983). The social significance of engaging in paid employment in order to secure adult status is perhaps lessened for female school leavers (Gaskell and Lazerson 1980). Yet, in the early years of post-school life, finding 'suitable' employment is important to both sexes.

Having shown the massive discrepancy between the ordinary kids' FOR and labour market realities, I want to show something of the personal troubles which this is causing the ordinary kids and their parents. Here are six short accounts of how life since leaving school has been experienced by the ordinary kids. Those who have been selected are in no sense exceptional, perhaps with the exception of Pat who has been in continuous employment since leaving school.

Mark

Mark did not work hard in school but enjoyed some of the lessons, particularly business studies, because he wanted to enter the retail trade. He passed seven CSEs but did not get any O levels. He believed that his chances of getting a job with his disappointing examination results were very poor, so he decided to try for more qualifications in the sixth form. He studied for four O levels and passed two. Mark recalls that when he left school at 17 he did not think that the:

> job prospects were going to be as bad as this, not as hard as this, I thought it would be slightly easier but it's not . . . I was just determined to get a job, really.

But despite adopting what he described as a 'more serious attitude' since leaving school, and applying for a number of jobs as a shop assistant in Middleport's large department stores, he did not find a job. He spent two months on the dole before going on a Government scheme in a shop in town. His two months on the dole when he first left school Mark recalls as being particularly 'difficult'. He spent most of the time when he was not looking for jobs 'hangin' around the 'ouse'. His father worked 25 miles out of Middleport in a large car plant, his mother was not in paid employment and his sister was still at school. Mark was conscious about always being around the house and not being able to contribute to the household income. He felt that he should not have to rely on his parents but be 'standing on his own two feet'.

The experience of being unemployed has changed him:

> I've grown more mature . . . and found life much harder, ah . . . I've just changed completely really. In school you're living off your mum really, but then it changed and you're waiting for your next payment from social security and waiting for the next phone call from the job centre.

His Government scheme proved to be interesting and worthwhile and made him all the more determined to get a job in the retail trade. He was told that he would probably get 'kept on' once the scheme finished but with little more than a week before the programme was due to finish, Mark was told that the company was intending to make further cut-backs and this meant no new staff were going to be employed. He was back on the dole.

Mark believes that Government schemes particularly in the retail trade had been substituted by employers for 'real' jobs:

I haven't got a chance, they can pay them £25 a week for doing the same work.

One of the reasons why he still thinks of his time on the Government scheme in a positive light is that he met his girlfriend at the shop, with whom he has been going out for a year and whom he hopes to marry. But he intends to live with his parents until he finds a job; as he says, 'my girlfriend's working but I don't want her to pay for me'.

Mark does not feel totally responsible for his unemployment; he feels that he has tried hard to find a job but cannot find one. He now sees the situation as very bleak, but says that he will 'keep trying and one may come along':

> If I get a job that's a good year . . . you've got money for a start and em, it fills your life and you're learning more like, em . . . you can learn more through the training and really enjoy it . . . it feels like you're doing somethin'. Right now I'm not doing nothin', nothin' at all, sittin' around, but with a job you'll get home and feel that you've done somethin'.

Despite not feeling completely responsible for his unemployment he is acutely aware of the way other people respond to him, particularly his girlfriend's parents, and he feels that:

> I've got to prove myself to them really, show that I'm not a lay-about and I can do the job.

He now feels that his only hope is a job working in the same factory as his father, which would include working nights. His father has agreed to 'put his name down' and 'put in a good word for him'.

> It's terrible ent it . . . but I can't stay on the dole all my life.

Jane

Jane lives at home with her mother, who has a part-time job, and sister, who's on a Government scheme. When Jane left school she was unemployed for seven months before she decided she had no choice but to go on a Government scheme,

> I was determined not to go on a scheme because, you know, the money for a start, £25 a week it's nothin' is it? The way that people were takin' advantage of them, I was determined not to go on one. But in the end it got so bad, you know, it was terrible, you know, you never realize it's going to be that bad . . . when I came out of school, and no job, I

thought it couldn't be that bad and I could get a job easy . . .
thought easy you know. Just have a nice long holiday, stay in bed, but
my mother she was havin' me up before nine every morning and goin'
down to the job centre, but it was just useless, so I didn't have no
alternative, it was either a Government scheme or just you know, laze
about on the dole and do nothin' about it.

The year after leaving school was the worst year of Jane's life. It
was 'that age where everything went wrong'.

When I was on the dole everything was getting on top of me, you
know. I was gettin' really depressed cos I couldn't get a job and my
mother and I we weren't getting on very well.

After her daily trip to the job centre Jane would come home and
help her mother with the housework and:

I was bored then for the rest of the day. I was too old to hang 'round
street corners and too young to go to discos. I was just stuck in the 'ouse
all the time it was just terrible. It was a really bad time.

The Government scheme did get Jane off the dole and out of the
house during the day. But her dislike of the Government scheme
she was on, which involved her working as a shop assistant in
Tesco, made her feel very frustrated. Coupled with the fact that
her mother's new boyfriend was virtually living at home with
them, which led her to leave and find a flat on the other side of
Middleport, her life grew more difficult. She felt lonely, but did
not want to return home because she had left after a big argument
with her mother and felt she had been in 'the right'. For straightforward economic reasons Jane found it impossible to survive
living by herself. The money she received from the Government
scheme and Social Services combined was £33, and her rent was
£32 a week. Her grandmother fed her and tried to act as mediator
between Jane and her mother.

The Government scheme at Tesco confirmed Jane's worst fears:

it just got so bad there (at Tesco's), they were really takin' advantage of
the scheme. There was no one being 'kept on' no matter how good you
were.

Jane left the scheme after four months and went back on the dole
for another two months. Things were now very bleak. However,
her grandmother put a good word in for her at a hair salon in town
where her grandmother was friendly with the owner. They were
unable to offer her permanent employment, but were prepared to

take her on a Government scheme. Jane told me that she had always been interested in hairdressing,

> but I never really was that keen, like I always wanted to be a hairdresser. But all of a sudden I thought well, you know, better if I could get a trade, you know, but it's just getting in.

After four months on her second scheme Jane did 'get in'. Her boss put her in touch with another hairdresser who wanted an apprentice, and she was offered the job. She felt that when it comes to looking for jobs you are either lucky or you're not:

> It's not what you knows it's who you knows. I would never have got that job if my grandmother didn't know the hairdresser. I just fell lucky . . . qualifications are important but if you are in the know, who needs qualifications?

The sense in which Jane felt that she was lucky also found expression when she told me that she no longer kept in touch with many of her school friends because they were 'courting strongly'. Many of the people she knew from school had been on Government schemes and some were on the dole and some were now

> married with children and weren't doin' nothin', but it was very rare you'd bump into somebody who had a proper job.

During the first year of her apprenticeship Jane's relationship with her mother improved, and she has recently returned home to live with her mother and sister.

Tom

Tom left school at 16 with 5 CSEs and an O level in Art. He applied for many jobs including British Telecom, the Post Office, and the Fire Service. They all rejected him:

> I was determined not to go on the dole straight from school. I was really determined that I was going to find a job before I left school, because I didn't want to face the prospect of just sittin' 'round the 'ouse on my backside all day . . . and was lucky enough to find one.

He found a job as an apprentice scaffolder. The first year was spent at college in the south east of England. He was only paid £10 a week plus board, which made regular trips back home impossible:

> I was looking forward to going away but leaving home at my age, at sixteen, was a big step to take. I didn't know what to expect or what. I

did get a bit upset and I wanted to come home, but I didn't. I reckon I
wasted a year of my life.

The reason why Tom felt that he had wasted a year of his life was
that he left the job when he was 'on site' back in South Wales,
which made his training year now seem pointless. Although there
were occasions where he could earn up to £150 a week, he believed
that it was not worth the risks involved as a scaffolder. On
occasions he had asked the foreman for a safety harness but the
other workers had laughed at him:

> It was completely different on site, you know. I didn't feel as safe as I
> did when I was in college . . . I felt I wasn't suited for the job . . .
> It's a mug's game, scaffolding.

Despite hating his time on site, he did not want to leave, because
he knew that his chances of finding another job were bleak. He
also felt obliged not to break his contract with the company. So
one day when he was asked to climb a section of scaffolding which
he thought to be too dangerous he deliberately refused and was
sacked.

Tom found himself on the dole and living at home with his
parents and brother who was still at school. His father sold car
spares and thought he could find Tom a job in the same line of
work but Tom refused to allow his father to make the necessary
enquiries because he wanted to 'stand on his own two feet'. Tom
also refused to go on a Government scheme because he

> reckon's they're slave labour for what they are paying you. I was on
> slave labour for £10 a week, but you know I had somethin' to look
> forward to at the end because it was an apprenticeship.

While he was on the dole he realized that more people who had
messed around in school were in jobs compared with those who
had 'made an effort' and passed examinations, but:

> it's just how life goes 'ent it, you can have ten CSEs and ten O levels
> and still not get a job.

The one highlight for Tom since leaving school was that he had
passed his driving test and bought an old car, which was currently
off the road because he could not afford the road tax. Tom recalls
the time on the dole as the worst time of his life. He became very
depressed. He met a girl who was also unemployed and they spent
every day together for four months, during which time she

became pregnant. He felt that it was his responsibility to 'stand by her', and they arranged to get married.

His aunt found him a job working behind a bar in a hotel so he could begin to earn some money. The job only lasted one month because Tom believed the landlord wanted to get rid of someone so they sacked him. Despite trying to get reinstated by taking his case to a tribunal for unfair dismissal, he was back on the dole. In this situation the extreme tension between him and his fiancée resulted in her calling off the wedding. Tom told me that:

> she can't work because she's got problems so I'll be keeping her for the rest of my life. I don't mind that cos it's what I want to do, but the way she hurt me then, I don't want to make the same mistake twice.

He went to the doctor to try to rid himself of the depression he was still experiencing. Shortly afterwards his aunt found him another job worth £85 a week, working nights at a film processing factory about five miles outside Middleport. The job is only for six months, but Tom is hopeful that he will be made permanent. He enjoys the work, everything's getting better for him and he hopes to have his car back on the road soon:

> It's not my fault, perhaps, that I couldn't find a job. I'm surprised I had three jobs though, in two years. Not a lot of people have had one job in those two years, you know, I've been very lucky. I know I've made a mistake with my girl friend and all that, but you can't change that can you.

And although Tom now feels much happier, he knows that he could be back on the dole at the end of his six-month contract.

Sue

Sue lives at home with her parents and older brother in a small terrace house not far from Thomas High School. Her father is a crane driver and her mother a housewife. Living so close to the school serves as a constant reminder of her time at the school and of her friends who she now rarely sees because 'they're all going steady'.

Although pleased to have left school she enjoyed her school days:

> it was good really, if you wanted to learn you could learn, they do help you really, with exam results and that, but that doesn't really help you with a job now, cos you've got to have A levels to get certain jobs.

Sue took seven CSEs and passed six, including two at Grade 1. Despite not feeling that her qualifications would get her a job as a nursery nurse, two days after leaving school she found a job through an employment agency as a nanny in London. When she arrived at her first job she felt:

> they were exploiting me, it was only £20 a week and for the first night she left me on my own with the children until 2 o'clock in the morning.

Two days later she was on her way back to South Wales, and in retrospect she feels that she was too young to leave home. Back in Middleport she went on the dole for two months, during which time she went to the careers service and was offered a Government scheme working with children. Despite not wanting to go on a YOP while at school:

> I changed my mind, it's a bit more than the dole and you are learnin' somethin' . . . but the main reason was because of that Government scheme, I could be with children, but I couldn't be with them otherwise.

Sue still feels that most Government schemes exploit young people but feels that hers was okay. However, it did not lead to a job and she was back on the dole, where she stayed for another nine months.

> When I was first unemployed I thought I wouldn't be unemployed for long. I was applying for jobs and eh . . . I did have replies from them . . . well one of them did, but the rest didn't. I couldn't be bothered then, if they're not replying to me what's the point writin' to them, and I thought because I've only got 2 O levels I'd never get a job cos there's so many with A levels going for these jobs . . . shorthand typin' and I couldn't go for childcare because I don't have the experience . . . I was fed up, I was really disheartened. I went down the job centre, there was nothin' there.

She felt aggrieved that she had O levels and was unemployed, whilst some of the girls she knew, and who had not bothered at school, had found jobs. However, she feels responsible for being unemployed, 'It's my fault, I could have helped myself', because she thought she should have worked for more qualifications by taking a shorthand typing course. She did not undertake the shorthand and typing course at the local technical college because they put her onto the wrong course, so she did not bother going.

While Sue was unemployed she rarely got up before ten o'clock, and would occasionally go into town with her boyfriend. She also had a casual cleaning job for a couple of hours a day, which she hated, but it at least got her out of the house. After nine months on the dole, and having almost given up hope of finding employment, she found a temporary job for a year. The job involves writing out lists from micro-film and collecting the office mail. 'I hate it down there, I can't stand it, it's borin', it's terrible', but she knows that it gives her money, gets her out of the house, and provides a sense of independence so that she hasn't 'got to rely on other people'. Sue also knows only too well that there simply are not any other jobs around, and intends to 'stick at it in the hope that the work will get more interesting', although she would still like to do nursery nursing but 'I know I can't do that now'.

Pat

During her time at Thomas High School Pat had to help 'bring up' her younger brother because her mother no longer lived at home. Her father had been unemployed for six years, but had recently entered a retraining programme to learn to be a motor mechanic. Pat had considered going to the technical college, and although her father getting out of the house was a great relief for the whole family, the financial problems remained, so she gave up the idea of going to college and left school at 16 to look for employment.

Pat had eight CSEs to her credit when she left school but was disappointed, although not surprised, that her best grade was only a grade two. She told me that while at school she had been getting to 'the stage where in some lessons I couldn't care less'. Pat also felt that because she wanted to join the army and qualify as a driver, she should be studying something which would help her to realize her ambition. She knew that girls could do this job just as well as boys.

'When I left school I was pretty frightened. I didn't want to go on the dole or get anything like that'. Unlike many of her contemporaries she did not have to settle for 'anything like that', because two weeks after leaving school the careers teacher recommended her for a job, and after two interviews she started work as a receptionist/typist in a car showroom:

> I'm in work at 8.30, greet customers, receive paper work ready to be typed, complete bills and check them, and give customers back their cars.

She thought the move from school to work had been a big move.

> I was petrified about starting work. My father took me backwards and forwards for the first week. The first day I got there I didn't want to go in. It was terrible . . . they make me feel alright but I was petrified when I got there.

Despite her initial uncertainty about what the world of employment had to offer, she does not think that life has changed that much since the time she was in school. The one thing she does miss are her school friends whom she now rarely sees because she has been 'courting for five months' and attends the local sub-aqua club twice a week. This leaves her little time for socializing with old school friends.

Pat told me that she had always felt more ambitious than many of her school friends. She felt that many of them did not want to get 'good' jobs with 'good' money:

> for many girls their ambition is to get married and have children . . . mine is a good job and good money . . . although any job now is clearly somethin'.

It was a recognition of the fact that some of her school friends were unemployed which led her to believe that life since leaving school had been very good to her – 'not what I wanted, but never mind'.

After two years in the job and having moved from a starting salary of £34 to £62 a week she felt that she was 'going nowhere'. After just a year in the job it no longer presented a challenge. Moreover, someone she liked working with had left and the girl she particularly disliked was moved to work alongside her. She decided to apply to the army – the job she had wanted ever since an army careers talk in the fourth year at school. Her day-to-day existence in the car showroom became increasingly dreary, particularly when she thought about spending more than the next five minutes with the girl she now worked with. Thoughts of the army had her increasingly restless. After her final army interview she decided to hand in her notice without knowing if her interview had been successful. It was. Despite having a boyfriend in Middleport whom she wants to continue to see at weekends, Pat will leave Middleport next month to join 'the Professionals'.

Martin

Martin lives at home with his parents and younger brother, who is currently on a Government scheme, and his sister, who is still at school. The daily life of the whole family has changed recently from a situation where all the males in the household were unemployed to one where his father found paid employment for the first time in two years and Martin is now an apprentice hairdresser. His brother remains less fortunate and is on a second Government scheme.

When Martin left school he had passed the six CSEs he sat. During the last year of secondary school he wanted to be a welder, and applied to all the firms he knew of to try for an apprenticeship, but without success. He had sent off approximately twenty letters of application, received only three replies and had two interviews. After three months on the dole, stuck in the house with his parents and in the knowledge that his chances of getting an apprenticeship were virtually non-existent, he decided to go on a Government scheme and work in a shoe shop. He did not want to go on a Government scheme but realizing that his situation was:

> the same as everyone else, couldn't find a job anywhere else, so that was the only thing I could do. So I went on one.

Martin believed that Government schemes are being used by employers as cheap labour, and feels that the scheme he went on was 'a waste of time':

> I didn't think it's worth going on the scheme, but em . . . I didn't have a job, it was experience and gets you out of the 'ouse anyway.

Martin did not particularly enjoy working in a shop, but he was broadening his occupational horizons in the attempt to find a job. He turned his hand to hairdressing and was taken on for a three-month trial on a wage of £29 a week, having got the job through a friend who was already in the trade. I asked him about the shift from wanting to be a welder when he was at school to working in hairdressing:

> Well I sort of dressed a bit different. Started from school, started dressing a bit different from everyone else, em . . . when I was in the shoe shop I was just normal I wasn't dressin' different. Then all of a sudden I just changed the way I was wearing clothes and I just fancied being a hairdresser . . . I found it interesting. I wanted to do it . . . I would never go into welding.

After his three-month trial they were unable to keep him on and Martin was back on the dole. It was during this spell on the dole that Martin's relationship with his parents deteriorated to the point where he felt he had to leave home. He went with his girlfriend and two other friends to London. They were all unemployed, and he only stayed three weeks before returning to Middleport with his girlfriend, whereupon they found a flat. It was then that he wrote to me and stated:

> At the moment my hair is orange. There is very little chance of me getting a job, not because of my exam results, but my appearance. I am not scruffy or nothing like that, in fact I pay up to £30 for a pair of trousers – it's my hair. But I'm not changing it. I know I dress a bit different, but for me or anyone else who dresses like me, there isn't hardly any jobs around. Since leaving school I have had a job in a shoe shop and in a hairdressers, but none were successful. It's not because I didn't like them, I loved hairdressing, but as every manager says, 'I'm very sorry, but we can't keep you on'. There are no chances for school leavers, they either have to go on a course or go on the dole.

Shortly afterwards he did begin to tone down his appearance:

> I used to get some stick . . . got called all the gay names, but you get used to it in hairdressing.

However, it did get on his nerves when he was unemployed, and this contributed to his decision to dress more conventionally.

It was at this time that Martin responded to an advert for an apprentice hairdresser which he had spotted in a local newspaper. This application led to his first permanent job, but he left after nine months because he was being underpaid and had not been given apprentice papers. He continued his apprenticeship on a salary of £30.40 a week, at the hairdressers where he had previously worked for three months.

Martin split up with his girl friend and went to live with his parents, because things had improved considerably since he and his father had found employment. He also now sees most of his school friends settling down:

> They're never out in the nights. I'm always out. I'd never think of going out serious with anyone now. I think it's best to enjoy it while you're younger. There's always time for women later on.

After finishing his apprenticeship Martin hopes to return to London, but his most immediate concern is to buy a car.

One of my reasons for including these case studies stemmed from a desire to locate the ordinary kids' labour market experiences in terms of their more everyday concerns about relationships with parents, or insufficient money to buy clothes or to go to public houses in the town centre. In addition, they help us to make sense of the final concern of this chapter, namely the way in which the ordinary kids have subsequently interpreted the relationship between their educational and labour market experiences, and how they have interpreted the fact that some of them have been able to find jobs, while others have not and seem to have little chance of doing so.

THE ORDINARY KIDS' UNDERSTANDING OF SCHOOLING
AND THE LABOUR MARKET

The above discussion shows clearly that the ordinary kids have not abandoned their desire to enter 'tidy' working-class jobs, although their expectations of entering such jobs, particularly among the ordinary kids who are unemployed, are not high. The gap between preferences and expectations does not rule out the possibility that a considerable number of ordinary kids may be developing disaffected attitudes towards their educational experiences. In order to assess this possibility the ordinary kids were first asked how important they thought qualifications were, while they were at school, and eighteen months later.[7] Table 6.8 shows the changes that have taken place in the ordinary kids' perception of the importance of qualifications since reaching school leaving age.

The proportion of ordinary kids stating that qualifications had become of *little* importance *increased* by 10 percentage points, from 13 to 23 per cent. Despite almost a quarter of the ordinary kids now believing qualifications to be of little importance, half suggested that qualifications were 'very' important at both times. What these figures obscure are differences between ordinary kids with labour market experience and those who have remained in

Table 6.8 *The perceived value of qualifications at school and 18 months later* (%)

	At school	After 18 months
Very important	52	49
Fairly important	36	28
Of little importance	13	23
Total (number)	159	158

Table 6.9 *The importance of qualifications as seen by the ordinary kids with labour market experience and those remaining in full-time study 18 months after attaining school-leaving age (%)*

	Labour market experience			Full-time study		
	M	F	Total	M	F	Total
Very important	29	49	38	83	71	78
Important	36	24	30	17	29	22
Unimportant	36	27	32	—	—	—
Total (number)	62	51	113	24	21	45

full-time study, and differences between the sexes. In Table 6.9 we find that double the proportion of ordinary kids who remain in full-time study believe qualifications to be 'very' important (78 per cent) compared to those with labour market experience (38 per cent), and that almost one-third of those who have left full-time study believe that qualifications are unimportant.

Table 6.9 also shows important variations between the sexes in each category. Among the ordinary kids in full-time study it was the boys who were more likely to believe qualifications to be 'very' important (83 per cent), whilst among those with labour market experience it was the girls (49 per cent) who were more likely to express the continuing value of qualifications.

Differences between male and female ordinary kids with labour market experience may reflect the variations found between qualifications and the chance of being in employment. Of those *in* jobs, under half of the boys compared with over three-quarters of the girls had at least one O level (or equivalent), and under one-third of the boys unemployed or on Government schemes had a similar qualification compared with over 60 per cent of girls. This finding tentatively suggests that female school leavers require better qualifications than boys to stand a chance of gaining the types of employment they are applying for. This finding may also give some support to the view that studying for additional qualifications until the age of seventeen may well enhance girls' but not boys' chances of finding employment (Raffe 1984: p. 188).

The ordinary kids do perceive a change in the importance they attach to qualifications, but such changes are not uniform. The ordinary kids who remain in full-time study show an increase in the proportion now believing that qualifications are very important, while those ordinary kids with labour market experience have registered a substantial decline in the perceived value of qualifications. It can be hypothesized that the declining importance attached to qualifications among the ordinary kids with labour market experience is the result of the unemployed ordinary kids' feeling that qualifications will not help them get employment. A further breakdown of the ordinary kids' responses to this question shows, contrary to expectation, that it was those in employment rather than those who have been unable to find jobs who showed a greater tendency to question the value of school certificates. Under a third of those in employment believed qualifications to be 'very' important, against 46 per cent of those who were unemployed. A similar trend emerged when those with labour market experience were asked whether their schooling had proved to be a waste of time – two-thirds of the ordinary kids unable to find jobs felt their schooling had been something other than a waste of time, compared with 57 per cent of those in employment.

The continuing importance of qualifications recognized by a large proportion of the unemployed ordinary kids, as opposed to those in jobs, suggests that although approximately a third of ordinary kids unable to find jobs feel that qualifications are unimportant, these unemployed school leavers may be adopting individualistic accounts of their fate in the labour market (Kelvin 1981; Jahoda 1982). There is general agreement within the unemployment literature that the effect of being unemployed on one's sense of dignity and social identity will be greater among those who cannot attribute their unemployment to external causes, which a number of studies of unemployed youth have found them unable to do. For example, a study by Youthaid (1981a) found that the:

> general concepts of the problem of unemployment were highly individualized, focusing on personal characteristics very much more than any shortage of jobs in the economy.
>
> (p. 12)

A partial measure of how much the ordinary kids who are unable to find jobs may be engaging in self-recrimination was gained by considering responses to the statement, 'I now wish I'd worked harder in school to get more qualifications'. Once again it was those in employment who were least likely to agree (42 per cent) and most likely to disagree (37 per cent), compared with 54 per cent and 32 per cent respectively for those unemployed, although the proportion now wishing that they had worked harder while at school is much smaller than the 75 per cent of the sample reported by Rathkey (cited in Roberts 1984).[8]

The finding that it is the ordinary kids in employment who are most sceptical about the connection between educational and labour market performance raises the possibility that it is they who are most likely to *externalize* reasons for unemployment (e.g. because there are so few jobs it does not matter how many qualifications you have), rather than those now unemployed. Whether this conclusion has any substance can be further investigated by showing how the ordinary kids responded to the statement, 'there are jobs if you make an effort to find one'. In Chapter 3 it was shown that, at school, two-thirds of ordinary kids agreed that jobs were available if an effort was made to find them and a further quarter were unsure. The proportion disagreeing with the statement has increased from under 10 per cent to over one-third of ordinary kids as the realities of the labour market become apparent. But in this instance it was the ordinary kids *in* employment who were the *most* likely to believe that 'jobs *are* available if an effort is made to find one' rather than the unemployed ordinary kids.

Table 6.10 shows that *under* half the ordinary kids looking for jobs *now* believe that no matter how hard they try they cannot find a job, compared with under a quarter of those in employment. The conclusions to be drawn from Table 6.10 are at best tentative but have major significance for understanding the post-school experiences of these ordinary kids. Braun (1979) has argued for example, that:

> While no one can deny that there is an economic crisis, the crisis on the labour market is transferred into a crisis of values and deficient attitudes on the part of the individual. The feeling of guilt, self-contempt and self-aggression among the young unemployed are thus the equivalent of a general social climate that has put the burden of the blame on those who are unable to defend themselves. (p. 53)

It is true that there is little in the way of an ideology which would help the ordinary kids to link their personal predicament to political actions (Scholzman and Verba 1980), but at least during the initial transition from school into the labour market, the ways the ordinary kids understand their unemployment are probably

Table 6.10 *There are jobs if you make an effort to find one: all ordinary kids with labour market experience (%)*

	In jobs	Unemployed	All ordinary kids
Agree	60	46	50
Not sure	18	6	15
Disagree	23	48	35
Total (number)	62	54	161

more various and less inconsistent than the quotation from Braun implies, and they clearly differ between the ordinary kids who found jobs and those who did not. Differences between school leavers in jobs and those on the dole in the way unemployment is understood were also found by Gurney (1981), who concluded that 'leavers who were out of work were found to favour more external attributions than their employed peers' (p. 79).

The study of the ordinary kids supports Gurney's conclusion, and also highlights a need to avoid treating the distinction between 'individual' and 'collective' explanations given by people for being unemployed as synonymous with those distinguished as 'internal' and 'external' explanations. What this study of ordinary kids reveals is not that those in jobs adopt a collective account of why people are unemployed and the unemployed an individualistic account (or vice-versa), but rather that they emphasize different elements of an individualistic explanation. The ordinary kids who are unemployed, although registering a decline in the perceived importance they ascribe to school performance for finding jobs, remain more likely than those in jobs to emphasize *technical* differences in 'human capital' (i.e. having enough qualifications) as a reason for their failure to find jobs, rather than a *moral* failing involving a willingness to 'make an effort'. Alternatively, those *in* jobs emphasize that the reason why some of their peers are unemployed is not a *technical* but a *moral* issue. They are unemployed because they have not been willing to 'make an effort'.

The belief among the ordinary kids who are in employment that finding employment depends primarily upon a willingness to 'make an effort' is consistent with the way in which the ordinary kids in school legitimized their right to whatever jobs were available, compared with the rems who had not bothered to 'make an effort'. It is the same cultural understandings which allowed the ordinary kids to distinguish different types of 'being' in the school which now threaten to divide the ordinary kids.

It has been argued that differences between jobs in terms of level of skills, training, working conditions, and money, previously represented a division between 'respectable' and 'rough' working-class youth. In a period of decline in occupational opportunities, the manifestation of a willingness to make an effort increasingly depends upon being in a job whether or not it is the one preferred. Sennett and Cobb (1977) have argued that there is no more urgent business in life than establishing a sense of personal dignity, and this certainly appears to underly the attitudes of the ordinary kids who are in jobs. They may not be in the jobs they want, but at least they have made the effort to find a job rather than being on the dole. It is through employment that the ordinary kids can demonstrate their moral worth both to themselves and to others. The experience of unemployment therefore circularly reinforces the attitude that to be unemployed is not to show willing, because by definition you can only show willing once you are in a job.

As the duration of unemployment increases it is also increasingly difficult to do – and to be seen to be doing – something to demonstrate one's social worth: leaving the vagaries of the market to determine an increasingly uncertain and bleak future. It is also becoming increasingly difficult for the unemployed ordinary kids to sustain an understanding of their present and future lives in terms of 'getting on'. Moreover, a major problem in the experience of unemployment is the threat of falling to a postion normally felt below one, such a social descent may be seen as a moral descent in the eyes of other ordinary kids. Being unemployed is interpreted as a moral descent among the ordinary kids in jobs, but those on the dole largely reject the view that their unemployment is the result of a failure to 'make an effort'.

There was a substantial increase in the unemployed ordinary kids coming to believe that there are no jobs regardless of how hard they try to find one, and it may well be that a small proportion of the ordinary kids who are currently unemployed may not be prepared to take jobs they do not want. However, although the ordinary kids recognize the lack of occupational opportunity for school leavers, their response to unemployment is fatalistic (if only they had better qualifications, had worked harder at school, or if only mum or dad could put a 'word in' for them). The crucial link between personal predicament and labour market condition is rarely made in a consistent manner. However, there may be a growing sense of alienation among the ordinary kids in employment as well as those in the dole. The ordinary kids have not simply accommodated previous understandings of who they are and what the future has to offer according to changing circumstances, or according to labour market conditions. Despite the tendency to understand personal experiences in individualistic and fatalistic terms, 'their apparent acquiescence should not be confused with contentment' (Runciman 1966: p. 26). Sennett and Cobb (1977) have also noted that the psychological motivation instilled by a class society is to heal a doubt about the self rather than to create more power over things and other persons in the outer world. Despite the fact that what has happened to many of the ordinary kids since leaving school directly challenges their sense of social justice based on a willingness to 'make an effort', their transition from school seems set to lead to increasing divisions amongst working-class youth, rather than to the creation of a collective understanding of their collective problems.

7 · Unemployment and educational change

The first task of this chapter will be to consider what a study of ordinary kids has to contribute to existing sociological accounts of working-class educational behaviour. The second is to assess the consequences of a social and educational climate which has given rise to the new vocationalism.

EDUCATION AND THE WORKING CLASS

The empirical findings of this study challenge much of our existing knowledge about education and the working class. They also show why new ways of thinking about these questions are required at a time when economic restructuring is changing the ground-rules for both teachers and taught. In Chapter 2 it was argued that working-class educational experiences have hitherto been explained in terms of a process of either educational or cultural differentation, but that both these accounts are inadequate because of their one-sidedness. The educational system does not simply fail pupils from a working-class background, nor do these pupils simply 'fail' themselves. It is rather the interplay between class culture (understood as a set of resources which gives rise to different FORS among working-class youth) on the one hand, and the school's selection processes on the other, which provides the key to understanding patterns of educational behaviour amongst working-class youth.

An attempt has been made to understand both this relationship and variations in pupil response in terms of several factors: firstly, orientations to the formal culture of the school, secondly the way in which these different orientations are associated with different ways of being a working-class pupil within the informal pupil culture, and thirdly the interrelationships between pupil and social identities which have been called FORS.

The importance of working-class FORS is that they capture the pupil's sense of being in the world; educational identity is a key part in this sense. FORS are the historical product of the shared social and educational experiences of working-class people, which are imbued with social significance and convey varying degrees of social status. At the heart of these social experiences are the economic activities of adults living in the locality. It is therefore hardly surprising that occupational identity has had an important impact on the demand for education, and that this limited demand is a consequence of class inequalities. Such a belief is supported by the conclusions drawn by Goldthorpe *et al.* (1980) from their study of social mobility in contemporary Britain:

> Where inequalities in class chances of this magnitude can be displayed, the presumption must be . . . that to a substantial extent they do reflect inequalities of opportunity that are rooted in the class structure, and are not simply the outcome of the differential 'take-up' of opportunities by individuals with differing genetic, moral or other endowments that do not derive from their class position. (p. 252)

However, this does not preclude some working-class pupils developing a FOR in terms of 'getting out' of the working-class neighbourhoods of Middleport, a FOR which places a considerable premium on school success. Neither does it rule out the possibility that the school has an important impact on who develops which FOR.

The FORS exhibited by particular pupils are not simply the result of early childhood socialization. The educational system does play a part in reinforcing or transforming pupil dispositions. There is a loose fit between family background and pupil FORs because of the interaction between 'institutional context and the processes of class cultural production' (Hogan 1982: p. 61). A recognition of the school's role in framing the life chances of working-class youth is important because it avoids the tendency of 'cultural' accounts to drift into forms of voluntaristic explanation, which underplay the significance of the school and its ability to determine the life chances of pupils whether or not large numbers of working-class children were to be convinced of the value of academic success. It ignores the way in which the school is structured and organized and the differential power relations which pupils from a disadvantaged background confront.

It is in terms of the school's selection processes that we can understand why the school has the potential to transform the FOR of particular pupils, and why it has failed to offer much of a challenge to the educational and social identities of working-class children who have used the school for their own purposes. This study supports the view that, in order in win pupil compliance, teachers do try to convince all pupils that 'swotting' is worthwhile, and that if they work hard they can achieve a better future than that which confronts their school friends. However, swotting has a social and moral significance which means that it incurs social costs. Moreover, swotting is irrelevant to their present and future lives unless 'real' opportunities for educational and social advancement are seen to exist (and even then they may be rejected). The majority of working-class pupils are unlikely, therefore, to consider it as a viable option.

It is this interrelationship between class culture and school structure which provides the key to understanding intra-class variations in the demand for education, prior to, and as a result of, the collapse of occupational opportunities for working-class youth. Changing economic and social conditions have led to a crisis in the classroom, producing personal troubles for ordinary kids and professional troubles for teachers.

In this study it has been shown that the ordinary kids have remained invisible from sociological view, due to a propensity to lump together all those pupils who did not exhibit anti-school behaviour as conformists. Surprisingly this problem was particularly evident in Willis' 'cultural' explanation of working-class resistance to school which was billed as a challenge to the deterministic and over-socialized versions of earlier accounts. He not only failed to challenge the view that the vast majority of working-class pupils did conform to the normative order of the school, but reinforced this assumption by the way he contrasted the creativity and rationality of the non-conformist 'lads', with the passive, and in his terms, irrational responses of other working-class pupils.

The fact that a large proportion of pupils from a working-class background may 'make an effort' in school while at the same time not harbouring ambitions beyond those of their working-class neighbours in Middleport, appears to have remained largely beyond sociological comprehension. However, a study of the ordinary kids leads to exactly that conclusion. The alienated instrumentalism of the ordinary kids was not a response to academic 'failure'. The ordinary kids' response to school never involved a commitment to academic success as a way of 'getting out' of their class of origin, seduced by a knowledge that a few do succeed. Their educational and social ambitions have remained firmly rooted in the concerns of the working class.

The failure to distinguish different types of compliance to school among working-class pupils, results in a blindness to the signficance of the ordinary kids' response as being one which is as distinctively a 'working-class' cultural response as that which leads to a rejection of the school. It also leads to the underplaying of the school's failure in its attempt to manage the contradictions inherent in the schooling process between the school's selection processes and its need to incorporate the vast majority of working-class pupils in order that the daily routines of school life can be achieved. Despite a limited demand for, or access to, academic success, the ordinary kids' willingness to make an effort was 'less the outcome of a process of ideological incorporation or class determinism than of the very efforts of working-class people to take control of their lives' (Hogan 1982: p. 52). This attempt by the ordinary kids to take command of their lives often had contradictory and unintended consequences.

The ordinary kids complied with the daily routines of school life because modest levels of effort and achievement were instrumental to their advancement within the working class, but it is precisely because academic success has never been necessary to 'get on' that the school has not had to actively legitimate the outcomes of its selection process. This raises serious doubts about the importance which Marxist accounts (Bowles and Gintis 1976; Bourdieu and Passeron 1977) have attached to the school's legitimation function. The inevitability of working-class failure has led them to emphasize the way the school legitimates its outcomes by convincing working-class pupils that the 'fixed' contest is a 'fair' one. The greater the degree of inequality believed to exist in the school, the greater the importance of legitimating outcomes is seen to be. However, it can be argued that it is only where academic success is a goal desired by the majority of pupils, and all pupils are willing to take part, that the outcomes of the school's selection process need to be actively legitimated. It is precisely this condition which has been absent in many schools like Thomas High School. Yet the same FORs which have contributed to the reproduction of the working class have also confronted the school with the problem of legitimating its daily routines because the FOR exhibited by the ordinary kids provided the basis for a collective resistance to the school's definition of 'success' and 'worthwhile knowledge'.

The educational incorporation of the ordinary kids involved contest *and* negotiation, resistance *and* accommodation. They did define much of the academic curriculum as irrelevant and boring; and because their FOR was predicated on future performance in the labour market and transition into working-class adulthood, such understandings enabled them to maintain a sense of personal worth and dignity in an institution in which they were modestly placed, and where people are hierarchically ordered and accordingly rewarded on the basis of school performance. In consequence their collective resistance to school was always fragmented and limited in scope. To enter into open conflict with teachers not only threatened their ability to 'get on', by endangering their chance of examination success and getting a good school reference, it was also greeted with moral censure from other ordinary kids who were continuing to make an effort. Making an effort stood as a testimony to one's social and moral worth. A consequence of this understanding is that the ordinary kids defined those who did not bother to make an effort as morally inferior – as rems. The existence of such social and moral divisions among working-class pupils effectively inhibits the development of any class consciousness of the structural location of working-class people in school and in the labour market.

One of the conclusions to be drawn from this study of ordinary kids is, therefore, that the incorporation of large numbers of working-class pupils has depended upon the existence of economic and social conditions which generated enough working-class jobs for school leavers, which were regarded as more, or less, desirable and entry into which modest levels of academic success were seen to facilitate. So long as this situation prevailed the school was able to manage the contradictions underlying the schooling of ordinary kids. The current levels of youth unemployment and economic restructuring have not, therefore, directly caused the crisis in the classroom, but they have brought these contradictions to a head. Such a situation is making it extremely difficult for teachers to contain working-class alienation from school, given the existing structure and organization of schooling.

Family and economic life in South Wales have been seriously disrupted in the working-class neighbourhoods of Middleport. Such changes have struck at the heart of the transition from childhood to adulthood. The material bases of the FORS exhibited by the ordinary kids (and rems) can now be seen to reflect past processes rather than current practices. It is making it increasingly difficult for the ordinary kids to see why they should continue bothering to 'make an effort' in school if it is no longer the basis for personal survival in the labour market. Consequently, the same class-culture/school structure mechanisms which in the past had facilitated the reproduction of working-class FORS are now, under present market conditions, central elements in the current classroom crisis which threatens the reproduction of social inequalities.

Because sociologists have failed to provide an historical analysis of the relationship between class formation and educational behaviour (Hogan 1982), they have been unable to recognize that it is the ordinary kids, rather than those working-class pupils who have traditionally rejected the school (i.e. male anti-school subculture), who pose the biggest threat to the school in the late 1980s. This is not only because of their great numbers, but also because it is those who have made an effort in school and who have developed expectations of the future involving more than a series of 'shit' jobs, who are likely to threaten the existing social order when these aspirations remain unmet. The government's response to what it sees to be the problems both in the schools and in the labour market has led to the vocationalization of working-class education. This is a policy which will do little to solve the crisis in the classroom, but which will extend the inequalities already confronting ordinary kids.

THE NEW VOCATIONALISM AND SOCIAL INEQUALITY

In Chapter 5 the political and classroom contexts of the new vocationalism were examined. It was shown that one of the main arguments for the new vocationalism was the belief that the school was failing to prepare its pupils for economic realities. This belief was challenged there because, among other things, it fails to take any account of working-class experiences of school. In agreement with Watts it was argued that while youth unemployment is not an educational problem, it is a problem for education. It may be argued that like its diagnosis of the school's contribution to Britain's economic and social problems, the Thatcher Government's prognosis of how this situation can be changed is equally misconceived.

The Middleport study shows that youth unemployment is resulting in different motivational responses to school. Whereas a large proportion of ordinary working-class pupils who were previously willing to make an effort have come to question the value and purpose of school, the swots, particularly those from a middle-class background, are interpreting unemployment (and government cuts in higher education) as a situation which increases the stakes for academic success and therefore they have attached greater instrumental importance to the school as a means of achieving desired occupations and access to higher education.

The Government's response to the intensification of middle-class demands for 'education' (legitimated under the guise of parental choice) has been an increasing willingness to allow the rapid spread of private educational establishments as a response to market forces,[1] whereas the new vocationalism is being used to reform the education of the working class to meet the 'needs' of industry. The Government's desire to be 'doing something' about the comprehensive school and youth unemployment is therefore creating the ideological space it needs to reintroduce early segregation and selection,[2] and to move towards its ultimate goal: the privatization of British education, of which the city technology colleges are a forerunner. The new vocationalism is a doctrine for 'other people's children' because it leaves the academic education of the middle classes completely untouched. As Watts (1983) has noted, 'vocational-preparation programmes . . . tend to deprive their students of access to what in terms of status and income must be regarded as the *real* vocational prizes' (p. 14). Moreover, by focusing on reforming the school system rather than the labour market and the economy, vocational reformers address the symptoms rather than the sources of the conditions they hope to eliminate (Kantor and Tyack 1982: p. 2).

The main reason why working-class youth are unable to find employment is a result of a collapse in the *demand* for young workers. The study of ordinary kids in Middleport leads to the conclusion that the current crisis in schools results from the fact that there has been a decline in the type of employment opportunities through which the ordinary kids can 'get on' in working-class terms and become adult in a respectable fashion. Its conclusion was *not* that these school leavers must be educated once more to know their place: it was that they already *do* know their place. They saw school as a useful aid in attaining it, but became increasingly frustrated and angry when they discovered that there are insufficient places to accommodate them. If there are anti-industrial attitudes (Wiener 1981) harboured among Britain's youth today, they are to be found not among ordinary kids but within the middle classes. Yet it will be middle-class parents and pupils who will resist any interference with the school curriculum which affects the acquisition of paper qualifications giving access to higher education and the professions.

The class interests which underly the right's programme of educational reforms can be seen from the fact that we are told we need to prepare working-class school leavers for jobs which are massively over-subscribed, while we have skill shortages. These shortages are for more highly educated technologists and engineers, which require a specialist education in polytechnics or universities. Yet it is precisely the middle classes, who have dominated places in higher education, who have rejected a career in industry – not the ordinary kids. However, it is the victims of Britain's industrial decline who must suffer the personal, educational, and social consequences in order that educational and social inequalities can be maintained.

There are a number of other reasons why the new vocationalism is seriously flawed. The attempt to restructure the educational system in order to meet the 'needs' of industry must be treated with considerable scepticism. As long ago as 1947 the Central Advisory Council for Education stated:

> Schools can prepare their pupils for industry only to a very limited degree, because it is in practice almost impossible to do more and would be highly undesirable on the grounds of educational principle. The practical objection to basing education on the needs of the scholar's future employment is the variety and frequent change of occupations, and rapidity of technical change. (p. 50)

Indeed when it comes to specifying what the 'needs' of industry are and how they can best be met, employers express considerable uncertainty (Central Policy Review Staff 1980). What they do seem to agree about is the need for a flexible and adaptable workforce capable of responding to changes in the work process (Parsons 1985; MSC 1985b). The same Central Advisory Council report also stated that, 'the greatest thing which the schools can do for industry is to provide a good general education to as high an age as practicable' (p. 56). The attempt to find vocational solutions to economic and social problems has been popular in America since the turn of the century. The Thatcher Government has frequently looked across the Atlantic Ocean for guidance on economic and social policy, but they obviously missed the conclusion drawn by Kantor and Tyack (1982) that:

> fifty years of major evaluations of vocational training have shown that

there is little economic advantage to vocational training, as opposed to non-vocational education at the high school level. (p. 2)

In Britain, Ashton and Maguire (1986) have argued that a more vocationally orientated curriculum is unlikely to improve the employment prospects of 'non-academic' pupils.

If we are going to meet the social and economic demands of an advanced capitalist democracy, we will require young women and men to be capable of responding to new opportunities, which will include periods of retraining, but also allow them to benefit constructively from a shorter working week and a shorter working life (Watts 1983; Handy 1984; Williams 1985). If Britain is to meet these demands it is not more *vocational* education which is required during the compulsory school years, but a more *general* education for *all* pupils.[3] The way to ensure the provision of a workforce to meet the *social* and economic needs of the late twentieth century requires that we *break down class and gender inequalties. The new vocationalism will impose them.*

This conclusion is grounded in the unsurprising finding that pupils construct their social identities (to which occupational identity is central), in class- and gender-specific ways. For example, although the ordinary kids shared a FOR towards the future in terms of 'getting on' in working-class terms, the types of employment and ways in which they can become adults in a respectable fashion varied between the sexes. If we are genuinely interested in producing the 'labour force of the future', the educational system must attempt to break down sexism in schools which operates against both boys and girls and fosters the development of gender-specific occupational preferences and expectations by, for example, *reinforcing* the processes through which boys enter metalwork, woodwork, and design, craft and technology and, for girls, home economics, childcare and office practice (Whyte *et al*. 1985).

A study of the ordinary kids in Middleport also shows that because categories of pupils are so closely related to class-cultural understandings of being a working-class adult, it is only when the school offers an 'out' both subjectively and objectively that the costs and benefits of being defined as a swot and 'getting out' of the working class are truly posed for the majority of these pupils. Conservatives such as Hampson (1980), however, have argued that:

Young people's perceptions of jobs are often outdated and their aspirations circumscribed by social and cultural factors. The problem is to overcome the pupil's family, background and peer group influences. (p. 93)

This lack of openness to new possibilities he considers to be a problem of 'ignorance' to be overcome by better careers advice and sources of occupational information. But when ordinary kids discuss school and adulthood they are not expressing attitudes based on an *ignorance* of alternatives; they are expressing collective *knowledge* of ways of being a working-class pupil and becoming a working-class adult. Their orientations are grounded in the material practices of working-class people, transmitted from generation to generation, and are the basis for establishing personal dignity, social identity and social status in a class society. They will not easily give up understandings which serve to define who they are, and maintain a sense of social dignity, unless there are genuine opportunities to make a *new* future. The importance of this point reminds us that the educational system cannot compensate for society (Bernstein 1969), and so long as sexual discrimination is practised by employers against any application for employment which does not conform to appropriate gender specification, or as long as the attempt to encourage the ordinary kids to conceptualize their future in 'new' ways is not supported by equal access to a comprehensive education or genuine opportunities beyond the school gate, the school's impact on pupil attitudes and preferences will be small.

However, the structure and organization of schooling *does* make a difference to the way the ordinary kids respond to school. If we are going to overcome the growing alienation of the ordinary kids, educational equality is particularly important in the present economic and social circumstances. In order to achieve greater educational equality it will be necessary to build on the advances which have been made in the post-war period (Simon 1986). This is not to deny that there are many things which are wrong with the educational system which pre-dates the new vocationalism, for example, the failure to abolish private schooling; and the willingness to allow the universities to dictate the structure and content of the secondary school curriculum which has caused early specialization and an emphasis on the academic at the expense of other educational considerations.

The tragedy today is that we have lost sight of the advances that were made in the post-war period. Yet if it is true that working-class demands for education must be understood in terms of the interplay between identity and institutional structure, there is nothing inevitable about the contemporary patterns of working-class educational behaviour. The only thing which is certain is that if we do not develop an alternative politics of education to Thatcherism, the attempts which were made to generate educational opportunities for the working class will be lost.

What is paradoxical about this situation is that it was a sociology based on liberal democratic assumptions which had an important impact on educational policy in the 1950s and 1960s. The liberal democratic approach to educational issues has been correctly criticized by Marxist writers for its naivety in believing that by reforming the school you can create a more equal society. The Marxist response is based on a belief that anything less than fundamental change in the constitution of society is a reformist strategy destined to fall foul of the logic of capitalism. Therefore, they have little to say to the classroom teacher, or about more general questions about educational policy. The best we can hope for, and place our faith in, is the oppositional character of the male anti-school subculture of working-class 'lads' ('tidy' or otherwise) – which recent Marxist accounts have somewhat unconvincingly interpreted as a resistance to capitalism (see Chapter 4). This resistance is seen to offer the potential for widespread civil disobedience which in turn may help to destabilize British society.

However one interprets the 'resistance movement' in Marxist educational sociology, the sociology of education has evacuated the political stage which has proved to be an act of political suicide. The contemporary lack of realism on the left has allowed the right to dominate educational debates and policy. As Giller and Covington have noted in the sphere of juvenile justice:

> if the left is to do anything other than stand as critical commentators on the sidelines of the slide into Repression, there is a need to participate in and contribute in a tangible way to the current policy debate.
>
> (quoted in Clarke 1985: p. 407)

The absence of any critical realism in the sociology of education has consequently contributed to the right's ideological supremacy in its interpretation of the classroom crisis, the implications of which we are now witnessing in British classrooms.

I have already suggested that the educational system cannot compensate for society. But it is not an all or nothing situation and the attitude 'if we cannot change the unequal basis of British society there is little point in trying to reform the school', is not justifiable. In a society which will remain capitalist for the foreseeable future, there are important political and ideological battles over the structure, organization and content of secondary education which need to be fought and won in order to secure the ground we have gained, let alone to advance toward socialism. Within capitalist societies there are important differences in the degree of inequality and the degree of repression. There are also important differences in the structure, organization and content of the educational system, which offer varying degrees of opportunity to different social classes, genders and racial groups.

What the right's political assault on the educational system has surely taught us is that, if liberal educational reforms are difficult to implement and if it is difficult to demonstrate that they have conferred a positive advantage on the working class, it is relatively easy to restructure schooling to the disadvantage of those who are already disadvantaged.

The educational policies of the right not only operate at the expense of the mass of people, but also at the expense of an educational policy which could offer some hope to both school and society. It is for this reason that an alternative politics of education is required. One of the reasons why the teaching profession and others concerned with present trends in British education have failed to mobilize popular support for an alternative politics of education is their apparent inability to counter the argument that liberal democratic reforms have both failed to alter significantly patterns of working-class educational performance, and failed to meet the 'needs' of industry. I have tried to address both these charges.

An alternative educational strategy must confront the issue of the relationship between the educational system and the economy for a number of reasons. First, popular support for educational reform and investment in education has always been couched in terms of its beneficial impact on Britain's economic development (Halsey, Floud and Anderson 1961; Vaizey 1962). Second, many of those whom the school serves will evaluate being in school with an eye to their future economic and social roles beyond the school gates (Ashton and Field 1976; Griffin 1985). Third, unless the limitations as well as the potential of the school as a source of social and economic change are clearly specified, exaggerated demands will continue to be made on the school, and the school and its pupils will continue to be the scapegoat for Britain's social and economic problems (Clarke and Willis 1984). Fourth, it is not a question of whether there should be a connection between education and industry but of how the connection is made. It is obvious that elements of technical education are essential for *all* young people if they are going to take advantage of advanced communication systems, computer technology, etc. But there is a considerable ˌdifference between teaching *all* pupils *about* industry and training particular groups of pupils *for* industry (Jamieson and Lightfoot 1981).

The debate about education and the economy must, however, be conducted in a wider context. As Tawney (1982) stated several decades ago, appreciation of the deficiencies of what is and the character of what ought to be, requires an appeal to some standard more stable than the momentary exigencies of our commerce, industry or social life: 'it must in short have recourse to principles'. The importance of this point is easy to recognize if we consider that recent debate about education and industry has almost completely lost sight of issues about social justice. An appeal to principles of social justice is therefore essential because the reduction of social and educational inequalities is a political not an educational goal. 'It has to be set *for* education, not just *in* education (Hall 1983: p. 6). And in order to meet the challenge *to* the comprehensive it will be necessary to win the ideological battle for 'education', because, as Tawney (1982) remarked:

> An appeal to principles is the condition of any considerable reconstruction of society, because social institutions are the visible expression of the scale of moral values which rules the minds of individuals, and it is impossible to alter institutions without altering that valuation. (p. 10)

It is for these reasons that the direction and determination of educational policy *is* the business of teachers. To deny this is a denial of professional responsibility because of the inherently political nature of education. If anyone doubted this belief in the past, they cannot do so in the 1980s. As D. Hargreaves (1982) has noted, the attempt by teachers to hide behind an apolitical mask is a fraud, and:

> By depoliticizing their work, the teachers make their task more, not less, difficult for they are thus prevented from developing an explicit philosophy of the relation between education and society. (p. 226)

Until teachers convert their professional troubles into issues of social structure they will fail to solve their troubles and will be continually forced into taking courses of action which will deepen the classroom crisis.

CONCLUSION

> Secondary education has for more than half a century been undergoing a serious crisis which has by no means reached its conclusion. Everybody feels that it cannot remain as it is, without having any clear idea about what it needs to become. . . . Everywhere educationalists and statesmen are aware that the changes which have occurred in the structure of contemporary societies, in their domestic economies as in their foreign affairs, require parallel transformations, no less profound, in the special area of the school system.
>
> (Durkheim 1977: p. 7)

This is how Durkheim described the problems surrounding secondary education in France at the beginning of the century, and if he were to visit Britain in the 1980s he would probably make a similar assessment. Comprehensive schooling in Britain is in a serious crisis which has by no means reached its conclusion. Most observers now believe that fundamental educational change is required. The debate about what the school needs to become has been dominated by the right, whilst the teaching profession laments the demise of the post-war dream, and sociologists and educationalists wonder why they no longer dominate educational debates.

I have tried to show why the right's assessment of the classroom crisis is at best perfunctory, if not dishonest; why its policy initiatives (i.e. the vocationalization of working-class education) is both a policy for inequality and will not meet the educational challenge of the late twentieth century. I have also tried to show why an alternative politics of education – or perhaps what might be called the 'new education' (Ranson et al. 1986) is necessary, and why the fight for the 'new education' cannot be fought, let alone won within the confines of the classroom and staffroom.[4] It can only succeed if it is based on the principles of social justice. Therefore to fight for a new education must, at the same time, be a fight for wider social change which will serve the development of human potential among the whole population rather than the narrow and selfish interests of those who are already over-privileged. Yet as recent educational policies have shown, and Simon (1986) has correctly noted:

> The historical record clearly shows that there is nothing inevitable about educational advance. Far from progress being linear, advances are more ofteɪɪ met by setbacks, by new crises, by ideological and political struggles of all kinds. Our present age is no exception. The chances of success will be greater . . . the more clearly we recognize the obstacles that must be overcome if we are to turn existing potentialities into reality. (p. 52)

Some of the obstacles and potentialities have been highlighted in this book,[5] but obviously these require further elaboration and detailed discussion. Yet it is evident that an unwillingness to take up the challenge *to* the comprehensive school will have far-reaching implications for teachers and working-class parents and pupils. Despite the fact that the data on which this study is based derives from the detailed investigation of the attitudes and experiences of working-class youth in one locality, and despite the fact that contemporary social and economic change defies anything more than calculated guesses and judgment even on the part of those who are supposed to know 'best' (i.e. sociologists, economists, and educationalists), the conclusion of this study is that the 'writing is on the wall' not only for Thomas High School but for many other schools like it in working-class areas with high rates of youth unemployment.

The problem is that the burden of the growing contradictions within capitalist Britain – which in Marxist terms can be expressed as a contradiction between the forces and relations of production – have fallen heavily on 'traditional' working-class neighbourhoods such as those in Middleport, which in turn highlight the contradictions underlying the schooling of working-class children. Many of the ordinary kids feel increasingly alienated from school and from a society which offers them little more than a choice between a plethora of training schemes and the dole queue (Coffield *et al.* 1986). Among younger working-class pupils who are entering secondary education with a knowledge that there is little hope of their getting a job when they leave school, making an effort will refer to a much longer time-span. If they were to calculate whether it's worth making an effort for five years when there is little chance of a job at the end of it, the answer from a growing number of 'respectable' working-class pupils may be 'no'.

In these circumstances there is likely to be a fundamental change in the attitudes of even junior school pupils which will lead large numbers of pupils who would previously have complied with the school to reject it. Moreover, even if some working-class parents are led to see the school as the only way out of their present predicament for their children, their aspirations will clash with the declining opportunities for educational and social advancement on offer to their children (Connell *et al.* 1982). Also, the rejection of school by a growing number of respectable working-class youth is not based on the same cultural understandings of the rems (i.e. not upon a belief that they can achieve social and adult status without having to make an effort in school), but because both the school's day-to-day practices and its selection processes are believed to be illegitimate. Hence, although the allocation of middle-class pupils to middle-class jobs has not led to working-class revolts, the school's attempt to determine who gets a job and who is unemployed on the basis of school performance will meet with far greater resistance.

To what extent the vocationalization of working-class education will succeed in leading the ordinary kids to continue to make an effort remains unclear but it has been shown that teacher complicity with the new vocationalism will exacerbate rather than resolve the crisis in the classroom and ultimately contribute to a further decline in the credibility of the teaching profession and to the extension of educational and social inequalities. The right will no doubt respond to the growing problems of control in the school as further evidence that the only way to overcome the current educational crisis is through 'market solutions' (i.e. educational vouchers) and early selection and segregation. The combination of inegalitarian educational policies and the economic circumstances confronting working-class parents and children will, therefore, lead to increasing class conflict over education, and problems of order in the classroom. Consequently, in one way or another the battle for 'education', like the ordinary kids' attempt to become adult in a respectable fashion, is only just beginning.

Notes

1 INTRODUCTION

1 This is how one of the teachers in this study described some of the ordinary kids.
2 The CTCs involve increasing efforts to reduce the power of Local Education Authorities who have usually been responsible for the provision of public secondary education, and to expose the educational system to market forces in the belief that this will make schools more responsive to the demands of parents and employers, and fuel a further growth of the private education sector. They will also result in the reintroduction of early selection.

3 PUPIL ORIENTATIONS AND YOUTH UNEMPLOYMENT

1 In some schools, particularly those where most of the pupils are from middle-class backgrounds, the connection between the rems, swots and ordinary kids and different orientations to school may be somewhat different. For example, some of the ordinary kids in Greenhill (which caters for middle-class pupils), may be taking a number of O levels, and some of those 'making an effort' for CSEs may be seen as rems. However, the O level pupils selected for Greenhill where the swots *even* in that school and the CSE pupils were similar to the ordinary kids found in Thomas High School and St Birinus who have an alienated instrumental orientation.
2 A major problem with the data collection was the failure to gain complete information about pupils' social class background. The first problem was having to reply on pupils' accounts of the occupational activities of parents, when almost 20 per cent of the sample had parents who were unemployed or were 'no longer living at home'. The second problem (involving gaining access to information) resulted from one of the schools (St Birinus) refusing to allow questions about parental employment. This forced me to ask respondents from St Birinus about parents' occupations in the follow-up postal questionnaire, which provided occupational data for a little over half of these respondents.

The social class composition of the sample by school (%)

	Thomas H.S.	St Birinus	Greenhill
Social class			
I–II	11	16	55
III Non-manual	15	9	15
III Manual	58	56	25
IV–V	17	20	5
Total (number)	152	82	85

If those with parents who are unemployed or no longer living at home had offered an occupation for their fathers, the proportion of pupils from categories III manual and IV and V would be approximately 80 to 85 per cent in Thomas H.S. and St Birinus.

3 In Thomas High School and St Birinus even pupils who were not working for CSEs were encouraged to register for 1 or 2 examinations.
4 The teachers in Thomas High School believe it to be important to offer 'equality of opportunity' to both boys and girls, allowing them to undertake whatever subjects they want, but felt it was not part of their role *actively* to direct pupils. Given the cultural resources available for boys and girls to make sense of who they are and what they might become, and the structural organization of the school, the call for equality of opportunity between the sexes is a conservative ideology if it is non-interventionist, and ensures the continuation of overt sexual dscrimination in British schools.
5 This conclusion also challenges those who have argued that when *mental* is understood as 'academic' and *manual* as 'practical' that mental and manual are translated into spheres of male and female activity (Macdonald 1981; Willis 1977).
6 This was established on the basis of a number of criteria – qualifications, attitude to school, whether pupils thought school was a waste of time. The number of pupils in the sample adopting an alienated orientation to school is under-represented as a result of a number of Easter leavers remaining away from St Birinus at the time the questionnaire was administered. The sample from Greenhill was also skewed given the need to ensure a middle-class and academically successful category within the sample. Moreover, the way the alienated category was identified may also lead to their under-representation, resulting from the necessity for respondents to qualify for inclusion along a number of dimensions rather than by default.

7 Environmental responses are partially inflated as a result of combining the importance of having good work mates with the desire for good working conditions.
8 This is a poor question because it does not differentiate between attitudes of pupils about their future job prospects and whether they feel qualifications are a waste of time regardless of the job situation. However, when the two questions are combined this difficulty is largely overcome.

4 REMS, SWOTS, AND ORDINARY KIDS

1 The informal pupil culture must be distinguished from class or gender-specific 'youth subcultures'. Pupils will draw upon different aspects of 'street' and 'pop media culture' but there will be qualitative and quantitative differences in their use and significance (Ball 1981).
2 Parsons (1954) has noted that at the line between childhood and adolescence 'growing up' consists precisely in the ability to participate in youth culture patterns (p. 93). Growing up in the school involves the participation in youth subcultures. This process is recognized by one of the tidy lads in this study:

> *Larry*: I feel sorry for the pupils who are comin' to this school next year, cos it will be crap . . . it's just the fourth year, they look up to the fifth year and they imitate all the fifth year lads, muckin' about, you know. The fourth and third year muck about, but the fifth year seem to be the worst, don't they . . . in their behaviour, than the fourth year. They'll be exactly the same next year and it will go on and on unless they put a stop to it, like.

The younger pupils may lead them to identify with particular groups of older pupils who are themselves oriented to the formal culture of the school in different ways. For younger pupils this is a *side-bet* (Becker 1964; Ashton 1975) which does not necessarily involve a commitment to a particular way of 'being' in the school. However, as pupils move into examination channels these earlier side-bets may lead the pupil to develop stronger peer group affiliations that consolidate an acknowledgement of being academic/practically non-academic. This may increasingly make other ways of understanding being/becoming and what is necessary for these to be materialized, unfeasible, even if 'thinkable', alternatives.
3 However, Willis takes class consciousness as underlying the counter-school culture even though it is not articulated in a coherent fashion by the lads. One of the reasons for this, according to Willis, results from the view that 'words and considered language' is an expression of mental

life which is rejected by the lads as being too much like what is expected of them at school. However, the quality of his transcriptions on other topics suggests otherwise. Ultimately, the political significance of the counter-school culture depends upon a particular 'reading' and 'decoding', premised upon an 'act of faith', that we can examine the counter-school culture to reveal the *rational class impulse* which underlies it (pp. 125–6). In this sense, his thesis suffers from the same difficulties confronting the majority of work connected with 'reading' youth cultures at the Centre for Contemporary Cultural Studies and elsewhere (Cohen 1980; Murdock and Mcron 1976.) in the attempt to contextualize and explain working-class youth subcultures in terms of the 'parent' culture.

5 ORDINARY KIDS AND THE NEW VOCATIONALISM

1 Careers education will be taken to include careers guidance.
2 Hayes and Hopson (1971) argue that if the results of the manpower forecasts are to be used it is essential that the counsellor must not be concerned in any way with the need to meet national manpower requirements. This view challenges the 'official' view of careers education since the 1970s, see Schools Council (1972). For a good review of the historical development of careers education in Britain, see Bates (1984).
3 The brief of the careers service as understood by the ordinary kids can be further illustrated by comparing Thomas H.S. with St Birinus. In Thomas H.S. we have noted that there is little careers provision in school, in St Birinus careers education does appear to a regular slot on the timetable. Both schools have the same careers officer. When the ordinary kids from the two schools were asked to evaluate the helpfulness of careers teachers and officers, 61 per cent from Thomas H.S. compared with 53 per cent from St Birinus, reported them as 'very helpful'. In the evaluation of the careers interview there was virtually no difference between the schools (62 per cent and 64 per cent respectively). The fact that pupils from St Birinus do not believe careers provision to be any more helpful than those in Thomas H.S. further suggests that official careers provision is primarily viewed by the ordinary kids as a source of labour market information.

6 ORDINARY KIDS IN THE LABOUR MARKET

1 The quantitative data were collected using a postal questionnaire administered a little over eighteen months after the fifth secondary year of schooling. Three-quarters of respondents who could have responded did so (see Chapter 1). There was little difference in the response rate of the ordinary kids and swots, but only 57 per cent of the rems responded.

A breakdown of the numbers responding to the questionnaire and the proportion with labour market experience is set out below.

	Rems	Ordinary kids	Swots	Total
Labour market experience	28	118	50	194
In full-time study	—	45	76	123
Missing cases	21	62	51	134
Response rates %	57.1	72.4	71.2	70.3
Total (number)	49	225	177	451

2 In other words: the decision to undertake further study was not based on a positive evaluation of current and further academic performance for other than a small number of ordinary kids, it was rather the result of a negative evaluation of their chances of finding 'suitable' or 'any' employment. Many of those who did stay on would have applied for jobs while at school and during the summer holidays, but it was those with better qualifications who opted to stay on in full-time study because they thought it might be of benefit – over 80 per cent of ordinary kids who did not get any O levels or equivalent left school, as did half of those with up to three O levels and under 30 per cent of those with four or more equivalent O levels.

3 This is the longest period of unemployment, not total time unemployed.

4 Ashton and Maguire (1980b) note that 'there are still jobs that are generally thought of by both employers and employees as women's or men's work . . . and this is pervasively tied up with gender identity' p. 121). There is some evidence to suggest that employers would welcome more girls applying for apprenticeships (Ashton and Maguire 1980b), although Bennett and Carter (1981) have found that girls who want to enter male-dominated occupations have had their aspirations frustrated.

5 68 per cent of ordinary kids believed that having the 'right attitude' was the most important thing employers looked for when recruiting school leavers.

6 There was little difference between the sexes, 12 per cent boys against 16 per cent girls stating job security and 34 per cent of the boys and 32 per cent of girls interesting/enjoyable work.

7 The adequacy of retrospective accounts of the value they place on qualifications while at school is not of crucial importance, given that our primary concern is that of measuring the degree of change between what they believed about qualifications between two periods. Indeed it is interesting that the attitudes of the ordinary kids while in the fifth year at school vary considerably and are becoming polarized. Two-thirds of the ordinary kids remaining in full-time study reported

qualifications to be 'very' important in the fifth year at school compared to 46 per cent with labour market experiences.
8 Rathkey (1978): study of 86 unemployed 16–19 year olds on Teeside, reported in Roberts (1984: p. 66).

7 UNEMPLOYMENT AND EDUCATIONAL CHANGE

1 Which is an even more effective way of excluding the working class than the now discredited 11+ examination (see *The Daily Telegraph* 29/12/86).
2 The basis for selection can no longer rely on arguments about three different types of intelligence, which informed the 1944 Education Act. Arguments for this sort of organization are now stripped of their scientific veneer to reveal the utilitarian and social basis for such divisions.
3 This argument is strengthened by the fact that school leaver unemployment is generating ample time for vocational training beyond the age of 16!
4 Ranson, Taylor and Brighouse (1986) suggest that:

We are experiencing a Janus-headed revolution. In one of its forms – *the new vocationalism* – the reworked process of education and training merely replaces one unilinear focus of learning (academic) with another (practical and vocational). While the other form – *the new education* – eschews selection and seeks to design learning experiences which meet the needs of each young person or adult (p. 9).

Janus is an ancient Italian deity, regarded as having doors and entrances under his protection, represented with a face on the front and another on the back of his head. If the 'educational revolution' is Janus-headed, then it seems to me that the 'new vocationalism' represents the main entrance and the 'new education' the service entrance for local traders. They are not of equal standing or visibility in contemporary educational debates. It may well be more comfortable for teachers to feel that what they are doing is part of the 'new education', but this does nothing to change the political and classroom context which is dominated by the new vocationalism.

5 For a more detailed account of what a left realist strategy for education might involve, see Brown, P. (forthcoming 1988) 'Education and the working class: A cause for concern', in H. Lauder and P. Brown (eds) *Education: In Search of a Future*, Lewes: Falmer Press.

References

Abrams, P. (1982) *Historical Sociology*, London: Open Books.

Althusser, L. (1972) 'Ideology and ideological state apparatuses', in B. R. Cosin (ed.) *Education: Structure and Society*, Milton Keynes: Open University.

Anderson *et al.* (1982) *Educated for Employment?* London: The Social Affairs Unit.

Apple, M. W. (ed.) (1982a) *Cultural and Economic Reproduction in Education: Essays on Class, Ideology and the State*, London: Routledge & Kegan Paul.

Apple, M. W. (1982b) *Education and Power*, London: Routledge & Kegan Paul.

Arnot, M. and Whitty, G. (1982) 'From reproduction to transformation: recent radical perspectives on curriculum from the USA, *British Journal of Sociology of Education* 3: 93–103.

Ashton, D. (1975) 'The transition from school to work: notes on the development of different frames of reference among young male workers', in G. Esland *et al.* (eds) *People and Work*, Edinburgh: Holmes McDougall/Open University.

Ashton, D. and Field, D. (1976) *Young Workers: From School to Work*, London: Hutchinson.

Ashton, D. and Maguire, M. J. (1980a) 'The function of academic and non-academic criteria in employers' selection strategies', *British Journal of Guidance and Counselling* 8: (2): 146–57.

Ashton, D. and Maguire, M. J. (1980b) 'Young women in the labour market: stability and change', in R. Deem (ed). *Schooling for Women's Work*, London: Routledge & Kegan Paul.

Ashton, D. and Maguire, M. J. (1986) 'The structure of the youth labour market: some implications for educational policy', paper prepared for *Economics and Education Management*: A National Seminar.

Ashton, D., Maguire, M., and Garland, V. (1982) *Youth in the Labour Market*, Department of Employment Research Paper No. 34.

Ball, S. J. (1981) *Beachside Comprehensive: A Case-Study of Secondary Schooling*, Cambridge: Cambridge University Press.

Bates, I. (1984) 'From vocational guidance to life skills: historical perspectives on careers education', in I. Bates *et al. Schooling for the Dole?*, London: Macmillan.

Bates, I., Clarke, J., Cohen, P., Finn, D., Moore, R., and Willis, P. (1984) *Schooling for the Dole?*, London: Macmillan.

Becker, H. S. (1961) 'Schools and systems of stratification', in A. H. Halsey *et al.* (eds) *Education, Economy and Society*, New York: Free Press.

Becker, H. S., (1964) 'Personal Change in Adult Life', *Sociometry* 27: 41–53.

Bennett, Y. and Carter, D. (1981) *Sidetracked? A Look at the Career Advice Given to Fifth-Form Girls*, Manchester: Equal Opportunities Commission.

Bernbaum, G. (1977) *Knowledge and Ideology in the Sociology of Education*, London: Macmillan.

Bernstein, B. (1969) 'A critique of the concept of compensatory education', in *Class Codes and Control*, vol. 2, London: Routledge & Kegan Paul.

Bernstein, B. (1975) *Class, Codes and Control, vol. 3*, London: Routledge & Kegan Paul.

Bernstein, B. (1977) 'Class and pedagogies: visible and invisible', in J. Karabel and A. H. Halsey *Power and Ideology in Education*, Oxford: Oxford University Press.

Blackburn, R. M. and Mann, M. (1979), *The Working Class in the Labour Market*, London: Macmillan.

Blackman, S. J. (1987) 'The labour market in school: new vocationalism and socially ascribed discrimination', in P. Brown and D. Ashton (eds) *Education, Unemployment and Labour Markets*, Lewes: Falmer Press.

Bloxham, S. (1983) 'Social behaviour and the young unemployed', in I. R. Fiddy (ed.) *In Place Of Work*, Lewes: Falmer.

Bourdieu, P. (1974), 'The school as a conservative force: scholastic and cultural inequalties', in J. Eggleston (ed.) *Contemporary Research in the Sociology of Education*, London: Methuen.

Bourdieu, P. (1977) *Outline of a Theory of Practice*, Cambridge: Cambridge Unversity Press.

Bourdieu, P. and Passeron, J. C. (1977) *Reproduction: in Education, Society and Culture*, London: Sage.

Bowles, S. and Gintis, H. (1976) *Schooling in Capitalist America: Educational Reform and the Contradictions of Economic Life*, London: Routledge & Kegan Paul.

Boyson, R. (1975) *The Crisis In Education*, London: Woburn Press.

Braun, F. (1979) 'Youth unemployment in West Germany: the psychosocial aspect', *Research in Education*, 21: 41–54.

Bridges, D. (1981) 'Teachers and "the world of work"', in J. Elliot *et al. School Accountability*, London: Grant McIntyre.

Brown, P. (1987a) 'Schooling for inequality? Ordinary kids in school and the labour market' in P. Brown and D. Ashton (eds) *Education, Unemployment and Labour Markets*, Lewes: Falmer.

Brown, P. (1987b) 'The new vocationalism: a policy for inequality' in B. Coles *Young Careers: The Search for Jobs and the New Vocationalism*, Milton Keynes: Open University Press.

Bulmer, M. (ed.) (1975) *Working Class Images of Society*, London: Routledge & Kegan Paul.

Burgess, R. G. (1982) *Field Research: A Sourcebook and Field Manual*, London: Allen & Unwin.

Burgess, R. G. (1983) *Experiencing Comprehensive Education*, London: Methuen.

Byrne, E. M. (1978) *Women and Education*, London: Tavistock.

Carter, M. (1962) *Home, School and Work: A Study of the Education and*

Employment of Young People in Britain, London: Pergamon Press.

Carter, M. (1966) *Into Work*, Harmondsworth: Penguin.

Cashmore, E. E. (1984) *No Future: Youth and Society*, London: Heinemann.

Central Advisory Council for Education (1984) *School and Life*, London: HMSO.

Centre for Contemporary Cultural Studies (1981) *Unpopular Education*, London: Hutchinson.

Central Policy Review Staff (1980) *Education, Training and Industrial Performance*, London: HMSO.

Central Statistical Office (1985) *Social Trends*, London: HMSO.

Cherry, N. (1976) 'Persistent job-changing: is it a problem? *Journal of Occupational Psychology*, 49: 203–21.

Clarke, J. (1985) 'Whose justice? The politics of juvenile control', *International Journal of the Sociology of Law* 13: 407–421.

Clarke, J. and Willis, P. (1984) 'Introduction', in I. Bates *et al. Schooling for the Dole*, London: Macmillan

Clarke, L. (1980a) *Occupational Choice: A Critical Review of Research in the United Kingdom*, London: HMSO.

Clarke, L. (1980b) *The Transition from School to Work: A Critical Review of Research in the United Kingdom*, London: HMSO.

Coffield, F., Borrill, C., and Marshall, S. (1986) *Growing Up At the Margins*, Milton Keynes: Open University Press.

Cohen, P. (1982) 'Schooling for the dole', *New Socialist* 3: 43–7.

Cohen, S. (1980) *Folk Devils and Moral Panics*, Oxford: Martin Robinson.

Coleman, J. S. (1961) *The Adolescent Society*, New York: Free Press.

Connell, R. W., Ashendon, D. J., Kessler, S., and Dowsett, G. W. (1982) *Making the Difference: Schools, Families, and Social Division*, Sydney: George Allen & Unwin.

Corrigan, P. (1979) *Schooling the Smash Street Kids*, London: Macmillan.

Cousin, G. (1984) 'Failure through resistance: critique of learning to labour', *Youth and Policy* 10: 37–40.

Cox, C. B. and Boyson, R. (eds.) (1977) *Black Paper*, London: Temple Smith.

Culley, L. and Demaine, J. (1983) 'Social theory, social relations and education', in S. Walker and L. Barton (eds) *Gender, Class and Education*, Lewes: Falmer.

Dale, R. (1983) 'Thatcherism and education', in J. Ahier and M. Flude (eds) *Contemporary Education Policy*, London: Croom Helm.

Dale, R. (ed.) (1985) *Education, Training and Employment*, Oxford: Pergamon Press.

Dale, R. (1986) 'Examining the gift-horse's teeth: a tentative analysis of TVEI', in S. Walker and L. Barton (eds) *Youth, Unemployment and Schooling*, Milton Keynes: Open University Press.

Davies, L. (1979) 'Deadlier than the male? Girls' conformity and deviance in school', in L. Barton and R. Meigham (eds) *Schools, Pupils and Deviance*, Driffield: Nafferton.

Davies, L. (1984) *Pupil Power: Deviance and Gender in School*, Lewes: Falmer Press.

Deem, R. (1978) *Women and Schooling*, London: Routledge & Kegan Paul.

Delamont, S.(1980) *Sex Roles and the School*, London: Methuen.

Department of Education and Science (1980) *A Framework for the School Curriculum*, London: HMSO.

Department of Education and Science (1985) 'Education and economic activity of young people aged 16 to 18 years in Great Britain from 1974 to 1984 '*Statistical Bulletin* 5.

Department of Employment (1981) *A New Training Initiative: A Programme for Action*, London: HMSO.

Donovan, A. and Oddy, M. (1982) 'Psychological aspects of unemployment; an investigation into the emotional and social adjustment of school-leavers', *Journal of Adolescence* 5: 15–30.

Downes, D.(1966) *The Delinquent Solution*, London: Routledge & Kegan Paul.

Durkheim, E. (1977) *The Evolution of Educational Thought*, London: Routledge & Kegan Paul.

Eggleston, J. (ed.) (1982) *Work Experience in Secondary Schools*, London: Routledge & Kegan Paul.

Equal Opportunities Commission (1982) 'Gender and the secondary school curriculum' *Research Bulletin* 6.

Equal Opportunities Commission (1985) 'Occupational segregation by sex', *Research Bulletin* 9.

Erikson, E.(1968) *Identity: Youth and Crisis*, London: Faber & Faber.

Etzioni, A. (1961) *A Comparative Analysis of Complex Organizations: On Power, Involvement, and their Correlates*, New York: Free Press.

Everhart, R. B. (1983) *Reading, Writing and Resistance: Adolescence and Labour in a Junior High School*, London: Routledge & Kegan Paul.

Finn, D. (1983) 'A new deal for British youth? The new vocationalism and the Youth Training Scheme', *Social Science Teacher* 13: 42–45.

Floud, J. and Halsey, A. H. (1958) 'The sociology of education: a trend report and bibliography', *Current Sociology* 3: (3): 165–93.

Floud, J. and Halsey, A. H. (1961) 'English secondary schools and the supply of labour', in A. H. Halsey *et al.* (eds) *Education, Economy and Society*, Glencoe: Free Press.

Fox, A. (1980) 'The meaning of work', in G. Esland and G. Salaman (eds) *The Politics of Work and Occupations*, Milton Keynes: Open University.

Fromm, E.(1962) 'Personality and the market place', in S. Nosow and W. H. Form (eds) *Man, Work and Society*, New York: Basic Books.

Fuller, M. (1983) 'Qualified criticism, critical qualifications', in L. Barton and S. Walker (eds) *Race, Class and Education*, London: Croom Helm.

Gamble, A. (1981) *Britain in Decline*, London: Macmillan.

Gaskell, J. and Lazerson, M. (1980), 'Between school and work: perspectives of working-class youth', *Interchange* 11: 80–96.

Gaskell, J. (1983) 'The reproduction of family life: perspectives of male and female adolescents', *British Journal of Sociology of Education* 4: 19–38.

Giddens, A.(1986) *The Constitution of Society*, Cambridge: Polity Press.

Ginzberg, E. *et al.* (1951) *Occupational Choice: An Approach to a General Theory*, New York: Columbia University Press.

Giroux, H. (1981) *Ideology, Cutlure and the Process of Schooling*, Lewes: Falmer Press.

Gleeson, D. (ed.) (1983) *Youth Training and the Search for Work*, London: Routledge & Kegan Paul.

Goldthorpe, J. H., Lewellyn, C., and Payne, C. (1980) *Social Mobility and Class Structure in Modern Britain*, Oxford: Clarendon Press.

Goldthorpe, J. H., Lockwood, D., Bechhofer, F. and Platt, J. (1969) *The Affluent Worker in the Class Structure*, Cambridge: Cambridge University Press.

Griffin, C.(1985) *Typical Girls?: Young Women from School to the Job Market*, London: Routledge & Kegan Paul.

Grubb, W. N. and Lazerson, M. (1982) 'Education and the labour market: Recycling the youth problem', in H. Kantor and D. B. Tyack (eds) *Work, Youth and Schooling*, Stanford: Stanford University Press.

Gurney, R. M. (1981) 'Leaving school, facing unemployment, and making attributions about the causes of unemployment', *Journal of Vocational Behaviour* 18: 79–91.

Hall, S. (1977) *Review of the Course (E202), Schooling and Society*, Milton Keynes: Open University.

Hall, S.(1983) 'Education in crisis', in A. M. Wolpe and J. Donald (eds) *Is There Anyone Here From Education*, London: Pluto.

Hall, S. and Jacques, M. (eds) (1983) *The Politics of Thatcherism*, London: Lawrence and Wishart.

Hall, S. and Jefferson, T. (eds) (1976) *Resistance Through Rituals*, London: Hutchinson.

Halsey, A. H., Floud, J., and Anderson C. A. (eds) (1961) *Education, Economy, and Society*, New York: Free Press.

Halsey, A. H., Heath, A. F., and Ridge, J. M. (1980) *Origins and Destinations: Family, Class, and Education in Modern Britain*, Oxford: Oxford University Press.

Hammersley, M. and Turner, G. (1980) 'Conformist pupils?', in P. Woods (ed.) *Pupil Strategies*, London: Croom Helm.

Hampson, K. (1980) 'Schools and work', in H. Pluckrose and P. Wilby (eds) *Education 2000*, London: Maurice Temple Smith.

Handy, C.(1984) *The Future of Work*, Oxford: Robertson.

Hannon, V. (1981) *Ending Sex-Stereotyping in Schools: A Sourcebook for School-Based Teacher Workshops*, Manchester: Equal Opportunities Commission.

Harary, R. (1966) 'Merton revisited: a new classification for deviant behaviour', *American Sociological Review* 31: (5): 693–7.

Hargreaves, A.(1982) 'Resistance and relative autonomy theories: problems of distortion and incoherence in recent marxist analyses of education', *British Journal of Sociology of Education* 3: 107–26.

Hargreaves, D. H. (1967) *Social Relations in a Secondary School*, London: Routledge & Kegan Paul.

Hargreaves, D. H. (1982) *The Challenge for the Comprehensive School*, London: Routledge & Kegan Paul.

Harris, C. C. (1983) *Social Transition and the Deconstruction of the Family: Reflections on Research into the Domestic Circumstances of the Victims of Economic Change*, paper presented at the *Tocqueville Society Seminar* on

'Work and the family in Europe and the US' Arc-et-Semams, June 1983. A much abbreviated version of the paper appeared in the *Tocqueville Review*, Fall-Winter, 1983.

Harris, C.C. *et al.* (1987) *Redundancy and Recession in South Wales*, Oxford: Blackwell.

Hayes, J. and Hopson, B. (1971) *Careers Guidance*, London: Heinemann.

Hayes, J. and Nutman, P. (1981) *Understanding the Unemployed*, London: Tavistock.

Hillard, J. (1986) 'Thatcherism and decline', in D. Coates and J. Hillard (eds) *The Economic Decline of Modern Britain*, Brighton: Wheatsheaf.

Hogan, D.(1982) 'Education and class formation: the peculiarities of the Americans', in M. W. Apple (ed.) *Culture and Economic Reproduction in Education*, London: Routledge & Kegan Paul.

Holland, G. (1986) 'Training young people for the future', in S. Ranson, B. Taylor and T. Brighouse (eds) *The Revolution in Education and Training*, Harlow: Longman.

Hopkins, A. (1978) *The School Debate*, Harmondsworth: Penguin.

Hopper, E.(1971) 'Notes on stratification, education and mobility in industrial societies', in E. Hopper (ed.) *Readings in the Theory of Educational Systems*, London: Hutchinson.

Hyman, H. H. (1953) 'The value systems of different classes: a social psychological contribution to the analysis of stratification', in R. Bendix and S. Lipset (eds) *Class, Status and Power*, Glencoe: Free Press.

Jackson, B. (1968) *Working-class Community*, London: Routledge & Kegan Paul.

Jackson, B. and Marsden, D. (1966) *Education and the Working Class*, Harmondsworth: Penguin.

Jackson, M. P. (1985) *Youth Unemployment*, London: Croom Helm.

Jahoda, M. (1982) *Employment and Unemployment*, Cambridge: Cambridge University Press.

Jamieson, I. and Lightfoot, M. (1981) 'Learning about work', *Educational Analysis* 2: 37–51.

Jenkins, R. (1982) 'Pierre Bourdieu and the reproduction of determinism', *Sociology* 16: 270–81.

Jenkins, R. (1983) *Lads, Citizens and Ordinary Kids*, London: Routledge & Kegan Paul.

Jenkins, R. and Troyna, B. (1983) 'Educational myths, labour market realities', in B.Troyna and D. I. Smith (eds) *Racism, School and the Labour Market*, Leicester: National Youth Bureau.

Kahl, J. A.(1961) 'Common man', in A. H. Halsey *et al.* (eds) *Education, Economy and Society*, New York: Free Press.

Kantor, H. and Tyack, D. B. (1982) 'Introduction: Historical perspectives on vocationalism in American education', in M. Kantor and D. B. Tyack (eds) *Work, Youth and Schooling*, Stanford: Stanford University Press.

Keil, T. and Newton, P. (1980) 'Into work: continuity and change', in R. Deem (ed) *Schooling for Women's Work*, London: Routledge & Kegan Paul.

Kelly, G. P. and Nihlen, A. S. (1982) 'Schooling and the reproduction of patriarchy: unequal workloads, unequal rewards', in M. W. Apple (ed) *Cultural and Economic Reproduction in Education*, London: Routledge & Kegan Paul.

Kelvin, P. (1981) 'Work as a source of identity: the implications of unemployment', *British Journal of Guidance and Counselling* 9: (1): 2–11.

King, R. (1971) 'Unequal access in education: sex and social class', *Social and Economic Administration* 5: 167–75.

Kirton, D.(1983) 'The impact of mass unemployment on careers guidance, in the Durham coalfield', in R. Fiddy (ed) *In Place of Work*, Lewes: Falmer Press.

Kogan, M. (1978) *The Politics of Educational Change*, Manchester: Manchester Unversity Press

Kornhauser, W. (1960) *The Politics of Mass Society*, London: Routledge & Kegan Paul.

Lane, M. (1972) 'Explaining education choice', *Sociology* 6: 25–66.

Lavercombe, S. and Fleming, D. (1981) 'Attitudes and duration of unemployment among sixteen year old school leavers', *British Journal of Guidance and Counselling* 9: (1): 36–45.

Lee, D. *et al.* (1987) 'Youth training, life chances and orientation to work: a critical case study', in P. Brown and D. Ashton (eds) *Education, Unemployment and Labour Markets*, Lewes: Falmer.

Leonard, D. (1980) *Sex and Generation: A Study of Courtship and Weddings*, London: Tavistock.

MacDonald, M. (1981) 'Schooling and the reproduction of class and gender relations', in R. Dale *et al.* (eds) *Education and the State: Politics, Patriarchy and Practice*, Lewes: Falmer/Open University.

McCulloch, G. (1986) 'Policy, politics and education: the TVEI', *Journal of Education Policy* 1: (1): 35–52.

McRobbie, A. (1978) 'Working-class girls and the culture of femininity', in Centre for Contemporary Cultural Studies, Women's Studies Group, *Women Take Issue*, London: Hutchinson.

Maizels, E. (1970) *Adolescent Needs and the Transition from School to Work*, London: Athlone Press.

Maguire, M. J. and Ashton, D. N. (1981) 'Employers' perceptions and use of educational qualifications', *Educational Analysis* 3: (2): 25–36.

Manpower Services Commission (1977) *Young People and Work*, London: Manpower Services Commission.

Manpower Services Commission (1985a) *Manpower Services Commission: Corporate Plan 1985–1989 Wales*, Sheffield: MSC.

Manpower Services Commission (1985b) *TVEI Review 1985*, Sheffield: MSC.

Marshall,T. H. (1950) *Citizenship and Social Class*, Cambridge: Cambridge University Press.

Massey, D. (1985) 'Geography and class', in D. Coates, G. Johnson, and R. Bush, *A Socialist Anatomy of Britain*, Cambridge: Polity.

Merton, R. K. (1957) *Social Theory and Social Structure*, New York: Free Press.

Millman, V. (1985) 'The new vocationalism in secondary schools: its influence on girls', in J. Whyte *et al.* (eds) *Girl Friendly Schooling*, London: Methuen.

Mills, C. W.(1970) *The Sociological Imagination*, Harmondsworth: Penguin Books.

Murdock, G. and McCron, R. (1976) 'Youth and class: the career of a confusion', in G. Mungham and G. Pearson (eds) *Working-Class Youth Culture*, London: Routledge & Kegan Paul.

Murphy, J. (1981) 'Class inequality in education: two justifications, one evaluation but no hard evidence, *British Journal of Sociology*, 32: 182–201.

Parsons, D. (1985) *Changing Patterns of Employment in Great Britain: a Context for Education*, Sheffield: MSC.

Parsons, T. (1949) *The Structure of Social Action*, New York: Free Press.

Parsons, T. (1954) *Essays in Sociological Theory*, New York: Free Press.

Parsons, T. (1961) 'The school class as a social system: some of its functions in American society', in A. H. Halsey *et al.* (eds) *Education, Economy and Society*, New York: Free Press.

Plowden Report, Central Advisory Council for Education (1967) *Children and their Primary Schools*, London: HMSO.

Raffe, D. (1983) 'Employment instability among less-qualified young workers', *British Journal of Guidance and Counselling* 11: (1): 21–34.

Raffe, D. (ed.) (1984) *Fourteen to Eighteen: The Changing Pattern Of Schooling in Scotland*, Aberdeen: Aberdeen University Press.

Raffe, D. (1987) 'Youth unemployment in the UK 1979–84' in P. Brown and D. Ashton (eds) *Education, Unemployment and Labour Markets*, Lewes: Falmer.

Ranson, S. (1984) 'Towards a tertiary tripartism: new codes of social control and the 17+', in P. Broadfoot (ed.) *Selection, Certification and Control*, Lewes: Falmer Press.

Ranson, S., Taylor, B. and Brighouse, T. (eds) (1986) The Revolution in Education and Training, Harlow: Longman.

Reeder, D. (1981) 'A recurring debate: education and industry', in: R. Dale *et al.* (eds) *Schooling and the National Interest*, Lewes: Falmer.

Rees, T. L. and Atkinson, P. (eds) (1982) *Youth Unemployment and State Intervention*, London: Routledge & Kegan Paul.

Rees T. L. and Gregory, D. (1981) 'Youth employment and unemployment: a decade of decline', *Educational Analysis* 3: (2): 7–24.

Rees, G. and Rees, T. L.(1980) 'Educational inequality in Wales: some problems and paradoxes', in G. Rees and T. L. Rees (eds) *Poverty and Social Inequality in Wales*, London: Croom Helm.

Reid, I. (1978) *Sociological Perspectives on School and Education*, London: Open Books.

Roberts, K. (1974) 'The entry into employment: an approach towards a general theory', in W. M. Williams (ed.) *Occupational Choice*, London: George Allen & Unwin.

Roberts, K. (1975) 'The developmental theory of occupational choice: a critique and an alternative', in G. Esland *et al.* (eds) *People and Work*, Edinburgh: Holmes McDougal/Open University.

Roberts, K. (1983) *Youth and Leisure*, London: George Allen & Unwin.

Roberts, K. (1984) *School Leavers and their Prospects: Youth and the Labour Market in the 1980s*, Milton Keynes: Open University.

Roberts, K., Dench, S., and Richardson, D. (1987) 'Youth rates of pay and employment', in P. Brown and D. Ashton (eds) *Education, Unemployment and Labour Markets*, Lewes: Falmer.

Roberts, K., Duggan, J. and Noble, M. (1981) *Unregistered Youth Unemployment and Outreach Careers Work, Part One, Non-registration*, London: Department of Employment Research Paper 31.

Rogoff, N. (1961) 'Local social structures and educational selection', in Halsey, A. H. *et al.* (eds) *Education, Economy and Society*, New York: Free Press.

Rosser, C. and Harris, C. C. (1965) *The Family and Social Change*, London: Routledge & Kegan Paul.

Runciman, W. G. (1966) *Relative Deprivation and Social Justice*, London: Routledge & Kegan Paul.

Rutter, M. *et al.* (1979) *Fifteen Thousand Hours*, London: Open Books.

Scholzman, K. L. and Verba, S. (1980) *Insult to Injury*, Harvard: Harvard University Press.

Schools Council (1972) *Careers Education in the 1970s*, London: Evans/Methuen.

Sennett, R. and Cobb, J. (1977) *The Hidden Injuries of Class*, Cambridge: Cambridge University Press.

Sharpe, S. (1976) *Just Like a Girl: How Girls Learn to be Women*, Harmondsworth: Penguin.

Silver, H. (ed.) (1973) *Equal Opportunity in Education*, London: Methuen.

Simon, B. (1986) *Does Education Matter?*, London: Lawrence and Wishart.

Sofer, C., (1974) 'Introduction', in W. M. Williams, (ed.) *Occupational Choice*, London: George Allen & Unwin.

Spender, D. and Sarah, E. (eds) (1980) *Learning to Lose: Sexism and Education*, London: The Women's Press.

Stafford, A. (1981), 'Learning not to labour', *Capital and Class*, 15, Autumn: 55–77.

Stewart, A. and Blackburn, R. M. (1975), 'The stability of structural inequality', *The Sociological Review*, 23: 481–508.

Sugarman, B. (1967) 'Involvement in youth culture, academic achievement and conformity in school', *British Journal of Sociology* 18: 151–64.

Sutherland, M. B. (1981) *Sex Bias in Education*, Oxford: Blackwell.

Swartz, D. (1981) 'Class, educational systems and labour markets', *Archives – European Journal of Sociology* 22: 325–53.

Tawney, R.H. (1982) *The Acquisitive Society*, Brighton: Wheatsheaf.

Thompson, E. P. (1977), *The Making of the English Working Class*, Harmondsworth: Penguin.

Tomlinson, J. (1981) 'Corporatism: a further sociologization of Marxism', *Politics and Power* 4: 237–47.

Turner, G. (1983) *The Social World of the Comprehensive School: How Pupils Adapt*, London: Croom Helm.

Turner, R. (1964) *The Social Context of Ambition*, San Francisco: Chandler.

Urry, J. (1981) 'Localities, regions and social class', *International Journal of Urban and Regional Research* 5: 455–74.

Vaizey, J. (1962) *Education for Tomorrow*, Harmondsworth: Penguin.

Veness, T. (1962) *School Leavers*, London: Methuen.

Venn, G. (1964) *Man, Education and Work: Post-Secondary Vocational and Technical Education*, Washington: American Council on Education.

Wakeford, J. (1969) *The Cloistered Elite: A Sociological Analysis of the English Public Boarding School*, London: Macmillan.

Walker, S. and Barton, L. (eds) (1986) *Youth, Unemployment and Schooling*, Milton Keynes: Open University Press.

Watts, A. G.(1978) 'The implications of school-leaver unemployment for careers education in schools, *Journal of Curriculum Studies* 10: 233–50.

Watts, A. G. (1981) 'Careers education and the informal economies', *British Journal of Guidance and Counselling* 9: 22–35.

Watts, A. G. (1983), *Education, Unemployment and the Future of Work*, Milton Keynes: Open University.

Welsh Education Office (1979) *Literacy and Numeracy and Examination Achievement in Wales: A Further Commentary*, Cardiff: Welsh Office.

West, M. and Newton, P. (1983) *The Transition from School to Work*, London: Croom Helm.

Whyld, J. (ed.) (1983) *Sexism in the Secondary Curriculum*, London: Harper & Row.

Whyte, J. *et al.* (1985) (eds) *Girl Friendly Schooling*, London: Methuen.

Wiener, M. J. (1981) *English Culture and the Decline of the Industrial Spirit, 1850–1980*, Cambridge: Cambridge University Press.

Williams, S.(1985) *A Job to Live*, Harmondsworth: Penguin.

Willis, P. (1977) *Learning to Labour*, Farnborough: Saxon House, Teakfield.

Willis, P. (1982) 'Cultural production and theories of reproduction', in L. Barton and S. Walker (eds) *Race, Class and Education*, London: Croom Helm.

Willmott, P. (1966) *Adolecent Boys of East London*, London: Routledge & Kegan Paul.

Woods, P. (1979) *The Divided School*, London: Routledge & Kegan Paul.

Woods, P. (ed) (1980) *Pupil Strategies*, London: Croom Helm.

Woods, P. (1983) *Sociology and the School: An Interactionist Viewpoint*, London: Routledge & Kegan Paul

Wrong, D. (1967) 'The oversocialized conception of man in modern sociology', in H. J. Demerath and R. Peterson (eds) *System Change and Conflict*, New York: Free Press/Macmillan.

Young, M. F. D. (ed.) (1971) *Knowledge and Control: New Directions for the Sociology of Education*, London: Collier-Macmillan.

Youthaid (1981a), *In and Out of the Programme*, London: Youthaid.

Youthaid (1981b) *Quality or Collapse?* London: Youthaid.

Name index

Subject index